GOVERNORS STATE UNIVERSITY LIBRARY
3 1611 00067 3233

USING WHAT WE KNOW ABOUT AT-RISK YOUTH

W9-BEP-359

HOW TO ORDER THIS BOOK

BY PHONE: 800-233-9936 or 717-291-5609, 8AM–5PM Eastern Time

BY FAX: 717-295-4538

BY MAIL: Order Department
Technomic Publishing Company, Inc.
851 New Holland Avenue, Box 3535
Lancaster, PA 17604, U.S.A.

BY CREDIT CARD: American Express, VISA, MasterCard

PERMISSION TO PHOTOCOPY–POLICY STATEMENT

Authorization to photocopy items for internal or personal use, or the internal or personal use of specific clients, is granted by Technomic Publishing Co., Inc. provided that the base fee of US $3.00 per copy, plus US $ .25 per page is paid directly to Copyright Clearance Center, 222 Rosewood Drive, Danvers, MA 01923, USA. For those organizations that have been granted a photocopy license by CCC, a separate system of payment has been arranged. The fee code for users of the Transactional Reporting Service is 1-56676/94 $5.00 + $ .25.

USING WHAT WE KNOW ABOUT AT-RISK YOUTH

LESSONS FROM THE FIELD

EDITED BY

ROBERT C. MORRIS

Professor, Secondary Education
School of Education, West Georgia College

Published in cooperation with
NATIONAL DROPOUT PREVENTION NETWORK
NATIONAL DROPOUT PREVENTION CENTER
at Clemson University

TECHNOMIC
PUBLISHING CO., INC.

LANCASTER • BASEL

GOVERNORS STATE UNIVERSITY
UNIVERSITY PARK
IL. 60466

LC 4091 .U75 1994

Using what we know about
at-risk youth

317504

Using What We Know about At-Risk Youth
a TECHNOMIC® publication

Published in the Western Hemisphere by
Technomic Publishing Company, Inc.
851 New Holland Avenue, Box 3535
Lancaster, Pennsylvania 17604 U.S.A.

Distributed in the Rest of the World by
Technomic Publishing AG
Missionsstrasse 44
CH-4055 Basel, Switzerland

Copyright © 1994 by Technomic Publishing Company, Inc.
All rights reserved

No part of this publication may be reproduced, stored in a retrieval system, or transmitted, in any form or by any means, electronic, mechanical, photocopying, recording, or otherwise, without the prior written permission of the publisher.

Printed in the United States of America
10 9 8 7 6 5 4 3 2 1

Main entry under title:
Using What We Know about At-Risk Youth: Lessons from the Field

A Technomic Publishing Company book
Bibliography: p.
Includes index p. 255

Library of Congress Catalog Card No. 94-60208
ISBN No. 1-56676-147-6

This Volume is sincerely dedicated to the Youth of Tomorrow, which includes our newest addition—Bobby

CONTENTS

IV. NETWORKING ACTIVITIES AND RESOURCES

FOREWORD

This volume marks the beginning of a series of publications that will examine what is known about youth at-risk of dropping out of school. The series editor, Robert Morris, has compiled within this first volume a unique general analysis of the field with appropriate current research in various areas of at-riskness. Individual authors have focused not only on the content of programs and methodology but on the *structure and process of change.* What they are looking for is dramatic change—in at-risk programs, in student achievement, and in the culture of the school—at all levels: district, building, individual, and university. They see restructuring—integrating the change effort at all of the various levels—as a requirement, not an option.

Change and growth are endemic in our complex modern society; the school or staff which does not change and grow is destined to atrophy; to become obsolete and to be a burden rather than a bulwark to us and to the communities we serve.

Using What We Know about At-Risk Youth: Lessons from the Field addresses the concerns of educators and society for what should be taught in schools today. It presents recognized experts' thoughts about such things as content and organization of disciplines and answers to questions about students at various levels of schooling. These answers provide fresh perspective because they are in a social context that recognizes current conditions as well as possibilities for the future. Also, because the authors are concerned with the continuing search for strategies that promote learning and thinking, they have considered what is known about how students learn and have related that knowledge to the nature of curriculum content, instructional practices and alternative programs. The authors maintain that the process of schooling must be rethought periodically to ensure that what is taught and how it is taught are both accurate and relevant to ensure that the entire school's population has an equal chance of graduating.

This book presents cogent, concrete and discipline-specific material in a way that should enable decision makers to translate the recommendations into workable interpretations. Other decisions appropriate for individual states, districts, and schools must be made with respect to implementation strategies, time allocations for each activity, and specific activities within programs. The interrelationships among alternative at-risk programs are left for local consideration, as are plans for community and business involvement and preparation required for innovative new programs.

Using What We Know about At-Risk Youth: Lessons from the Field offers a framework of specific concepts that can be revised or expanded in response to community expectations and needs of particular students. This volume is thus a starting point for addressing issues and serving students in at-risk situations. It is meant to serve as a beginning for planning the high-quality programs we all hope to see in our schools.

JAY SMINK
National Dropout Prevention Center
Clemson University

CONTRIBUTORS

Joseph Allen, *Assistant Professor, Department of Psychology, Gilmer Hall, University of Virginia, Charlottesville, VA 22903; (0) (804) 982-4727, FAX (804) 982-4766*

Maggie Bowden, *Assistant Superintendent, Meriwether County Schools, P.O. Box 70, Greenville, GA 30222; (0) (706) 672-4297, FAX (706) 672-1618*

John A. Bucci, *Associate Professor, Educational Leadership and Foundations of Education, Rhode Island College, 600 Mt. Pleasant Ave., Providence, RI 02908; (0) (401) 456-8063, FAX (401) 456-8379*

Joel L. Burdin, *Coordinator and Professor, Programs in Educational Administration and Supervision, Frostburg State University, Department of Educational Administration, Frostburg, MD 21532; (0) (301) 689-4352, FAX (301) 689-7032*

Marie Carbo, *Executive Director, National Reading Styles Institute, P.O. Box 39, Roslyn Heights, NY 11577; (0) (516) 248-8002, FAX (516) 248-8105*

Don Richard Castle, *Associate Professor of Education, Ashland University, 323 Bixler Hall, Ashland, OH 44805; (0) (419) 289-5203, FAX (419) 289-5097*

Margaree S. Crosby, *Associate Professor of Education, College of Education/Elementary and Secondary, Clemson University, 407-A Tillman Hall, Clemson, SC 29634; (0) (803) 656-5116, FAX (803) 656-1322*

Karla Driemeier, *Director of STARS Program, Rockwood School District, 1626 Hawkins Rd., Fenton, MO 63026; (0) (314) 225-3822*

Leona Eggert, *Associate Professor, Principal Investigator, Reconnecting At-Risk Youth, University of Washington, Psychosocial Nursing Dept. SC-76, T-417 Health Sciences Bldg., Seattle, WA 98195; (0) (206) 543-9455, FAX (206) 685-9551*

David E. Engel, *Heinz Professor of Education, University of Pittsburgh, 5 M 37 Forbes Quadrangle, Pittsburgh, PA 15260; (0) (412) 648-7115, FAX (412) 648-1784*

Dorothy Fielder, *Teacher Education Program, Westminster College of Salt Lake, 1840 S. 1300 East, Salt Lake City, UT 84105; (0) (801) 488-1623, FAX (801) 466-6916*

Kathy Herre, *Coordinator, Teen-Outreach Program, 660 First Ave., Association of Junior Leagues International, New York, NY 10016-3241; (0) (212) 683-1515, FAX (212) 481-7196*

Ladeen Howard, *Lead Teacher, Academic Education Services, Roosevelt Warm Springs Institute for Rehabilitation, P.O. Box 1000–Schoolhouse, Warm Springs, GA 31830; (0) (706) 655-5231, FAX (706) 655-5232*

Dennis N. Jackson, *Manager, Educational Opportunity Program for At-Risk Students, Indiana Department of Education, Room 229 State House, Indianapolis, IN 46204-2798; (0) (317) 232-0590, FAX (317) 232-9121*

Lyle C. Jensen, *Professor, Division of Education, Baldwin-Wallace College, 275 Eastland Rd., Berea, OH 44017-2088; (0) (216) 826-2166, FAX (216) 826-3779*

Gabriel Kuperminc, *Doctoral Candidate, U VA, 102 Gilmer Hall, Charlottesville, VA 22903; (0) (804) 982-5042, FAX (804) 982-4766*

Carolyn McKinley, *Lead Teacher–Academic Education Services, Roosevelt Warm Springs Institute for Rehabilitation, P.O. Box 1000–Schoolhouse, Warm Springs, GA 31830; (0) (706) 655-5231, FAX (706) 655-5232*

Cindy W. Moore, *Doctoral Candidate, University of Virginia, Department of Psychology, Gilmer Hall, Charlottesville, VA 22903-2477; (0) (804) 924-0670, FAX (804) 982-4766*

Robert C. Morris, *Professor of Education, Department of Secondary Education, West Georgia College, 1600 Maple Street, Carrollton, GA 30118; (0) (404) 836-6564, FAX (404) 836-6729*

Michael K. Newman, *Mental Health Counselor/Adult Educator, A-O-P Community Mental Health Center, 200 McGee Rd., Anderson, SC 29625; (0) (803) 260-2220, FAX (803) 260-2225*

Grace C. Osediacz, *Executive Director, Interagency Collaborative of Newport, RI, Thompson Junior High School, 39 Broadway, Newport, RI 02840; (0) 401 849-3426, FAX (401) 849-8770*

Emma M. Owens, *Assistant Professor, College of Education/Elementary and Secondary, 407-F Tillman Hall, Clemson University, Clemson, SC 29634; (0) (803) 656-3482, FAX (803) 656-1322*

Elizabeth C. Perna, *Dropout Prevention Education Research Assistant, Dropout Prevention, School District Poudre R-1, Fort Collins, Colo., 2540 LaPorte Ave., Fort Collins, CO 80521; (0) (303) 490-3241, FAX (303) 490-3247*

Susan Philliber, *Senior Partner, Philliber Research Associates, 28 Main St., Accord, NY 12404; (0) (914) 626-2126, FAX (914) 626-3206*

Vann Phillips, *Adult Literacy Instructor, Roosevelt Warm Springs Institute for Rehabilitation, P.O. Box 1000—Schoolhouse, Warm Springs, GA 31830; (0) (706) 655-5231, FAX (706) 655-5232*

Gail M. Powell-Cope, *Assistant Professor, College of Nursing, University of South Florida, 12901 Bruce B. Downs Blvd., Tampa, FL; (0) (813) 974-9208, FAX (813) 974-5418*

Alice E. Presson, *Associate Director for Evaluation, SREB—State Vocational Consortium, Southern Regional Education Board, 592—Tenth Street N.W., Atlanta, GA 30318; (0) (404) 875-9211, FAX (404) 872-1477*

Sandra Pritz, *Research Specialist, Center on Education and Training for Employment, The Ohio State University, 1900 Kenny Road, Columbus, OH 43210-1090; (0) (800) 848-4815, FAX (614) 292-1260*

Jack E. Rawlinson, *Director, Southeastern IL Vocational System, 112 N. Gum St., Harrisburg, IL 62946; (0) (618) 253-5581, FAX (618) 252-8472*

Rhonda Rowland, *S.T.A.R.S. Director, Schertz-Cibolo-Universal City ISD, 1060 Elbel Road, Schertz, TX 78154; (0) (210) 659-0133, FAX (210) 659-2388*

Jay Smink, *Executive Director, National Dropout Prevention Center, Clemson University, Box 345111, Clemson, SC 29634-5111; (0) (800) 443-6392, FAX (803) 656-0136*

Ellen M. Snow, *Education Consultant, Educational Associates, 745 East Mulberry Ave., Suite 750, San Antonio, TX 78212; (0) (210) 732-9955, FAX (210) 735-2286*

Edward B. Strauser, *Assistant Professor, School of Education, Armstrong State College, Victor Hall, 11935 Abercorn St., Savannah, GA 31419; (0) (912) 921-5541, FAX (912) 925-5209*

Wenifort C. Washington, *Executive Assistant, School Improvement/Special Services, Akron Public Schools, Staff Development Center, 65 Steiner Ave., Akron, OH 44301; (0) (216) 434-1661, X-3133, FAX (216) 434-9515*

John W. Wilson, *Regional Superintendent, Southeastern Illinois Vocational System, 112 N. Gum St., Harrisburg, IL 62946; (0) (618) 253-5581, FAX (618) 252-8472*

I

UNDERSTANDING STUDENTS AT-RISK

ROBERT C. MORRIS

1

Introduction: *The Problem, Its Difficulties, and Our Approaches*

If you believe you learn best by being involved in the process, if you are intrigued by the ambiguity and complexity of our age, our profession, our hopes and fears, this volume and subsequent volumes to follow are being written with you in mind. We live in a time of much conflict and uncertainty, a time of flagging confidence and mounting problems. The search for purpose in life as well as in education continues with little evidence of resolution. At the same time we live in an atmosphere of promise and excitement, a time of new break throughs and opportunity for personal and social fulfillment.

However one analyzes the frustration, behaviors and attitudes of troubled youth and their oftentimes seemingly "aimless existence," one fact is becoming increasingly clear. That is that in a society undergoing a revolution in its folkways, norms, and values, that its youth (quite possibly all of them to some degree) are at risk. Extrapolating selected perceptions from the entire spectrum of human behavior, one notices the fragility as well as the breakdown of traditional family life. Also, given the rise in numbers of structurally dysfunctional families, a rising divorce rate, the prominence of single-parent households, and childhoods victimized by violence, sexual abuse and incest, one can readily witness major impacts on a child's social and emotional development. These kinds of events all affect our youth's behaviors. They can twist, shape or disorient psychological and social functioning and the multiple relationships each of us has from childhood through young adulthood. They are often the essence of at-riskness.

While most young people successfully negotiate the transition from one life stage to the next by developing positive values and building strong relationships, for some it is an experience of pain, anger and uncertainty. And for what seems an ever-growing number of youth experiencing feelings of low self-esteem, isolation and depression, life-taking and self-harming behaviors are often the tragic consequences. As no surprise, a significant number of young people are mired in developmental problems. The school's task through it all remains that of educating the whole child, nurturing the personal and social aspects of a child's life and experiences. Since most children spend much of their waking hours in school during their maturing years, the school experience promises no panacea. It does, however, uniquely integrate resources of both educational and mental health. When offered in a systematic, long-term preventive approach, these resources can help to ensure assistance for all students toward building higher self-esteem, enabling students to cope with problems, develop healthy values, and nurture strong relationships from childhood into adult life. This, of course, is not always the case, but necessarily remains a major educational goal.

The effort this volume attempts to deal with is one of closing a "guidance gap" with current schools and community programs. The articles contained in this volume are directed at three basic areas: (1) health — that is, helping a student transfer learning to the real world through age-related activities and exercises; (2) Intermediate intervention where behavior having potential for undermining a student's progress is automatically a target for preventive/remedial intervention; and (3) Tertiary intervention, which involves the full range of school resources as well as the specialized resources of a community. These three conceptual areas of effort make up the content of this volume and are interwoven throughout the four sections that follow. Since many of the at-risk students who are currently in or will be coming to our secondary schools are well behind in basic academic skills development, it is highly likely that any and all of the three above-mentioned conceptual areas could be of importance in resolving student problems. The point is not to limit one's review of the contents of this volume to a title or heading that appears too narrow in scope or perspective, but to review and investigate any experience documented in this volume that might appear to affect a reader's concerns.

Precise topics within this text vary considerably, and interestingly only a few common definitions have emerged through the literature. The popular definition of students who are at risk is, by default, those students who are affected most by the risk factors. Those risk factors are: *low achievement, retention in grade, behavior problems, poor attendance, low socioeconomic status, and attendance at schools with large numbers of poor students.* All of these factors are closely related to dropping out of school which, as it turns out, is what the at-risk label is identifying.

Important research has found that by the time students are in the third grade, one can fairly reliably predict which students will ultimately drop out and those who will complete their schooling (Howard and Anders, 1978: Lloyd, 1978; Barber and McClellan, 1987; Hamby, 1989; Slavin, Karweit, and Madden,

1989). These risk factors are usually stress-related and ultimately affect the identification and predictability of dropouts with actual performance as the most reliable predictor.

With the above ideas concerning at risk in mind, this volume looks closely at the "classic dropout." That individual will likely be a member of a racial, ethnic, or language minority group and from a family where education is not a high priority; the individual will have academic difficulties, including the possibility of being behind in grade level; the individual will be bored or frustrated with school. The process of dropping out will often include a growing number of tardies and absences, disruptive classroom behavior, and a decline in academic performance. The classic dropout simply stops coming to school one day.

One common factor brought to light is that schools and school systems that are effective in reducing the numbers of dropouts **do not permit** this classic scenario to reach fruition. Through early identification, the high-risk student **is not permitted** to become just another statistic. Absences or behavior problems are not merely observed; action is taken to understand the causes and to prevent unnecessary repetitions. Where needed, the student is directed to the individual within the school (a counselor, a teacher, or an administrator) who is best prepared to understand the problems of the student and to work with that student in addressing those problems. Students should not be allowed to "disappear," but when the decision to leave school is not reversible, the school should point the dropout to alternative programs and options for keeping the door to an education open. The student, in general, needs to be made to feel that some individual cares, and also, that the school cares.

That individual within the school, (an administrator, counselor, or dropout coordinator), needs to assume responsibility as an advocate for the potential dropout, to insure that a resource response is mobilized in time and in sufficient manner to make a difference to the student. The burden should not however, rest on one individual, no matter how well meaning and skilled that individual might be. A support network of individuals, programs, and organizations must be in place to provide meaningful remedies and alternatives.

At-risk students need multiple resources. It is, therefore, important that schools and school boards network with multiple resources, such as a school/ community policymaking council, involving industrial leaders with a vested interest in children's school success. Groups to be considered include churches, businesses, schools, service clubs, universities, colleges, vociational and technical schools, youth service groups, chambers of commerce, health and social service groups, and local news media.

With a resource network in place, short-and long-range policies and plans can be developed for both in school and in the community. Policies and plans may include:

- Serving at-risk children through the resource network.
- Monitoring and evaluating both school and community programs serving at-risk children.
- Reviewing and monitoring the proactical function of the resource network.

A number of possible program formats offer simple but effective techniques for organizing and managing diverse school/community resources to develop and conduct programs for at-risk children. Numerous studies show that school programs alone are not well equipped to address those nonschool casues which place children at risk of school and life failure. It is therefore, imperative that school boards network with multiple resources (school, community, family, business, and industry) that can serve the needs of at-risk children both in school and outside of school.

The greatest value of the above kind of logic is the kind of effective use that can be made of it. Likewise it is hoped that the data, findings and experiences contained in this intial series volume can help improve activities and programs for at-risk students. Quite possibly the kinds of recommendations and reported information that follow can be used as benchmarks for program improvement, self-evaluation, and raising the levels of awareness in all segments of our communities.

REFERENCES

Barber, L.W. and McClellan, M.C. (1987). Looking atAmerica's Droupout: Who are they? *Phi Delta Kappan*, 69 (4), 264-267.

Hamby, J.V. (1989). How to get an 'A' on your dropout prevention report card. *Educational Leadership*, 46 (5), 21-28.

Howard, M.A.P. and Anderson, R.J. (19780. Early identification of potentioal school dropouts: Aliterature review. *Child Welfare*, 52. 221-231.

Lloyd, D.N. (1978). Prediction of school failure from the third-grade date. *Educational and Psychological Measurement,* 38, 1193-1200.

Slvan, R.E. Karweit, N.L., and Madden, N..A. (1989). *Effective programs for students at-risk*. Boston: Allyn and Bacon

DON RICHARD CASTLE

2

The Dynamics of Educational Systems and Low Achieving Dislocated Students: *An Intellectual Approach to School and Business Partnerships*

Historically education in the United States has served to support an achievement conscious and a merit ordered society. Evidence of merit and achievement is an essential criteria for acquiring social and economic benefits. Certificates, diplomas, and degrees set the standard for the distribution of the tokens of a meritocratic society and the subsequent organization and structure of the social hierarchy. Correlations between higher education attainment and social and economic success are undeniable. Those individuals who choose to spend more time and greater effort studying, should receive the benefits of educational success. The long term expectation of receiving benefits is a tradition of the educational system in the United States. Students committed to completing educational goals have been the traditional focus of school systems in this country. Much of the rationale for education emanates from the concept of equal opportunity for all students. They simply must take advantage of this opportunity and function on an equal basis with all others in the system. Yet students do not achieve at the same rate and level (Green, 1980).

The recent effort to increase opportunity for greater achievement for all students has become part of the national conscience of education. Special classes and intervention programs abound that are designed to tend to a variety of educational problems and issues. In most instances educational intervention of the last two decades has attempted to provide educational possibilities for the lower end students who chance suffering the misfortune of becoming social and economic liabilities.

Obviously education is important in sustaining the traditions, ideas, and values supporting the United States. Those citizens who attain high levels of education acquire the negotiability necessary to control their place in society and to acquire a greater share of the distribution of wealth and social status. Those who do not attain acceptable levels of education, subject themselves to society's pronouncements, tend to receive the inequities the country has to offer.

Educational response to the "ebb and flow" of the presence of high achieving and low achieving students is not a conscious process. Rather, educational systems are really dynamics that tend to be responsible to the presence of the largest category of student conditions. The systems have life and do gravitate toward focusing on the impact group. Driven by the desire for attainment and equal opportunity, educational systems expand, differentiate and intensifies in an evolutionary response to student populations. When education loses its importance, the reason tends to be the loss of social and economic attainment.

This characteristic of education in the United States may be viewed as a defect inherent in a "meritocratic society". This view of education may be especially predominant in deindustrialized urban settings of the United States where the presence of low achieving students is greater. Poverty and the related stress is a definite factor contributing to low educational achievement. Promoting the necessity of educational achievement to youngsters who see no connection between learning and economic and social benefits is difficult. The long term prospects of receiving the benefits of education fail to inspire low achieving students of poverty (Walker, 1990).

Often referred to as dislocated students, education seems to offer little hope and has little credibility for these youngsters. The dynamics of the educational systems do respond though. The subtle yet pervasive loss of industry in the United States produced and continues to produce dislocated students at an alarming rate. However, the educational dynamics begins as the systems responds to the necessity of re-establishing equal opportunity for all students. Logically, the increase in dislocated students diffuses equal educational opportunity and the hope for eventual negotiability (Fleisher & Kniesner, 1980).

One of the main problems is that low achieving dislocated students do not have a concise understanding of the relationship between education and earning powers. This relationship must be made clear to those in question in order to correct the social and economic conditions that plague the nation. The subject has important implications for the dislocated in that appropriate doses of schooling can improve their chances for employment. The human capital investment theory, which focuses on education and training, seems the appropriate course of action for a nation that faces a crisis in that area (Sheldon, 1987).

Another problem facing the training of the culturally different is illiteracy. A good number of low achieving dislocated students do not have the reading and writing skills necessary for retraining (Colander, 1981).

Solving the problem of illiteracy seems to rest on the idea that written and oral communication or language must be connected to solving problems. Children must understand the concept that language is for solving problems. The inability to understand the problem solving basis for language disconnects viable language use from the student and the educational setting. Consequently a number of conditions overtake children.

For example sensory use of language becomes primary in that children will continue to grow and develop while using language to deal with lower order needs. Even as children grow into adolescent and young adult stages, language function continues to be sensory based.

Higher order thinking and problem resolving strategies are not part of students at-risk thinking patterns. In essence the opportunity must be made available for thinking at higher levels to occur using language to solve problems. Pertinent to these strategies are numerous learning theories that instigate learning. Obviously one goal is to move these students from external sensory oriented thinking to the internalization of the process of language usage. This will likely begin to develop as the need to solve compelling problems take hold of the students. With teachers acting as coaches and facilitators students will be given just enough assistance to set the cognitive actions in motion necessary to find solutions. At lower functioning levels reading simple directions may require assistance while at the higher level researching material and recording findings may require assistance. Part of the strategy emerges when students make errors in their efforts to solve problems. Rather than viewing the errors as mistakes, teachers will see errors as evidence that language is being used and acquired in seeking solutions. Since one of the inherent concepts is that language skills toward higher thinking evolves, students will have ample opportunity to zero in on solution strategies. Appropriate and useful language will become part of the students growth and development through the various career stage sequences (Good & Brophy. 1990).

Much of the rationale for this approach emanates from the power of external cues to influence and control decisions made that decide intellectual capacities of students. The link between written verbal ability and intellectual ability is under tremendous scrutiny. Students at-risk are certainly in danger of being relegated to intellectually inferior educational stations due to the frustrations resulting from written verbal disfunctionality. Add the tendency to display negative behavior, students at-risk are deemed intellectually inferior. Notable to this plan for linking schools and business is the belief that language becomes useful for solving problems when comprehension takes place on a number of levels prior to use and application toward problem solving. Beginning with understanding simple step-by-step directions to complex higher understanding, students will be taught and learn enough about the problem to begin to search for a solution. At this point, teachers will begin assisting students on an individual basis (Dembo, 1991).

Much research has been devoted to what makes students want to learn. Their career education model includes essential tenets fundamental to well established research and conclusions reached during the development of this program.

(1) Students must have the opportunity to contribute to their own learning.

(2) Students are naturally curious and will search for answers to satisfy their curiosity.

(3) Students must feel a sense of accomplishment and have support for further accomplishment.

(4) Students must know that who and what they are is important to the unique contribution they bring to society.

(5) Students must learn in a manner where the traditional segmented curriculum is unified into a whole child learning interdisciplinary educational environment.

(6) Students learn better when others are involved with them in a cooperative setting with teachers being one segment of the setting.

(7) Students will learn better when they are in a learning environment that uses a team approach to teaching for solving the problems presented to students.

(8) Students may move about laterally to survey interests and curiosity before moving up sequentially.

(9) Students will learn better when time is not an element for evaluation.

(10) Students will learn when they understand that credentialling means criteria for negotiating with society for a better life economically, socially, emotionally and intellectually.

The intellectual approach to a school business partnership rests on the belief that students will make connections with learning when the learning represents a viable interest. Traditionally most school business partnerships involve the enhancement of psychmotor development while most components of cognitive and affective learning are diminished. This program involves three domains of learning using a multi-disciplinary integrated thematic approach. Based on the belief that the mind is always learning, field based career business issues will require an intellectual solution that involves math, science, and language.

For example part of the project is directed toward a medical technology in which science and math would likely be used to deal with the particular issue. The issue may be how to deal with people in a convalescent setting when only so much money is available. Add to the issue a contagious disease. The problem evolves. Literature may be incorporated into the learning to make students aware and sensitive to the situation. In the process of solving the problem students are finding connections. These connections between learning and careers begin to evolve for a number of well documented reasons. Being exposed to a variety of environments and experiences, learning from teachers and researchers and the interpretation of experience into symbols of meaning comprise the nature of this intellectual approach to career business partnerships.

Even though this program is in the planning stages, there is overwhelming evidence that implementation is essential for the challenges students must face. For those categorized as at-risk the challenge begins much earlier. In essence for them the challenge begins early in the formative years. Students at-risk must understand that learning is something that will give them freedom from poverty and deprivation.

A major problem facing the work force of the near future is the concept of credentialling which is having proof of qualifications for employment. This is extremely significant for those skill jobs to which the young and inexperienced will apply in that a minimum education will be required to get into the door while testing will permit the person to stay. It is likely that the testing will have little correlation with the job or job performance, for the idea is to test intelligence, not the ability to do a particular job. Schools will have to face this demand made by industry that intelligence is a requirement for employment. No longer will a diploma from an accredited high school guarantee the graduate permanent employment since schools will be required to prove that their graduates know what they have been taught. Their diplomas will have to represent a useful amount of learning (Gilder, 1981).

Clearly the diploma must once again represent something more than surviving thirteen years of formal education. The diploma must come to represent respect for those who earn them. Educational reform efforts of the last two decades have generated a great deal of chaos and contradiction about what should be taught, how it should be taught, how children best learn and even the idea that the concept of education in this country needs to be totally changed, a kind of a scrap heap approach. To strike a balance the outcomes of learning and effective child centered strategies must be part of the restructuring efforts. Philosophical differences among reformers appear equally significant when considering the necessity of content mastery and the cruciality of providing learning to students with a multitude of issues, problems, needs and perceptions regarding their place in the educational system.

Adding to the chaos has been a sense of desperation to change the educational system in the United States. These efforts have tended to lack vision and focus. However the educational big picture now seems to be coming into view as a result of this slow urgency and chaos. It appears that restructuring and reform now include all the school population. Dislocated students at-risk have become a viable ingredient in the educational process in that they are no longer the throw aways of the past. Their exit from the school system must include the credentials necessary to negotiate for a productive place in the economic mainstream.

Recent surveys conducted in a number of heavily deindustrialized urban settings indicate that dislocated students at-risk have definitive ideas about what school can do to provide necessary learning. Surprisingly, the results indicated that students at risk had more wide ranging visions than satisfying sensory economic needs. Responses showed that the arts and humanities are important to students at-risk. Essential to the educational process for students at risk is that what is taught must be compellingly interesting. As survey results showed, students are traditionally unable to make a compelling connection with what was being taught and how it was being taught. The dynamic of the educational system appears to have found direction in supporting the need for connections and compelling interest. Future world conditions play a major role in this dynamic according to demographers such as Harold Hodgkinson. This direction seems to focus on environmental concerns, communication and computation skills, creative thinking, human relations, analytical and problem solving skills and strategies, decision making, and values as part of the credentialling of students. Self esteem, self direction and motivation and intrinsics are part of this direction. Breaking the traditional time and organizational structures along with the evolvement of child centered, child enhancing teaching techniques is essential.

REFERENCES

Colander, David C. (1981). *Solutions to Unemployment.* New York: Harcourt Brace Jovanovich, Inc., pp. 156-158.

Dembo, Myron (1991). *Applying Educational Psychology in the Classroom.* Longman Press.

Fleisher, Belton M. & Kniesner, Thomas J. (1980). *Theory, Evidence and Policy: Labor Economics,* 2nd ed., Englewood Cliffs, N.J.: Prentice Hall, pp. 358-359.

Gilder, George (1981). *Wealth and Poverty.* New York: Basic Book, Inc., pp. 141-143.

Good, Thomas L. & Brophy, Jere E. (1990). *Educational Psychology: A Realistic Approach.* Longman Press.

Green, Thomas F. (1980). *Predicting the Behavior of the Educational System.* Syracuse: Syracuse University Press.

Sheldon, Scott C. (1987). Work and School Hand in Hand. *Mansfield News Journal,* 25 February.

Walker, Decker (1990). *Fundamentals of Curriculum.* Harcourt Brace Javonovick, San Diego.

DAVID E. ENGEL

3

School Leavers in American Society: *Interviews with School Drop-Outs/Stop-Outs*

Our principle reason for interviewing students who had to leave school before high school completion was to ascertain why they had done so. Previously we had not found clear data on that question. There was much quantitative evidence reporting numbers, such as, percentage by school district of drop-outs. So, while our interviews included a number of factors to provide us with a more complete profile of the early school leaver, our focus was on the reasons students could state for dropping out. Additional factors in our interview protocol included: family background, peer associations, perceptions of school personnel [e.g. teachers, administrators, counsellors, security and other ancillary personnel], school climate, neighborhood relations, media influences, recreational activities, field trips and travel. But the target was why the students left school before completion.

In aggregate a few factors stand out. Initially we found some predictable problems. Among teenage females, pregnancy was a major problem. The services the school district provide were not judged to be adequate. After delivery the number of in-school slots for child care were not up to the demand—a total of 150 for the school districts' 11 high schools, including such alternative schools as the high school for Creative and Performing Arts (CAPA). So it was not uncommon that a teenage mother left school because there was "no baby-sitter."

A second major problem among both males and females was failure in academic performance. Students reported that they fell behind in academic work. They missed turning in assignments and absenteeism increased. While it is difficult to identify such factors as causal, there is a clear conjunction between dropping out and absenteeism. Students who experienced increasing absenteeism were candidates for dropping out—what we have identified as "fadeouts."

Deeper analysis of interview transcripts suggests equally if not more troubling reasons for leaving school before completion. In a variety of ways and in several settings, students revealed a lack of support systems. Typically, in combination rather than singly, students experienced a lack of home reinforcement and in-school support. Predominantly the "stopouts" interviewed were from a single parent home with a mother as head of household. Education/schooling was not an obvious value communicated in the home environment. Sometimes the home was additionally complicated by "problems with a step-father" or with a mother's "boyfriend." In most instances, those interviewed felt that they were left on their own, at an early age.

We asked about student's perception of teachers. Our questions were open-ended eliciting comments on the best and worst. The best teachers, a distinct minority among those interviewed, were seen as caring individuals. For some teachers there was apparent appreciation. As one student put it, the best teachers "took time." One teacher was identified as a "big brother." Others, in general, tried to give extra help when students had difficulty understanding school subjects.

In contrast, the poorest teachers were portrayed as uncaring. Many said their worst teachers were mean [i.e. lacking in patience, talked at them, presumably, did not listen to them, or attempt to understand students' problems]. So, we have come to identify "caring" as a major discriminator of teachers.

A preliminary conclusion in this regard is that teachers can make a difference in minimizing the drop-out rate of a school district. One might conclude that school was a "turnoff" for students interviewed because many teachers were a "turn-off." More often than not teachers were perceived as favoring the brighter, achieving students as researchers we are cautious about this factor. We have not been inclined to indict teachers. We recognize, despite some negative reports in national studies, that elementary and secondary teachers experience some difficult circumstances, such as, full daily schedules, burdensome paper work, less than enthusiastic students. While increased compensation in recent years can offset such matters and reward the teacher's life, it is still not an easy profession.

Historical studies [e.g. Altenbaugh] have indicated that teaching is a kind of humanistic missionary work. There remains an important human connection between teacher and learner. And where the connection is made between what the teacher is there to impart and the learner can internalize for the development of a life career, teaching is a key contact, especially for adolescents, with the next generation. But when the contact is minimal or of perceived low quality a key support factor in the schools' support system is missing. Coupled with a lack of reinforcement in the neighborhood and home for the values of learning in the formation and development of life, students interviewed tended to exhibit patterns of drifting through and then out of school without any clear sense of why they were there in the first place.

Other studies [e.g. Cuban] have indicated that teaching has not changed over the years. As one teacher who played the role of student in colleagues' classroom for a year noted: Most teachers teach in much the same way they were taught—in an essentially didactic, teachercentered mode...The teacher knows the material and presents it to students, whose role is to absorb it. (Cuban p. 231) She went on to evaluate what was happening in class after class was the nurturing of "incredible passivity." (Ibid)

Without a sense of the importance of learning the "stop-outs" indicated their best subjects were those that were easy and/or where a teacher made it "fun"; while their worst classes were those that were "boring" or where the teacher did not sufficiently explain the material.

The bitter irony reflected in the interviews—and we will comment more on this later—was that students only began to develop a rudimentary sense of the value of education or an understanding of their lack of it after they had left school. The "stop-outs" upon returning to the educational program of the Job Corps did so very largely for reasons of employment not for the love of learning. As one stated: "I need an education to get a real job."

While teachers are a major influence on the experience of the "stop-outs," perceptions of other school personnel is not unimportant. Here we report student perceptions in descending order of authority of school personnel, not necessarily in importance. School administrators, essentially building principals and vice-principals were seen as those "who kept order" and occasionally walk hallways, in contrast to the district's definition of the principal as "instructional leader." Assistant principals, not surprisingly were identified as the enforcer of discipline codes. One interviewee, an exception not the rule, admitted that he had "pulled" a gun in school and later met with the building assistant-principal. His testimony was that he was treated fairly, despite the severity of the offense. Others, however, as we shall see are not so sanguine about their treatment by school administrators and security personnel.

Another conclusion for many females, not all, was pregnancy. Child care was the root problem. The Pittsburgh public schools have some limited child care options. One alternative high school, with a self-paced program has infant care for 28 and five regular high schools have 150 slots for child care and experiences in parenting. But those numbers do not adequately meet the need. Further, any recommendation to increase child care in the district would have to be made in the context of a 40 million dollar shortfall for 1993 and a series of personnel and program cuts. Accordingly, for many teenage mothers the Job Corps, which has a child care program, becomes the only alternative for high school completion.

Is racial discrimination a factor in dropping out of school? Here we had to do some digging in interviews. Most interviewed denied that race made a difference in their school experience. But we came to realize that these denials were based on what students believed should be, not what is. As we probed further we found that there were incidents of racial discrimination—teachers against students, students against students. One female student, African-American, reported that because of her race she was singled out as having stolen from a white female's locker. No evidence of theft was found, but she is convinced that racism was the basis of the charge and the investigation she underwent.

School environment was found to be another factor. Those interviewed reported that while the schools are well kept, they are noisy. In our most recent interviews this past October, 1992, a new factor emerged—teenage gangs. In one high school—really just outside the building—gangs have become a threat. Two rival gangs threaten each other and nonmembers alike. The head of security called for metal detectors to be installed in city secondary schools. Initially the school directors resisted the recommendation; but as the threat of gang activity persisted and as incidents of weapons in some schools was dictated, electronic devices were installed in some high schools on an experimental basis.

I asked one of the "stop-outs" whether this was a recent occurrence, because we had not heard of it until our most recent interviews. His cryptic response ["Since Rodney King"] is not difficult to interpret. Racial tensions seem to be on the increase.

Last May I travelled to New York for a meeting on the Friday after rioting broke out in south central Los Angeles. The bus from the airport crosstown on 34th Street was stalled for half an hour in gridlock about noon time. Sidewalks as well as roadways were jammed, more than the usual lunch time traffic. The bus driver told us that someone had been shot in downtown Brooklyn and that there was looting in a major department store. None of it was true and, despite Mayor Dinkins efforts to dispel them, rumors were flying. Rodney King himself had come on TV in Los Angeles pleading that the looting and rioting cease. New York was spared but only after the rumors had closed a majority of offices and sent workers home early. There was an afternoon of near panic in New York. Shops closed early. Subways were jammed. Lines at bus stops were a block or more long. Tension was high.

Now gangs have emerged as a sign of racial tension and unrest and can be a final threat to a student already uncomfortable in the school environment. But as a factor, the existence of gangs should be seen in combination with other factors enumerated herein. For some interviewees this seems to have been "the straw that broke the camel's back."

Further, to attribute racial tension as a causal basis for the rise of gangs strife is too glib a generalization. In most instances overt gang strife engages just one race. That indicates that another dimension of racial tension is operative. Could it be that frustration over the lack of racial equity is a major contributor to rise of gangs? Is territoriality and the illicit sale of drugs still another contributor to the gang phenomenon? At this point in our research we can only speculate and dig for more substantive evidence. Let me enter a caveat about these findings. They are preliminary but need to be noted. We are still interviewing "stop-outs." So this may be regarded as a progress report.

Further, I would say that what we have uncovered are student perceptions. Their lives have been problematic. Many blame themselves for dropping out of school. Their comments on teachers are not, in the main, excuses for what they have done. They do not blame their SES, although we would see that as a major factor along with a lack of family and community support.

The problem of school drop-outs or the "stop-outs" we have interviewed is more than a school problem. It is a large social problem. So we do not indict the public schools or its teachers and administrators. They have their failures, of course. But the failures are multiple: student failure, teacher failure, family failure, and community failure.

So when you put all of our qualitative data together you see a nest of problems. First, the students themselves. They admit in most cases that they had problems in school—cutting classes, sometimes disruptive, falling behind in school work, family difficulties including pregnancy and child care. Those we interviewed are trying to overcome these recognized difficulties.

Second, in the nest of problems is a lack of support systems. Although the students interviewed would not state it this way, their responses indicate that the home, the community, the school system did not provide either sufficient incentive or reinforcement to continue schooling. If such support is not present in their lives, where is a surrogate to be found?

In another group of questions we asked subjects about their experience with media. Questions probed students' reading, watching television, cinema, reading newspapers and magazines and books. Most interviewees read more than we had initially expected. AfricanAmerican "stop-outs" tended to read magazines oriented toward their experience, like Jet and Ebony. As one student put it, this was a way "to find out about...(her) heritage." Males tended to read the sports section of the newspaper. Movies and reading tended to focus on horror or "scary" subjects. Stephen King was a favorite author. Television viewing focused on news reports and entertainment, such as soaps and sit-coms [especially Cosby]. Viewing hours varied widely from 1-6 hours daily. Whether television viewing is an escape from other elements of life is an open question. But we did not detect excessive television dependency.

The tendency toward horror films and books is not statistically significant.

Still it raises several questions. Does such material speak to vicarious urges? Is "scary" material a healthy escape? Do "stop-outs" view such as representing reality?

CONCLUSION

At this juncture, we report a number of factors which make up the nest of problems derived from interviewed school leavers. No single factor can be regarded as the cause for leaving school before completion. In different ways, depending on the personal situation of subjects interviewed, one or more of these factors influenced the students' situation.

1. **Student Failure:** In many of the interviews students recognized that they did not complete school because they themselves had failed. They did not complete assignments. They could not cope with the school environment. In many cases, learning was not interesting. Why it was not will be examined shortly in terms of the relations with teachers. In general, however, students exhibited a failure to fit into the school environment, especially at the secondary school level. They applauded peers who have completed. In some instances, they voiced regret that they had done so. Had they been absent less from what they regard as a dull/boring regimen, would it have made a difference? Possibly. But apparently nothing sparked their sense of valuing continuance in schooling.

2. **Teacher Failure:** When interviewees were asked to identify good and bad teachers, "good" teachers stood out as a distinct minority. As we have reported earlier, teachers , with noted exceptions, were a turn-off and, hence, school was a turn-off. So, we question whether in general teachers have been sensitive to the need to make connections with their students. Are teachers sensitive to students who need reinforcement in their self-esteem? Do teachers recognize that some students who do not see learning as instrumental to their development as individuals or as social participants need greater care than those who achieve? Is there equal attention given to those who are not achieving? In any case, teachers are seen as a central factor in the retention of students.

3. **Family Failure:** A major influence in the retention of students for school completion seems to be the family. Most of those interviewed were from single parent homes. Often the home was a troubled environment. In some cases, a mother was intent on struggling to make ends meet. Or, there was discontinuity with a parent [usually a mother] for a variety of reasons, e.g. lack of communication, trouble with a "boy friend," sometimes the mother's,

sometimes the student's, controversy with mother sometimes leading to leaving the domicile. Apparently, lack of stability in the home is a factor in leaving school before completion.

4. **Community Failure:** In few of our interviews the community [defined as neighbors or community agencies] was a significant support factor. More often than not, interviewees had not availed themselves of community programs [e.g. church after school services, agency programs like YMCA or YWCA]. So, we question whether such programs are sufficiently attractive to the potential "stop-out"/drop out. Whether community programs can contribute to a support for the potential or actual school leavers remains an important question.

5. **The Media:** Here we look at subjects' involvement with electronic, print media, and cinema. Stop-outs do read, contrary to our early expectations. They read newspapers, magazines and books. Recreational reading of books tended to center on adventure/horror pieces. Stephen King was a favorite author. Magazine reading reflected African American students' need in Jet and Ebony to gain a sense of their heritage. Males tended to focus on sports reporting in newspapers and magazines. Current news events were not a topic of interest, nor were television documentaries or news oriented broadcasts [e.g. MacNeil-Lehrer, Washington Week in Review, This Week with David Brinkley, Nightline] given noticeable attention.

The hours of television viewing varied from one to six hours per day with an emphasis on entertainment, e.g. sports, soaps and sit-coms [esp. Cosby]. Both males and females read newspapers without any pattern of regularity or sense of interest in national or world affairs.

Overall, media outlets were used as means of escape or to reinforce identity. What seemed to be missing was desire to keep up with national and world affairs and intellectual/cultural awareness or enlightenment.

6. **Gang Threat:** Only in recent interviews did the threat od gangs to these students become apparent. Street gangs are a growing phenomenon and have become visible in the last year or so. Earlier the mayor of the city somewhat naively denied their existence. Similarly building administrators stated that gangs were not in existence inside their schools. Such testimony, of course, overlooked their presence outside and nearby. While security measures within buildings is not tax in general, the psychological presence of the gangs cannot be denied. Nor can the city deny the existence of gangs on the streets. In large measure, the gangs are clones of those in other cities, notably Los Angeles and Chicago, with common names and symbolism—names, such as Crips and Bloods, distinguishable by the color of attire. Although the gang members are distinctly from minorities and are a significant force in certain geographical

neighborhoods, one cannot overlook that their existence is attributable to the general racism in American society. Borne of frustration over a lack of opportunity for racial minorities, they seek outlets which are typically destructive.

The students who brought this to our attention were all African American males who were not gang members. Going to school, however, represented a threat somewhat in the form: "If you're not for us, you're against us." As a consequence, these students left school for reasons of gang threat, very possibly among others noted above.

Final Comment: The drop-out problem is not simply a school problem. It is a larger social problem of which the schools are a part. It involves students who recognize their own failure in schooling and also their own often unrecognized need for greater self-esteem. It involves teacher failure to regard their special needs and to devise ways to make contact with those outside the mainstream of students who achieve. Do we write them off as "losers?" Can we afford such waste of human life and reinforce the existence of a perpetual underclass?

But there is good news, as we have reported elsewhere. There is life after dropping out of school. If and when students recognize their need to complete high school and the available educational opportunities beyond, a better vision of life chances is potential. But the obstacles for those better life chances must be identified and confronted and become incorporated in whatever vision is promulgated for the nation's and, more importantly, their future.

This paper is a part of a larger ongoing study of students who have left the Pittsburgh Public Schools, Pittsburgh, PA before completing high school. Data from students are compiled from interviews with early school leavers who have returned to complete the GED at the Pittsburgh Job Corps Center.

REFERENCES

Richard J. Altenbaugh, *The Teachers Voice*. London: The Falmer Press, 1992.

Larry Cuban, *How Teachers Taught*. New York and London: Longman, 1984. p. 231

GAIL M. POWELL-COPE
LEONA L. EGGERT

4

Psychosocial Risk and Protective Factors: *Potential High School Dropouts Versus Typical Youth*

> *"Hey man! Let's skip class...let's go get high. School's a drag!...we're 10 minutes late for 3rd already anyway." It's cool I think, an' so I say "O.K." ...an' so we go out, wherever, ya know...an' 10 minutes goes by..an' I think, "Oh, Wow! I shouldn'a skipped today!" (Eggert & Nicholas, 1992)*

In an ethnographic study of high school students who skipped school, it was found that "skippin' an' gettin' high" was a cover term used to link the essential features of skipping school as a game (Eggert & Nicholas, 1992). These essential features included students' speech styles, rules for playing and scoring, and problems and consequences of the game for themselves as well as for key players in the school environment. Furthermore, "usin an' dealin" drugs was a cover metaphor students used to describe a major event that co-occurred with skipping (Eggert, 1993). It became clear that for this group of students at-risk of school failure, drug use was a critical dimension of their culture and interactions with peers. Findings from this ethnography led to further exploration of the school, personal, and social network characteristics of this high-risk group compared to students not at-risk of school failure, that is, "typical" students. Initially, Eggert and Herting (1993) found that high-risk youth reported greater drug involvement than did youth in two national surveys. In addition, an intervention study entitled Reconnecting At-Risk Youth (RAY), was initiated to prevent dropout, and decrease drug use and depression among high-risk youth (Eggert, Herting, & Nicholas, 1988).

Prevention studies that link dropout with drug abuse are critical. Alarming numbers of adolescents are at high-risk of dropping out of school (Rosenbaum, 1985) and are abusing drugs such as alcohol, cocaine, and inhalants (Johnson, Bachman, & O'Malley, 1990). While drug use among adolescents has shown recent declines, this appears to be mostly among casual or experimental users. Rates for frequent users have not dropped as sharply (Schinke, Botvin, & Orlandi, 1991) and potential school dropouts are at high-risk for progression toward drug abuse (Brown & Mills, 1987; NIDA, 1991; OSAP, 1989).

The goal of this study is to develop a risk/protective factors model for youth at-risk for school failure and dropout by elucidating factors in four domains that both increase and decrease their level of risk; (1) personal (e.g. emotional distress, drug involvement, emotional well-being), (2) peer (e.g. deviant bonding, peer support for school), (3) family (e.g. family distress, family bonding, family support for school), and (4) school (e.g. frequent changes in schools, truancy, academic failure, school bonding, and teacher support). In developing a risk/protective factors model of school dropout, we relied on literature from adolescent alcohol and drug abuse theory (Jessor, 1991; 1993) with its focus on individual, family, and network factors. Our assumption, that many of the same risk and protective factors present for drug abusers are also present for potential school dropouts, is based on evidence that school deviance (truancy, poor performance) and drug involvement are co-occuring behaviors within an adolescent risk lifestyle (Jessor, 1993).

Studies such as this that detail the features of high-risk students' lives are needed in order to develop effective and comprehensive prevention programs for potential school dropouts and to deliver effective intervention programs for those who already have dropped out. To date descriptive studies have focused on risk factors, or indicators of co-occuring problems. While these are necessary pieces of information, painting a complete picture requires examining the positive aspects of these youths' lives, and identifying potential strengths on which to build prevention programs.

The theoretical underpinnings for this study are derived from health promotion models and prevention literature (Bandura, 1977; Curtis, 1992; Dougherty, et al., 1992; Eggert & Herting, 1991; Hurrelman, 1990; Weissberg, Caplan, & Harwood, 1991) and Felner and Felner's (1989) transactional-ecological framework of risk and protective factors that posits common etiological roots for adolescent problem behaviors such as school dropout, substance abuse, and depression. Jessor (1991) explained that traditional epidemiology was concerned with the relationship between biological risk factors and morbidity and mortality (e.g. the link between cholesterol and hypertension) and as science progressed, the notion of risk expanded to include social environmental and behavioral factors, for example stress and dietary patterns. There is, however, a growing awareness of the need to specify protective factors, that is, those personal and social factors that buffer, attenuate, counter, or balance the effects of risk factors (Jessor, 1991). Interventions aimed at a specific health problem can then be targeted to reduce risk while at the same time to strengthen protection against these risks.

The purpose of this paper is to provide a comprehensive picture of potential high school dropouts' lives by comparing them to typical students on a number of risk and protective factors including: (1) personal problems and drug involvement, (2) school experiences, and (3) social network factors (friends, family, support). Understanding this picture is a crucial step in furthering intervention research and in developing effective strategies to curb adolescent school dropout.

Methods: The Reconnecting At-Risk Youth (RAY) Study

Data for these analyses come from an ongoing prevention study entitled, Reconnecting At-Risk Youth (Eggert, Herting, & Nicholas, 1988) which employs a longitudinal, panel design. A stratified random sampling procedure was used to select high-risk youth (potential school dropouts) and typical high school students from a population within one urban school district's four high schools. High-risk students were identified by a computer search of school records for students who were prior dropouts, in the top 25th percentile for absences/semester, and had a pattern of declining school performance. Herting (1990) demonstrated construct validity for this sampling method by finding that it accurately predicted other high-risk behaviors, low school achievement and school dropout over time. Typical youth were randomly selected from the pool of youth created by excluding students defined as high-risk and special education students in the high school population.

Subjects

The sample consisted of 541 youth (337 high-risk and 204 typical) in grades 9 - 12, randomly selected from the pool of high-risk students[1] and typical youth in the district's four high schools. Both the high-risk and typical youth were heterogeneous with respect to age and grade in school. Age ranged from 14 to 19 years (M = 16 years). Both groups contained similar proportions of males and females (51.4% males vs. 48.6% females). The majority were Caucasian (76.2%); minority groups (23.8%) included Asian-American, Native American, Hispanic and Afro-American youth. Conversely, because of sample selection definition high-risk and typical youth were distinctly different in their school performance. High-risk youth compared to typical youth had lower grade point averages (1.45 GPA vs. 3.01 GPA, respectively, on a 0.00 to 4.00 scale), fewer earned credits/semester (2.37 vs. 3.04) and more class absences (8.90 vs. 3.85 days/semester).

RAY Project Data Collection

The study was approved by the University and School District Institutional Review Board committees. After the project was explained both orally and in written form, informed consent was obtained from all youth and at least one parent (or legal guardian). Youth randomly selected to participate in the RAY prevention study were invited by personal interview to be involved in the research project, referred to as the High School Study in order to avoid inadvertent adverse labelling. This resulted in a high response rate for both typical students (98%) and high-risk (78%) youth[2] (Nicholas 1990). Data presented in this paper are from the baseline questionnaire, before the intervention, from both high-risk experimental and control youth, and from typical youth.

Data from the RAY project used for this study came from two sources: (1) the students' permanent school records (for school achievement and attendance indicators), and (2) an extensive 3-part questionnaire. Students were administered the questionnaire in small groups of 10 - 12. To enhance the validity of the data, care was taken to promote privacy during questionnaire administration and to protect the confidentiality of student information. Code numbers were used on questionnaires and once completed, the questionnaire was sealed in a separate envelope by the student. School district personnel did not have access to any of the questionnaire information supplied by the students.

Measurement

The High School Study Questionnaire (Eggert, Herting, & Thompson, 1988), which takes 50-90 minutes to complete, is a broad assessment of students' lives. The questionnaire includes a general assessment of the student's experiences related to school (e.g. teacher/classmate support), family (e.g. family stress, family goals met), and friends (e.g. conventional peer bonding). Students were encouraged to provide open-ended responses in each section of the questionnaire. All scales were computed by calculating the mean of scale items with higher scores indicating higher levels of the measured concept, unless otherwise noted.

Personal Problems and Experiences

All scales used to measure personal problems and experiences ranged from 0 (never) to 6 (always). Personal problems and experiences were conceptualized in terms of six commonly identified facets: (1) self-esteem, measured using a 4-item scale (α=.70) adapted from Rosenberg (1965), addressed perceptions of good qualities, feeling useless, wishing for more respect, and taking a positive attitude toward oneself; (2) stress, measured with a 5-item scale (α=.60), tapped the degree of pressure felt, feeling stressed out; (3) depression, measured by a 6-item scale (α=.86) adapted for use with adolescents from the Depressed Mood Scale (CES-D, Radloff, 1977; Ensel, 1986), tapped feeling lonely, sad, blue, and depressed; (4) suicide ideation was measured with 1 item indicating the frequency of suicide thoughts, (5) problems with anger control, measured with a 2-item scale (correlation between items = .44) adapted from Thompson and Leckie (1989), tapped loss of control and irritability; and (6) life satisfaction, measured with a 2-item scale (α=.81) adapted from Pettegrew and colleagues (1980), addressed feeling satisfied with life, and feeling that life is enjoyable.

Drug Involvement

Drug involvement was conceptualized in four components to tap into its complexity: pervasiveness of drug use, drug use frequency, problems with drug use control, and adverse use consequences (Eggert, 1990; Eggert, 1991; Eggert & Herting, 1992; Eggert, et al., 1988). Pervasiveness of drug use was measured using 6 dichotomous items that addressed the timing and context of use. Drug use frequency was defined as the frequency with which different types of substances (tobacco smoking, alcohol, marijuana, and hard drugs) were used within a specific time frame. Items were measured on an 8-point Likert-type scale ranging from 0 (no use) to 7 (use several times per day) and summed for a scale score. Problems with drug use control, defined as the adolescent's manageability of intended use or abstinence (e.g. inability to stop with one or two drinks, using alcohol and drugs for fun, using more than one drug simultaneously), was measured using an 8-item, 8 point Likert-type scale (α=.86-.88) with a possible mean ranging from 0 (not at all) to 7 (several times/day). Higher scores indicated poorer drug use control. Adverse drug use consequences (α=.86-.88) tapped four categories of consequences common to adolescent drug use: (1) physical (e.g. getting sick);

(2) psychological (e.g. feeling depressed, guilty, etc.); (3) interpersonal (e.g., problems with family and friends); and (4) social (e.g., problems at school or with the law). The possible mean of the 15-item Likert-type scale ranged from 0 (not at all) to 7 (several times/day) with higher scores reflecting more adverse consequences. Measurement models for drug involvement (consisting of drug use frequency, drug use control, and adverse use consequences) were established using data from a pilot study and then validated with two separate cohorts (Eggert, Herting, Thompson, & Nicholas, 1992).

School Experience and Attitudes

To assess perceptions of school experiences and attitudes toward school, students were asked to evaluate their overall attendance, the school atmosphere, and their school performance; and to rate their level of satisfaction with their school schedule. Items were rated on 7-point Likert-type scales ranging from 1 (totally unsatisfied/very bad) to 7 (outstanding/highly satisfied). Importance of school goals were rated on 7-point Likert-type scales ranging from 0 (not very important) to 6 (very important). Additionally, students were queried about changes or moves they made during junior and senior high school.

Characteristics of Close Friends

Deviant peer bonding, the degree of integration in a deviant peer group, was measured using a 5-item Likert-type scale (α=.80) ranging from 0 (none) to 6 (almost all), and taken from the work of Elliot, Huizinga, and Ageton (1985). The scale tapped the proportion of friends involved in alcohol and drug use, and deviant behaviors related to school (e.g. skipping school, getting into trouble). Higher scores indicated higher levels of deviant peer bonding.

Family Factors

Family factors included: (1) living situation (with whom the student currently lived); (2) parental divorce; (3) family (parental and sibling) drug use problems, and family discord (serious conflicts with parents), and (4) conventional family bonding (importance of family goals, success in meeting family goals, and time spent on family activities). Family drug use problems and family discord were measured on 7-point

Likert-type scales ranging from 0 (never) to 6 (always). Importance of family goals (α=.66) and family goals met (α=.82) were measured using 4-item scales that tapped having fair rules, doing things together, having a parent know I do well, and having parents to talk to (adapted from Elliot, Huizinga and Ageton, 1985). Time spent on family activities was measured by summing the number of weekend mornings, afternoons, and evenings, and weekday afternoons and evenings spent engaged in family activities (defined as talking with parents, eating dinner together, and going out together).

Social Support/Resources

Support for school was defined as another's listening and being available when happy or sad, and motivating and encouraging one to do one's best. Amount of support/help was measured using an 18-item scale (α=.86-.91) that tapped the amount of support ("someone you can count on") and help ("helping you with a task") received from family members, school sources and peers for school during the prior semester (Eggert, & Herting, 1991). Each source was rated on a 21-point scale ranging from -10 (nonsupportive/not helpful) to +10 (supportive/helpful).

Results

Data presented include subsets of scales, and individual items that tap different dimensions of each construct. Due to the number of comparisons in this analysis, the Bonferroni correction was applied to reduce Type I error; only p values of less than .001 were considered statistically significant. Quantitative data are supplemented with quotes taken from open-ended responses.

Personal Problems/Experiences

Figure 1 illustrates the personal problems and experiences of youth. Both groups tended to report moderate levels of self esteem and life satisfaction, and low levels of suicide ideation. High-risk youth experienced greater psychosocial problems than the typical students, i.e. greater stress and pressures, more depression, higher levels of suicide ideation, and greater difficulty in controlling anger. High-risk youth also experienced lower levels of personal protective factors including self-esteem and life satisfaction. However, the differences in levels of self-esteem, depression, and suicide ideation only approached significance.

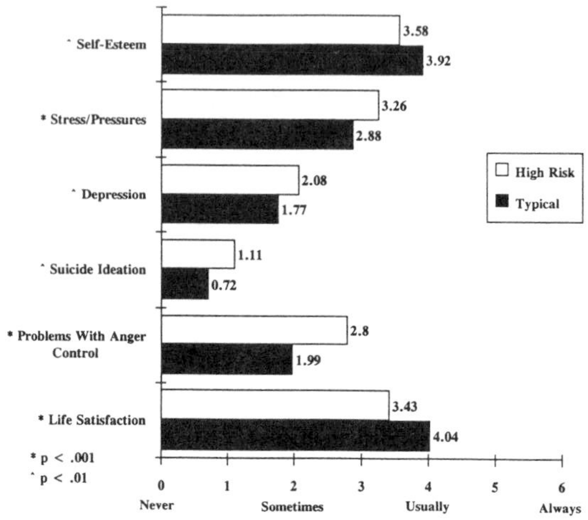

FIGURE 1. Personal problems and experiences: frequency of feelings/problems.

Drug Involvement

Figures 2 to 4 provide evidence for significant differences between high-risk youth in four aspects of drug involvement: pervasiveness of drug use, actual use of specific substances, problems with drug use control, and adverse consequences experienced due to drug use. Figure 2 shows that fewer high-risk youth (13%) claimed never to have used drugs than did typical students (39%). Also, high-risk students use significantly more on weekends (63% vs. 30%), when partying with friends (70% vs. 38%), at school (13% vs. 3%), and during the week (17% vs. 4%). Although not statistically significant, more high-risk youth tried to cut down on their drug use than did typical students as evidenced by more high-risk youth reporting "used in the past, but not now" (28% vs. 21%). One student said about the pervasiveness of drug use:

> *A lot of parents are so naive about where their kids are on weekends. Schools in this city have a lot of problems with pot and alcohol, and some schools have problems with coke. Everyone I know parties on the weekends.*

As the pervasiveness of use varied, so did the drug of choice. Figure 3 shows that compared to other substances, beer/wine and smoking tobacco were the highest for both groups followed by hard liquor and

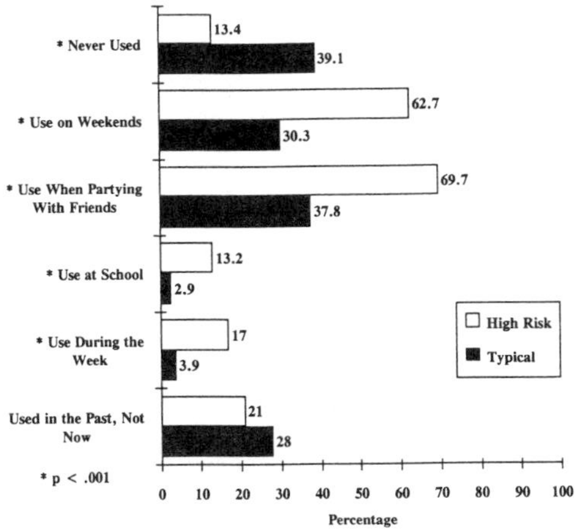

FIGURE 2. Pervasiveness of drug use: percentage of youth engaging in specific behaviors.

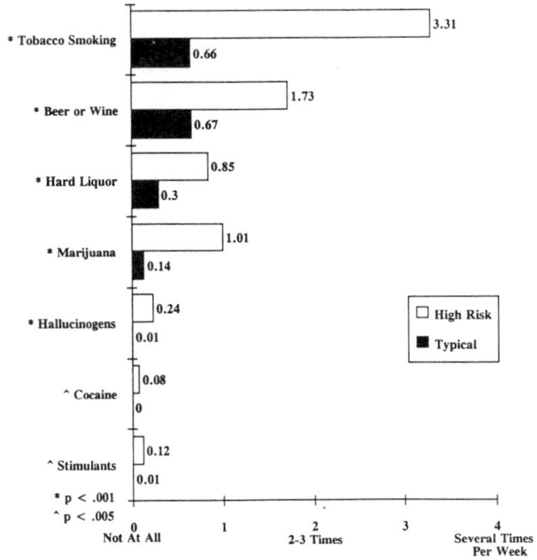

FIGURE 3. Use of specific drugs: frequency of occurrence in last four months.

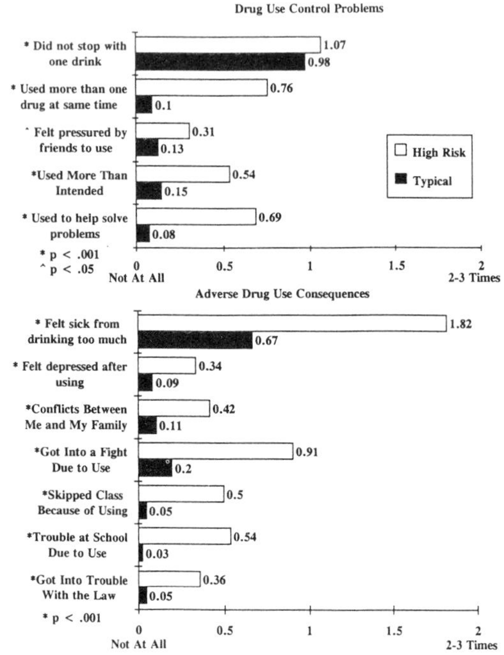

FIGURE 4. Drug use control problems and adverse drug use consequences: frequency of occurrence in last four months.

marijuana use. Use of smoking tobacco, beer/wine, hard liquor, and marijuana were significantly higher in the high-risk group compared to typical youth. The rate of use declined dramatically for the typical group as the severity of the substance increased. There was a similar decline for the high-risk group but differences among substances showed less dramatic declines. One youth described the changes in substance use over time:

> *I came here and didn't know anyone. Soon I met lots of people, but since I am easily talked into things, curious and self-conscious, I got into doing drugs. I first did pot a lot. Then toward the end of the year I started doing acid—a lot of it—approximately every other day for six months. I stopped after a bad trip. Now I don't drink or do drugs. I only smoke and I won't quit that!*

High-risk youth compared to typical youth also reported significantly more problems with drug use control (Figure 4) than did typical students including: not stopping after one drink, using more than one drug at the same time, using more than intended, and using to help solve problems.

Among the different problems, not stopping with one drink was reported most frequently in both high-risk and typical students. Figure 4 also shows that among both groups the most frequently reported consequence of drug use was feeling sick from drinking too much, followed by getting into a fight due to use. The least frequently reported consequences for high-risk students were feeling depressed after drug use and getting into trouble with the law due to drug use, and for typical students getting into trouble at school and with the law due to drug use. Overall, adverse consequences of drug use were more severe for the high-risk group; low levels of consequences were reported among typical youth. High-risk youth, more often than typical youth, reported significantly higher levels of drug use consequences across all items. One student felt explained the relationship between drug use and school performance and her expectations about the role of the school in preventing dropout:

> *Drugs have played a large part in my high school experiences. This is true for an alarming number of students. Because I believe that this issue is a driving factor for many failures and dropouts, I strongly believe the school system should go to extremes to help involve students, rather than threaten and hinder them. I believe that if the school system were more structured to help those in need, and be more understanding of the problems involved, less students would be dropouts and failures.*

School Experience and Attitudes

Figures 5 through 7 show differences between high-risk youth and typical high-school students on perceptions of school experiences and attitudes about school. Among perception ratings (Figure 5), high-risk youth rated most highly their satisfaction with their school schedules, compared to their attendance, which they rated the lowest. One high-risk youth explained his poor attendance as follows:

> *I haven't really been going to school much since the 8th grade. I didn't go then very much either. It's been about three years since I really went. I come back every semester and I promise myself that this time I'll try harder, but I don't even believe that promise anymore. I don't even know why I say it. So I stay at home, and stay in bed, and wait until my father finds out again.*

Typical students on the other hand rated most highly their attendance, and the school atmosphere lowest. Significant differences between groups were found on all indicators of perceptions of school experiences. Figure 6 shows that while students in both groups rated conventional school goals at least moderately important, high-risk students compared to typical students, placed significantly lower importance on all items. Figure 7 shows that high-risk students moved from school to school more often than typical students. Whereas 62% of typical students never changed junior/senior high schools, only 42% of high-risk students never moved. Thirty-two percent of high-risk students moved two or more times compared to only 12% of typical students.

Comparisons between high-risk and typical youth revealed a clear picture. High-risk youth had a much less satisfying school experience; they valued school less, evaluated their performance lower, and moved from school to school—all far more than did typical high school students. In short, these data point to low levels of "school bonding" for high-risk youth. One high-risk youth, a 15 year old male, summarized his school experiences and feelings of failure:

> *School has always been awful for me. I totally hate it. I don't think I ever liked school. I'm always getting F's and I hate that. It's always been like that. I don't try. I never try in school. Why try? The pressures at school just keep on. They don't ever stop! If you want to know the truth, I think a lot about dropping out. I don't need this. People are always picking on me, and I always feel stupid.*

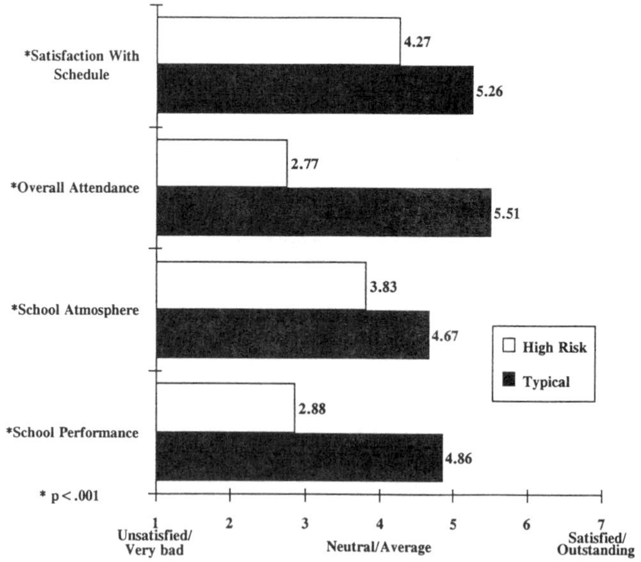

FIGURE 5. Evaluation of school experience.

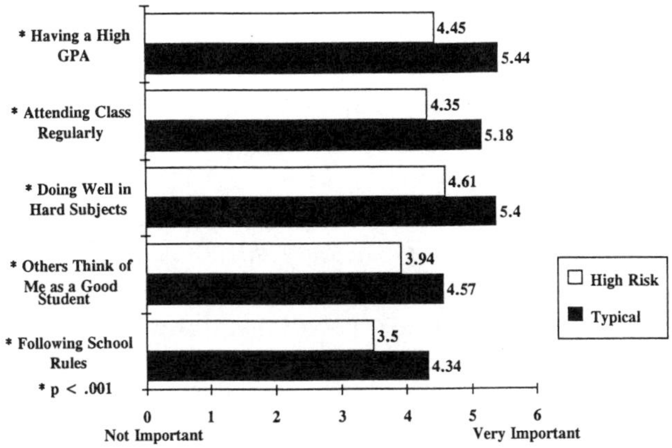

FIGURE 6. Importance of school goals.

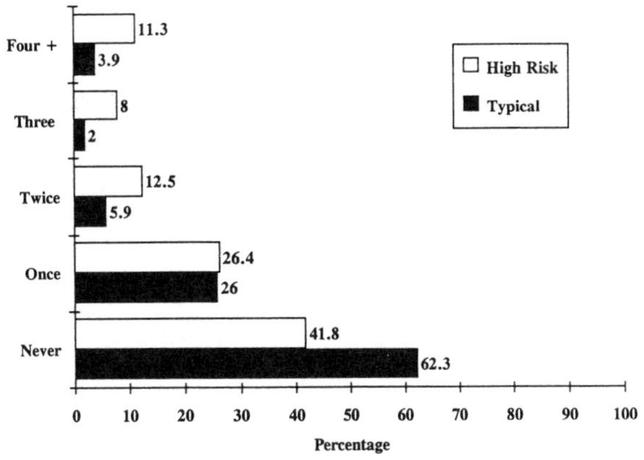

$X^2 = 32.42_{(df\ 4)}$; $p < .001$

FIGURE 7. Number of moves and school changes in junior and senior high school.

Social Network Factors: Peer Influences

Figure 8 shows that high-risk youth reported that over half of their friends used alcohol and skipped classes. One youth explained the problem with peer influences, "I love my friends and I love to party. Sometimes both of these conflict with school." In contrast typical youth were most likely to report that they had friends who were active in clubs. Both groups were least likely to report they had friends who often got into trouble with the law. Figure 8 demonstrates a greater negative influence from close friends for high-risk than for typical students. High-risk youth had significantly more close friends who skipped classes, used alcohol and other drugs, invited them to use drugs, did not really care about school, and often got into trouble. Conversely, high-risk youth had fewer friends who were active in school clubs. Thus, data about the characteristics of close friends suggests higher levels of "deviant bonding" for high-risk youth compared to typical youth.

Social Network Factors: Family Factors

Overall, figures 9 through 13 illustrate that high-risk youth experienced more family disruptions and problems than typical high school students. For example, significantly fewer high-risk youth (37%) than typical students (62%) lived with both natural parents (Figure 9) and more high-

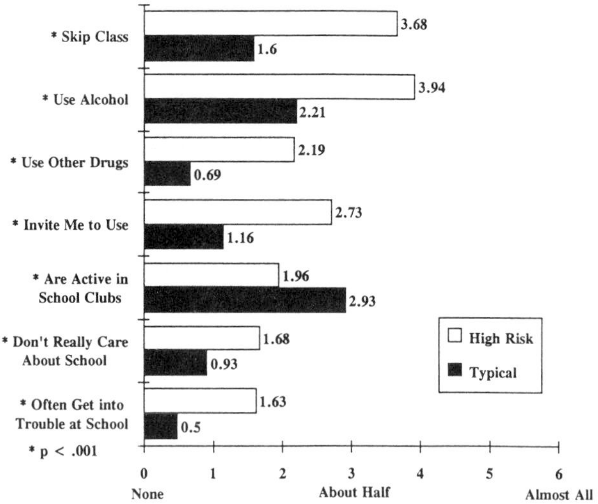

FIGURE 8. Characteristics of close friends: number of friends engaged in risky behaviors.

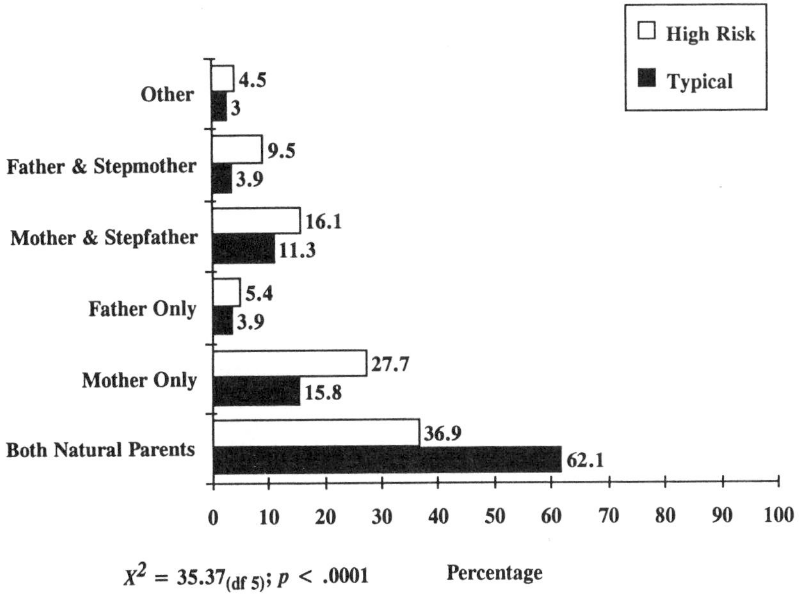

FIGURE 9. Living situation: percentage living with people identified.

risk youth experienced parental divorce (60% vs. 36%) (Figure 10). One 16 year-old high-risk youth said about her home life:

> *My parents are splitting up, you know, getting divorced. My father used to beat up my mother and stuff and now there's a court order saying he can't come near any of us. There was more stress at home than I could manage. I'm the oldest, and right now everyone is totally out-of-control....everyone is fighting and yelling.*

Also, high-risk youth, more so than typical students tended to endorse parent drug use (25% vs. 12%) and sibling drug use (35% vs. 21%) as problems (Figure 11); and reported significantly more serious conflicts with parents sometimes to always (89% vs. 74%) (Figure 12). Compared to typical youth, high-risk students reported significantly lower levels of conventional family bonding in three areas: importance of family goals, family goals met, and time spent engaged in family activities (Figure 13). Note that while high-risk youth and typical youth did not differ greatly in their ratings of the importance of family goals, the discrepancy between the groups is much greater in success in meeting family goals and in time spent on doing things together as a family.

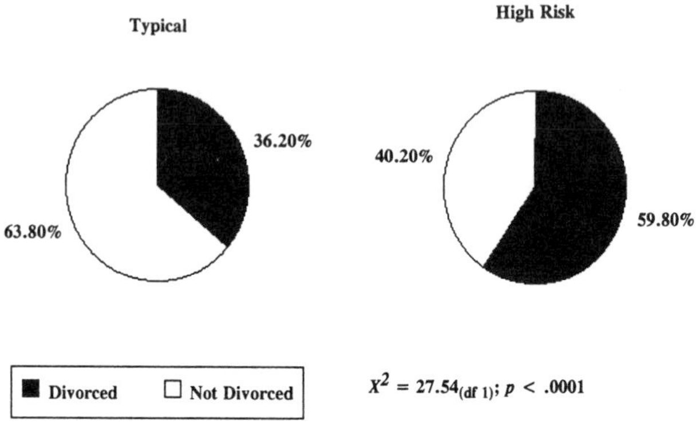

FIGURE 10. Parental divorce: percentage of students from divorced families.

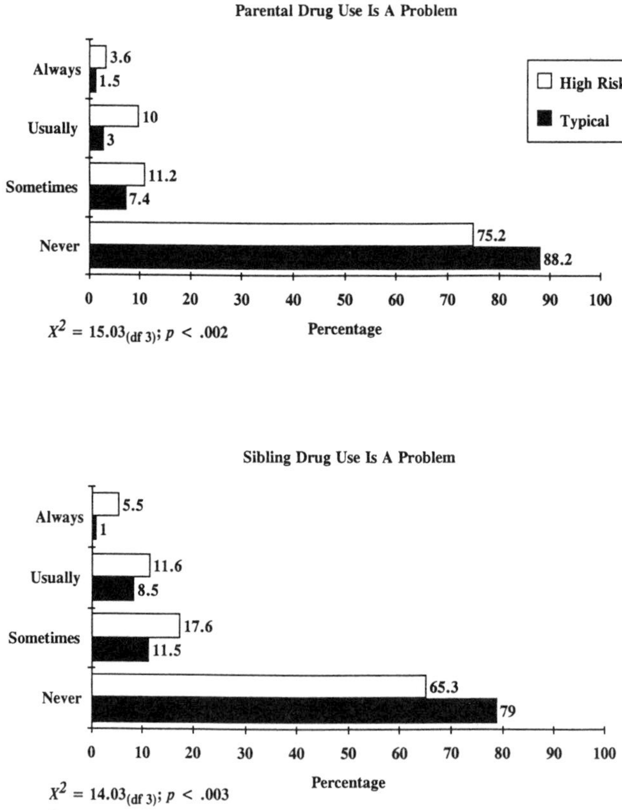

FIGURE 11. Family drug use problems.

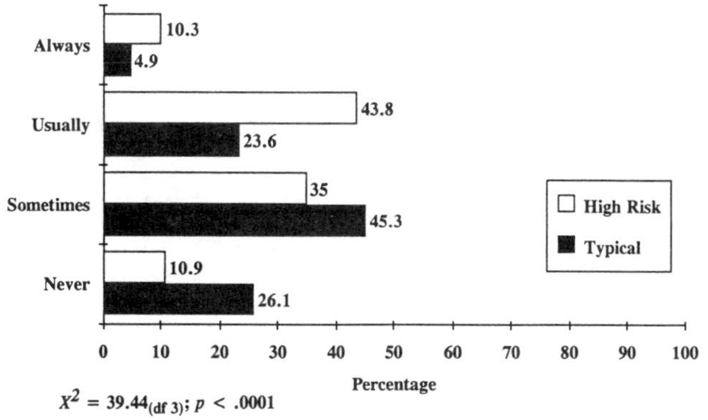

FIGURE 12. Family discord: percentage who have serious conflicts with parents.

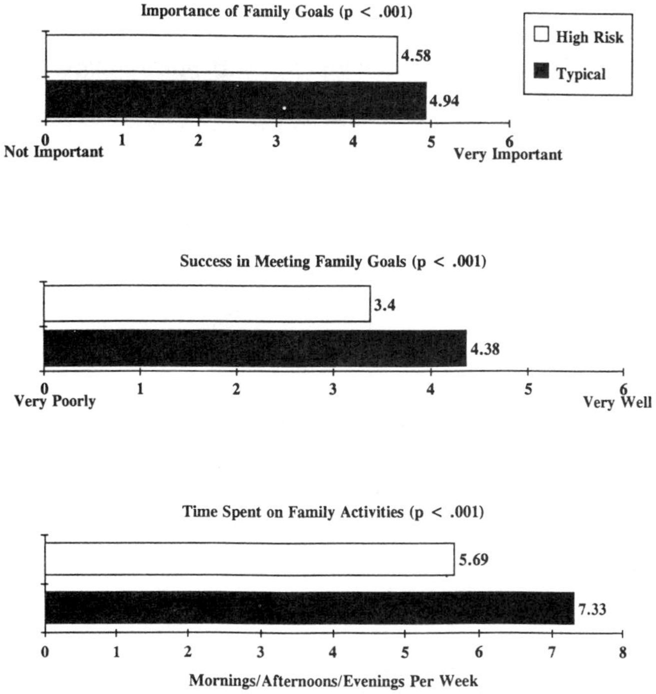

FIGURE 13. Conventional family bonding: importance of family goals, success in meeting goals, and time spent on family activities.

Social Network Factors: Social Support/Resources

Finally, Figure 14 shows similarities and differences in levels of social support and help received for school during the prior semester from themselves and important persons in their network. No differences existed in the amount of support received from best friends or brothers and differences for favorite teachers and sisters approached significance. However, high-risk youth perceived significantly less support from themselves, and from their mothers, and fathers than did typical students.

For high-risk youth, best friends, mothers, and favorite teachers were rated highest, whereas brothers, then sisters and fathers were rated lowest (in rank order). In contrast, typical students perceived the most support (in rank order) from best friends, mothers, and themselves; brothers, sisters, and favorite teachers were rated least supportive. The difference supportive teachers can make in one's school experience was explained by a student:

> *Teachers who really put themselves into their work are very interesting and that makes the class interesting to attend. I have two teachers I really like. I get encouragement from them and praise. One is a student teacher and she listens to my personal life, too.*

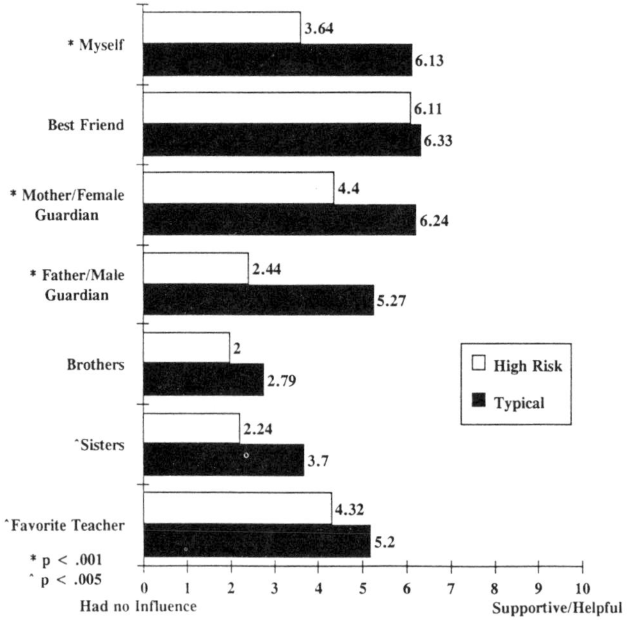

FIGURE 14. Social support/resources: amount of support received from network resource people.

Discussion

In short, all of the evidence points to significant differences across a broad range of dimensions between students at-risk for school dropout and typical high school students. On the average, high-risk youth, more than typical students, have more emotional problems, greater levels of drug involvement, more negative school experiences, more family problems, and receive less support from people in their social network.

Results from this study emphasize the relevance of protective factors, that is, resources that promote successful adolescent development and/or buffer risk factors (Jessor, 1993; Newcomb, 1992), in assessing adolescent risk and, therefore, in intervening with high-risk youth. Jessor (1993) argued that while risk factors of adolescents have been the focus of research and intervention, the role of protective factors has been understudied and undervalued. In this study, compared to typical students high-risk students had higher levels of risk factors and the anticipated lower levels of protective factors. This suggests targeting risk and protective factors in interventions such as those in the RAY project including: the importance of school goals, self-esteem, life satisfaction, importance of family goals, success in meeting family goals, time spent on family activities, and amount of social support from important people in the student's network.

Implications for Dropout Prevention

Study findings confirm that potential high school dropouts display a complex web of risk factors and deficits in protective factors that are significantly different from those of typical high school students. Understanding this complex web is crucial to appropriately plan prevention and treatment services. These data support the need for broad based interventions and policy that promote the health of adolescents by intervening on four levels: (1) personal; (2) peer; (3) school; and (4) family. This conceptualization suggests that interventions can target the individual to reduce personal risk factors (e.g. drug use, depression) and increase personal protection (e.g. self-esteem) as well as those factors that reduce social/environmental risk (e.g. family distress) and increase social protection (e.g. positive school bonding). Interventions and policy should be inclusive, that is supportive of altering personal and environmental conditions that adversely affect the health of adolescents, as well as promoting the personal strengths and environmental supports that buffer the negative effects of adverse conditions. While the focus of this paper is school dropout, Felner and Felner (1989) emphasized that because many problems of youth are co-occurring behaviors, many if not all can be best addressed with a common set of strategies such as mentorship and counseling, an array of social services, remedial and individualized instruction, school-business collaboration, and parental and community involvement (Han, Danzberger, & Lefkowitz, 1987). Comprehensive efforts that facilitating coordination of efforts are not only more likely to prevent dropout, but they are also efficient uses of resources (Felner & Felner, 1989). Therefore examples and recommendations for dropout prevention explained below are drawn from a range of prevention studies in adolescent health, most notably drug abuse prevention programs, and specifically from the ongoing school-based RAY project aimed at increasing school performance, and decreasing drug use and suicide behaviors.

Individual/Personal Level

Risk factors for potential school dropouts, in contrast to typical high school students in this study included:

- *drug involvement*—greater pervasiveness of use at school, during the week and weekends, and when partying with friends; more frequent use of tobacco, alcohol, marijuana and hard drugs; problems in controlling drug involvement (i.e. uncontrolled use, using more than intended and using to escape personal problems); and adverse drug use consequences (i.e. getting into trouble at school, with family and friends as a result of drug use); and
- *emotional distress*—greater perceived stress, more problems controlling anger, higher levels of depression and suicide ideation.

Deficits in personal protective factors included:

- *personal resources*—lower self-esteem, less self-support, and less life satisfaction.

Results from this study support Jessor's (1991) assertion: adolescent risk behaviors (such as drug use, unprotected sexual activity, withdrawal from the school environment) are in fact an organized and interrelated constellation of risk and protective behaviors. These behaviors are not isolated independent risk behaviors. Others also reported links between substance use and the noncompletion of high school (Mensch & Kandel, 1988; Weng, Newcomb, & Bentler, 1988) or between abuse and academic lifestyle, i.e. educational aspirations and academic achievements (Newcomb, McCarthy, & Bentler, 1989).

On an individual level, prevention efforts for potential dropouts that decrease personal risk and promote personal protective factors are needed. Dropout prevention programs that do not address the deleterious effects of drug involvement on school performance are inadequate. Specific to drug use, results support the use of assessments that measure multiple facets of drug involvement; doing so provides a more robust picture of high-risk youth's drug culture and therefore appropriately matched intervention. Characterizing drug involvement as pervasiveness of drug use, drug use frequency, drug use control, and adverse drug use consequences allows for differentiation among low-risk youth, low-risk users, and youth at-risk of school dropout (Eggert & Herting, 1993) which in turn facilitates triage to appropriate prevention or intervention programs.

Of particular concern was the trend toward higher levels of depression and suicide ideation reported by high-risk compared to typical youth. Evidence for the link between underachievement or poor school performance and adolescent suicide behaviors, however, is mixed; several studies of clinical populations reported this association (Wenz, 1979), others found no differences in school achievement between suicidal and nonsuicidal youth (Pfeffer, Zuckerman, Plutch, & Mizruchi, 1984). Lewis and colleagues (1988) found suicide attempters, relative to non-attempters, had significantly lower school achievement. Their data suggested links between poor school performance, depression, and suicide attempts. General reviews (Gans, Blyth, Elster, & Gaveras, 1990; Hawton, 1986; Swedo, Rettew, Kuppenheimer, Lum, Dolan, & Goldberger, 1991) and our preliminary results point to potential school dropout as a predictor of suicide behaviors. Hence, in planning services and research for students at-risk for school failure, the fact that this group may also be at-risk for depression and suicide must be taken into consideration.

Prevention services at the personal level for youth at-risk for school dropout should be directed toward reducing emotional distress and drug involvement, and enhancing life skills for coping with existing social and interpersonal risk factors that are not readily amenable to change. Enhancing self esteem lets youth know that they are valued. Learning is least likely to occur when unmet emotional needs for esteem and belonging are present. Thus, enhancing self-esteem lays the groundwork for effective prevention efforts. Approaches from the RAY project include offering a special elective class, called Personal Growth, to high-risk youth that provides a daily dose of support and caring coupled with skills training (e.g., in self-esteem enhancement, decision-making, personal control, and interpersonal communication). Other approaches to reduce personal distress in high-risk youth include mentoring programs and individual counseling services (Han, Danzberger, & Lefkowitz, 1987).

Peer Group Influences

Results from this study confirm that potential dropouts compared to typical youth experience both increased peer risk factors and decreased peer protective factors including more friends who:

- Use alcohol and other drugs, and invite them to use:
- Often get into trouble at school;
- Are not active in school; and
- Provide less support for school.

Increasingly, prevention research and theoreticians are recognizing the limitations of focusing solely on the individual to effect change; one's social environment is a critical determinant of behavior (Elliott, Huizinga, & Ageton, 1985; Ajzen, Fishbein, 1980; Hawkins, Lishner, Jenson, & Catalano, 1987). For adolescents, it is commonly recognized that peers provide a strong influence on their behavior, values, and attitudes through the establishment of normative beliefs (Schinke, Botvin, & Orlandi; 1991; Vorrath & Brendtro, 1985), particularly for adolescent drug involvement (Kandel, 1985; Kandel 1986; Newcomb, 1992). Findings presented in this present study suggest the same is true for potential school dropouts and point to multiple negative peer influences—a significantly different picture than for typical youth.

On a peer level, then, prevention efforts should focus on breaking the cycle of deviant peer bonding and promoting peer support and salutary peer relationships. Specific approaches would include a structured environment with cooperative learning opportunities with peers in the classroom, a structured positive peer culture to foster norms for learning, non-drug involvement, specific life skills training in resisting temptations to skip classes and use drugs, and encouraging involvement in school activities with peers (Vorrath & Brendtro, 1985). The RAY project tests a school-based intervention that combines a positive peer-group culture approach with life skills training to curb school dropout, drug use, and depression/suicide risk behaviors among potential drop-outs. Compared to a high-risk control group, at 5 month follow-up post intervention, intervention students showed increased school performance, decreased drug involvement, and decreased deviant peer bonding (Eggert, Thompson, Herting, Nicholas, & Dicker, 1993). In summary, fostering a positive culture with norms of valuing school goals and abstinence from drug use, and strengthening the bonds high-risk students' have with this culture could be a highly effective means to reduce school dropout and failure.

Family Factors

Another salient feature of the social network for youth is the family structure and support within the family. Compared to typical youth, potential school dropouts in this study experienced increased levels of risk factors including:

- *Family distress and disorganization*—serious conflicts with parents, parental divorce, multiple moves resulting in school moves for the youth; and
- *Family drug use*—parental and sibling drug use; as well as decreases in protective factors including;
- *Family support for school*—from both parents and siblings; and
- *Engaging in activities together as a family.*

These data support others' findings (Barrington & Hendricks, 1989; Clayton, 1992; Hawkins & Catalano, 1989; Newcomb, et al., 1986; Newcomb and Bentler, 1988) that youth are at greater risk for school failure, drug involvement, and emotional distress when there are serious conflicts in the home, family disorganization, and family stress and that parental and sibling drug use is one of the strongest predictors of adolescent drug involvement (Merikangas, Rounsaville, & Prusoff, 1992). These findings, then, extend what we know about adolescent drug use and families to the problem of adolescent school dropout.

Given the link between high-risk youth and troubled families, it is likely that stronger intervention effects will be realized when families are incorporated into prevention services. For prevention at the family level, then, the goal is to reduce family distress and enhance family support for the school. Specific strategies include involving parents as partners to improve the link between parents and schools (Han, Danzberger, & Lefkowitz, 1987), parent workshops to maintain their involvement, and skills training to help them help their children succeed in school (Bry, MacGreen, Schutte, & Fishman, 1991). We need to facilitate parents to enable their youth to succeed in school. This can be accomplished by helping parents demonstrate that school is important, model an interest in learning, use the home as a learning lab, and make school attendance a priority. Han and colleagues (1987) emphasized that parents should be involved with the schools in developing parent involvement programs to ensure their success. On the RAY project, research nurses conducted interviews with parents to determine acceptable content and approaches. Parents reported wanting: (1) a group for parents alone, (2) monthly combined groups with parents and youth, and (3) to meet in locations separate from school. In the RAY project one-to-one telephone and in-person contacts were widely accepted by parents whose youth were at-risk for suicide. Additionally, effective documented approaches (Bry, 1988) include meeting parents on "their turf" (e.g., home visits, meeting at lunch), and enlisting parents as "partners."

School Factors

Turning to the school level, compared to typical youth, potential school dropouts experienced increased levels of risk factors including:

- *Negative perceptions of the school environment*—low satisfaction with school schedule and school atmosphere;
- *Negative personal evaluations of school performance*—low ratings of overall attendance and school performance; and lower levels of school protective factors including
- *School bonding*—valuing positive school goals, and stability in living situation and therefore school stability; and
- *Teacher support*—support and help from their teachers.

Frequently low commitment to school means that youth cease to perceive the role of student as viable. Low commitment exacerbates academic failure, further weakens bonds to school, and results in an increased likelihood of dropping out. The present study confirms Eggert and Nicholas's (1992) ethnographic work on youth who skipped school.

Those high-risk youth demonstrated weak conventional school bonding, felt like "outsiders" to typical teacher support, perceived classroom activities as boring, and had low regard for education. Often these students were perceived by teachers as "losers." Additionally, in the RAY project one of the most important predictors of high-risk youth's success in improving school performance and decreasing drug involvement was perceived teacher support.

Intervention at the school level is critical to curb dropout. The goal of school-oriented intervention should be to enhance protective factors such as bonding to school and promoting school satisfaction. The RAY program includes the key elements of monitoring attendance weekly by providing youth with a record of their attendance, motivating youth to improve by capitalizing on conventional school goals, enhancing study skills and interpersonal communication skills for negotiating with teachers, and positively reinforcing youth for meeting school goals.

Intervention that targets teacher behavior is crucial. Training should focus on the development of interpersonal skills for working with disenfranchised high-risk youth. Specific strategies include proactive classroom management skills; effective instructional practices with these youth (e.g. cooperative learning, small group work, experiential learning opportunities); conflict management skills to prevent hostile teacher-student interactions; social support skills training to effect change with at-risk youth through caring interactions; and mentorship programs to provide students with important and empowering relationships (Smink, 1990).

In conclusion, results of this study support a multidimensional picture of both risk and protective factors that are related to potential school dropout versus academic success. This multidimensional model highlights the co-occurring problem behaviors and risk factors evident for potential dropouts in contrast to multiple protective factors for the typical high school student. It was shown that youth at high-risk of potential dropout have significantly greater risk factors and fewer protective factors in the domains of personal resources, peer influences, family influences and school environmental factors. Clearly the implication for preventive interventions is that no single approach or "quick-fixes" are bound to work; rather, comprehensive, multidimensional programs are needed to address the multiple causes and correlates of school dropout. Programs that include partnerships between youth, their peers, their family and caring and concerned school personnel are vitally needed to stem the tide of school dropout and its inevitable negative consequences for high-risk youth. High-risk youth deserve a second chance within environments similar to those found for the typical high school students in this study. It is hopeful that findings from this study will stimulate greater interest in developing dropout prevention programs to address this national concern.

REFERENCES

Ajzen, I., & Fishbein, M. (1980). *Understanding attitudes and predicting social behavior*. Englewood Cliffs, NJ: Prentice-Hall.

Bandura, A. (1977). Self-efficacy: Toward a unifying theory of behavioral change. *Psychological Review*, 84, 191-215.

Barrington, B.L., & Hendricks, B. (1989). Differentiating characteristics of high school graduates, dropouts, and nongraduates. *Journal of Educational Research*, 82(6), 309-319.

Brown, B.S., & Mills, A.R. (1987). At-risk populations: Some suggested directions. In *Youth at high-risk for substance abuse*. DHHS ADM-87-1537, Washington, D.C.: Supt. of Documents, U.S. Government Printing Office.

Bry, B.H. (1988). Family-based approaches to reducing adolescent substance use: Theories, techniques and findings. In Rahdert, E.R. & Grabowski, J. (Eds). *Adolescent drug abuse: analysis of treatment research*. Monograph 77, Washington, D.C.: Superintendent of Documents, U.S. Government Printing Office.

Bry, B.H., MacGreene, D., Schutte, C., & Fishman, C.A. (1991). *Targeted family intervention manual*. Unpububublished.

Clayton, R.R. (1992). Transitions in drug use: Risk and protective factors. In Glantz, M. & Pickens, R. (Eds). *Vulnerability to drug abuse*, pp. 15-51. Washington, D.C.: American Psychological Association.

Curtis, S. (1992). Promoting health through a developmental analysis of adolescent risk behavior. *Journal of School Health*, 62(9), 417-20.

Dougherty, D., Eden, J., Kemp, K.B., Metcalf, K., Rowe, K., Ruby, G., Strobel, P., & Solarz, A. (1992). Adolescent health: A report to the U.S. Congress. *Journal of School Health*, 48, 193-201.

Eggert, L.L. (1990). Conducting intervention research with high-risk youth. *Communicating Nursing Research*, 23, 175-182. (Abstract)

Eggert, L.L. (1991). Drug involvement and suicide ideation: prevention Research challenges. *Communicating Nursing Research*, 181-188.

Eggert, L.L. (1993). *Adolescents' metaphors for "Using an' dealin' drugs."* Unpublished manuscript. University of Washington, Seattle, WA.

Eggert, L.L., & Herting, J.R. (1991). Preventing teenage drug abuse: Exploratory effects of network social support. *Youth & Society*, 22(4), 482-524.

Eggert, L.L., & Herting, J.R. (1993). Drug Involvement among potential dropouts and "typical" youth. *Journal of Drug Education*, 23(1), 31-55.

Eggert, L.L., Herting, J.R., & Nicholas, L.J. (1988). *Reconnecting at-risk youth: drug users and dropouts* National Institute of Drug Abuse Funded Project. Unpublished manuscript.

Eggert, L.L., Herting, J.R., Thompson, E.A., & Nicholas, L.J. (1992). *Reconnecting at-risk youth to prevent drug abuse, school dropout, suicide lethality.* Technical Report, Advisory Council, National Institute of Mental Health & Prevention Research Branch. Unpublished manuscript.

Eggert, L.L., & Nicholas, L.J. (1992). Speaking like a skipper: "skippin' an' gettin' high." *Journal of Language Psychology*, 11, 75-100.

Eggert, .LL., Thompson, E.A., Herting, J.R., Nicholas, L.J., & Dicker, B. (1993). *Preventing adolescent drug involvement and school dropout.* Unpublished manuscript, University of Washington, Seattle, WA.

Elliott, D.S., Huizinga, D., & Ageton, S.S. (1981). *Adolescent peer pressure: Theory, correlates, and program implications for drug abuse prevention.* Rockville, MD: National Institute on Drug Abuse. Unpublished manuscript.

Elliott, D.S., Huizinga, D., & Ageton, S.S. (1985). *Explaining delinquency & drug use.* New York, NY: Sage.

Ensel, W.M. (1986). Measuring depession: The CES-D scale. In Lin, N. & Dean, A. (Eds). *Social support, life events, & depression*, pp. 51-70. Orlando, FL: Academic Press.

Felner, R.D., & Felner, T.Y. (1989). Primary prevention programs in educational context: A transactional-ecological framework and analysis. In *Primary prevention and promotion in schools*, pp. 13-49. Newbury Park, London: Sage.

Gans, J.E., Blyth, D.A., Elster, A.B., & Gaveras, L.L. (1990). *America's adolescents: How healthy are they?* Chicago, Il.: American Medical Association.

Hahn, A., Danzberger, J., & Lefkowitz, B. (1987). *Dropouts in America: Enough is known for action.* Washington, D.C.: Institute for Educational Leadership.

Hawkins, J.D., & Catalano, R.F. (1989). *Risk and protective factors for alcohol and other drug problems: Implications for substance abuse prevention.* Unpublished manuscript.

Hawkins, J.D., Lishner, D.M., Jenson, J.M., & Catalano, F. (1987). Delinquents and drugs: What the evidence suggests about prevention and treatment programming. In Brown, B.S. & Mills, A.R. (Eds). *Youth at high risk for substance abuse*, Rockville, MD: National Institute on Drug Abuse.

Hawton, K. (1986). *Suicide & attempted suicide among children & adolescents.* Newbury Park, CA: Sage.

Herting, J.R. (1990). Predicting at-risk youth: Evaluation of a sample selection model. *Communicating Nursing Research*, 23, 178.

Hurrelman, K. (1990). Health promotion for adolescents: Preventive and corrective strategies against problems behavior. *Journal of Adolescence*, 13(3), 231-250.

Jessor, R. (1991). Risk behavior in Adolescence: A psychosocial Framework for understanding and action. *Sociology of Adolescent Medicine*, 12, 597-605.

Jessor, R. (1993). Successful adolescent development among youth in high-risk settings. *American Psychologist*, 48(2), 117-126.

Johnson, L.D., Bachman, J.G., & O'Malley, P.M. (1990). *1989 National high school senior drug abuse survey: Monitoring the future survey.* Ann Arbor, MI: University of Michigan, Institute for Social Research.

Kandel, D.B. (1985). On processes of peer influences in adolescent drug use: A developmental perspective. *Advances in Alcohol and Substance Abuse*, 4, 139-163.

Kandel, D.B. (1986). Processes of peer influences in adolescence. In Silbereisen, R.K. & Eyferth, K. (Eds). *Development as action in context: Problem behavior and normal youth development*, pp. 203-227. Berlin, Germany: Springer-Verlag.

Mensch, B.S., & Kandel, D.B. (1988). Dropping out of high school and drug involvement. *Sociology of Education*, 61, 95-113.

Merikangas, K.R., Rounsaville, B.J., & Prusoff, B.A. (1992). Familial factors in vulnerability to substance abuse. In Glanz, M. & Pickens, R. (Eds). *Vulnerability to drug abuse*, pp. 75-97. Washington, D.C.: American Psychological Association.

Newcomb, M.D. (1992). Understanding the multidimensional nature of drug use and abuse: The role of consumption, risk factors, and protective factors. In Glantz, M. & Pickens, R. (Eds). *Vulnerability to abuse*, pp. 255-297. Washington, DC: American Psychological Association.

Newcomb, M.D., & Bentler, P.M. (1988). The impact of family context, deviant attitudes, and emotional distress on adolescent drug use: Longitudinal latent-variable analyses of mothers and their children. *Journal of Research and Personality*, 22, 154-176.

Newcomb, M.D., Huba, G.J., & Bentler, P.M. (1986). Life change events among adolescents: An empirical consideration of some methodological issues. *Journal of Nervous and Mental Diseases*, 174(5), 280-289.

Newcomb, M.D., McCarthy, W.J., & Bentler, P.M. (1989). Cigarette Smoking, academic lifestyle, and social impact efficacy: An eight-year study from early adolescence to young adulthood. *Journal of Applied Social Psychology*, 19(3), 251-281.

Office of Substance Abuse Prevention, (1989). *Prevention of mental disorders, alcohol & other drug use in children & adolescents* (Mono. 2) (DHHS-ADM-89-1646). Washington, D.C.: Department of Health & Human Services. Unpublished manuscript.

Pfeffer, C.R., Zuckerman, S., Plutch, R., & Mizruchi, M. (1984). Suicidal behavior in normal school children: A comparison with child psychiatric inpatients. *American Academy of Child Psychology*, 23, 416-423.

Radloff, L.S. (1977). The CES-D Scale: A self report depression scale for Research in the general population. *Journal of Applied Psychological Measures*, 1, 385-401.

Rosenbaum, P.R. (1985). *Dropping out of high school in the U.S.: The analysis of an observation study embedded in a complex sample survey.* Chicago, Il: Presented at the AERA Annual Meeting. Unpublished manuscript.

Rosenberg, M. (1965). *Society and the adolescent self image.* Princeton, NJ: Princeton University Press.

Schinke, S.P., Botvin, G.J., & Orlandi, M.A. (1991). *Substance abuse in children and adolescents: Evaluation and intervention.* Newbury Park, CA: Sage.

Smink, J. (1990). *Mentoring programs for at-risk youth.* The National Dropout Center.

Swedo, S.E., Rettew, D.C., Kuppenheimer, M., Lum, D., Dolan, S., & Goldberger, E. (1991). Can adolescent suicide attempters be distinguished from at-risk adolescents? *Pediatrics*, 88(3), 620-637.

Thompson, E.A., & Leckie, M. (1989). *Interpretation manual for symptoms of stress inventory*. Unpublished.

Vorrath, H., & Brendtro, L. (1985). *Positive peer culture*. 2nd ed. Chicago, Il: Aldine.

Weissberg, R.P., Caplan, M., & Harwood, R.L. (1991). Promoting competent young people in competence-enhancing environments: A systems-based perspective on primary prevention. *Journal of Consulting and Clinical Psychology*, 59(6), 830-841.

Weng, L.J., Newcomb, M.D., & Bentler, P.M. (1988). Factors influencing noncompletion of high school: A comparison of methodologies. *Educational Research Quarterly*, 12(2), 8-22.

Wenz, F.V. (1979). Sociological correlates of alienation among adolescent suicide attempts. *Adolescence*, 14, 19-30.

JOEL L. BURDIN

5

Unique Aspects of Rural At-Risk Youths

PART I: THE BIG PICTURE

One in every four U.S. students is "at risk." They are found in rural, suburban, and city areas. Action is urgent to reduce risk or else! Early action now or remedial actions later; reasonable corrective expenditures beginning in third grade at the latest or horrible cost later—for a long time. Salvaged lives or destroyed lives. The choices are quite clear. The sensible choice is a major and comprehensive program now to save our "at risk" students. Each community has them in large numbers. Rural communities can spot their at-risk youths, select from options the best remedial actions, and create networks for building communities which can solve their problems such as at-risk youths.

"At risk" is hard to define. Essentially, it is being in situations which are dangerous for normal well-being and development. It is a move toward characteristics and behaviors which put the young in harm's way and into anti-social or unsocial behaviors. "At-risk" means being in situations which are dangerous or restrictive of normal, healthy, full development. At-risk patterns can be spotted at a young age—in terms of mental, social, physical, emotional, and/or moral characteristics and behaviors.

Parents and various rural institutions, agencies, organizations, and enterprises (IAOE's) collectively can diagnose at-risk tendencies very early and take corrective actions. Needed is collaboration in which the special strengths and experiences of parents and various IAOE's are brought to bear in particular cases. Faced with tremendous, often burgeoning demands, no one IAOE can afford needless duplication of efforts. Faced with great needs, rural at-risks cannot suffer gaps in those efforts. Our rural areas have to work hard to create comprehensive services, especially if they are relatively isolated. A few years ago our society faced up to the fact that millions of handicapped peoples were not getting a fair shake; the Congress acted decisively and speedily. Services for the handicapped are now available throughout the land. That kind of action is essential today to serve those at-risk.

Nothing short of a crisis-level response will do. There are millions of 10-19-year-olds at risk. There are millions of younger school children, millions of pre-schoolers, and millions in womb who are in crisis. Their crises are our crises. No one parent or IAOE alone has the capacity to solve the problems.

An example of crisis is rural child-like youths having children by the thousands. Playing on the exploding drives of the young are sex- and violence-saturated popular music, TV, movies, and literature. Hedonism is the implied lifestyle of choice. Negative adult models and peer pressures accentuate the crises. Teen pregnancy strains educational systems, social services, and parents' resources. Too often, limited services and recreational outlets leave youth on their own. Often they turn to sex for pleasure and companionship. Babies are instantly at risk when they are born to youth who prematurely become mothers and fathers. Three of four children born to a single mother under 25 live below the poverty level (Ryan and Cooper, 1993, p. 386).

Financially and emotionally, teens are not ready to raise children. Sadly, such children are commonly doomed to become poverty's children and create other crisis cycles. That in turn yields a harvest of additional crisis situations. In some areas huge percentages of children are born to unwed mothers, often teens (or even worse to pre-adolescents). This is only one example of at-risk young persons.

Our children too often are in crisis before they are born. They do not receive adequate medical treatment (sometimes none at all until birth). They are exposed to mothers' destructive habits: poor nutrition, drugs, alcohol, tobacco, stress, and the like. One theory even holds that the jarring music which often envelopes mothers has a negative impact on the unborn! The early years leave scars that remain in adolescence.

After birth, immunizations are often neglected. Abuse and neglect are rampant. Latch-key kids and youth commonly are free to sample whatever catches their fancy: TV, music, reading materials, cigarettes, alcohol, drugs, and sex. For millions the world is a very dangerous place at home and beyond— and at ages which are totally inappropriate and when they are vulnerable.

Wait, you say! Millions of youth are properly supervised and sensibly restricted. Let's add a bunch of stars to the crowns of those who work hard outside homes and within to do the right things. Regrettably, our major concern in this chapter is the millions who are at great risk in homes and beyond.

That "beyond" danger zone sometimes includes the schools. There, some peers are endangering and corrupting. There, occasionally teachers are abusive and incompetent in creating positive environments for learning—academics, social skills, self-concept, and self-respect. Even a few cases of abuse and neglect are tragic, for their impact often extends throughout life. Too often, teachers in rural schools find them the least desirable places to work; teachers commonly place large urban and rural schools in the same "undesirable" category. Put another way, places with large concentrations of children at risk often are staffed by teachers who find their professional environments undesirable. Such teachers may leave many youth at risk!

Fortunately, caring and competent parents and professionals who serve the young can spot both abuse and developing at-risk conditions. Each has a role in eliminating problems and creating nurturing environments. No exceptions. No excuse for inaction as individuals or as community or as society. We act now, or we pay very big prices later, in dollars, in wasted human lives, or in inadequately developed potentiality. Each is, all are, tragedies. Corrective actions in rural areas may be a big challenge. Often, there are scattered populations, isolation factors, limited social services, limited public transportation, and many more challenges to meet. With commitment and resources, sound programs can be undertaken for rural America (Helge, 1991).

The Nature of "Risk"

There are some tell-tale signs to watch for in youth, warning signs of at-risk characteristics and behaviors in the bud: low learning levels; repeating grades; hating school; excessive absences; alienation from others; withdrawing from family and other children; dropping out of school; using drugs; criminal behavior; early sexual activity; acceptance of failures as normal; consequences of poverty; experiencing discrimination based on race, ethnicity, and gender; and long-term welfare dependency (List derived from American Association of School Administrators, 1989, 1990). The AASA monograph organizes at-risk factors into categories such as poverty, ethnic/racial origins, schools and schooling, home and family, and students themselves. There's a whopping list of 47 big subcategories. The diversity and magnitude of the crises we face with our young who are at risk are frightening. Our other crises make the youth at-risk situation even more scary. To fuel some nightmares, consider the economic situation, health care reform, and international competition, all with impacts on youth and potent in themselves.

We have to say that at-risk peoples, both young and old, are overwhelming us. When one-fourth of your young are at-risk, we are in crisis. We simply have to place as-high-as-any priority on the tragic 25 percent of youth who are at risk. That means school-by-school study and action; community-by-community revitalization to provide adequate nurturance for youth; coordination of institutions, agencies, organizations, enterprises, and individuals; and local, state, national, and international cooperation.

Additional monies are essential. Better use of existing funds is important. Fine-tuning present programs and inventing new ones are called for. Now or later, the price of at-risk characteristics and behaviors will be paid by individuals and by our society. My continuing assertion is that the most decisive action can best be taken at the local level, in our homes, neighborhoods, and close-at-hand IAOE's. Locally, there's a face to the crisis in the lives of our young. Locally, individual needs cry out, and we can hear them. Locally, we can develop the will and the ways for responding to the cries, to the crises.

A colleague recently wrote on the role of humor in education. After writing about at-risk crises, I'm almost ready to exchange my sad analyses for his light-hearted ones. His topic is more pleasant than mine. Yet at the same time, I will carefully continue to watch for the sad signs of at-risk young people— the haunted among us— who sometimes silently and often-times loudly call out for our love, caring, and competence. It's time to mobilize at all levels of our great society. Now it's time for both short-term and long-haul mobilization to rescue millions of our young from their horrible present lives and their frightening futures. That response could make projects such as landing on the moon pale by comparison.

PART II: WHOLE POPULATIONS AT RISK

Whole populations are at risk. The previous paragraphs dealt with the nation in general. Now it's time to provide examples of specific sub-groups with disproportionate at-risk youth populations. There follows an examination of several populations. Their youth share at-risk conditions of the nation in general. Additionally, there are unique racial, ethnic, and circumstantial factors to address.

Native Americans at Risk

Europeans and their American counterparts have been confused about "Indians" from the earliest days when the Western Hemisphere was "discovered," after Indians had been here thousands of years! Misnaming the Indians/ Native Americans was understandable, granted the geographical knowledge available at the time. Mistreating and exploiting them, the pattern which emerged early, was indefensible.

Other patterns were counterproductive. One was idolizing them. For example, they were pictured, at various times in U.S. history, as the ultimate peaceful people. They were the perfect custodians of the land. They were wonderfully religious. They were the practitioners of human rights and human relations. Some were correctly stereotyped—positively or negatively. There were many exceptions. There were dozens of variations among the tribal groups and within each. There were good and not-so-good people everywhere among the Indians.

Variations were—and still are—as great as can be found among Europeans, Africans, Asians, and Pacific Islanders. Found among Indians in America's vast East-West stretches of land and our North to South great land masses were warriors, land plunderers, enslavers, torturers, and contentious peoples. Indeed, all Indians were not praiseworthy.

Granted a realistic picture of Indians in their diversity, they and their fellow Americans can realistically look at this small subgroup of the population. They can accept the enriching contributions of these peoples. They can see Indians as a unique part of the variegated fabric of American life. Importantly, they can see the potentialities of Indians when their problems are minimized or resolved, when their positives are expressed.

There are in the picture many crises. Indian youths' crises are varied, real, and extensive! Urban and rural Indians share the crises of other Americans and have some which are uniquely their own.

Out of sight and largely out of mind are the rural Indians. Scattered across our vast continent are the "reservations," which were in spite of treaty obligations originally concentration camps. Indians who left them were hunted down and returned. Things have improved. Tribal governments now rule in major matters. They function as states in many ways. Their governments still are limited in some ways. An example is the FBI's jurisdiction over murders in Indian lands.

Indian governments are responsible for crisis management and human services. They have agencies to provide education, social services, roads, detention centers, and other normal governmental services. Like other government operations across America, they vary in role and effectiveness. They are staffed by professionals who labor to solve crises— of individuals, of Indian communities, and of our nation.

The crises can be grouped into broad categories(AASA, 1989, 1990). A pervasive concern is the loss of indigenous languages and cultures. Even in remote areas there is the bombardment of the young by broadcast or cable TV, radio, videotapes, audiotapes, and CD's, newspapers, and magazines. These manipulative media have several negative effects. The Anglo culture undermines Indian values and ways:

(1) Open advocacy of non-traditional ways— values, languages, behaviors,clothing, and lifestyles— put the young in direct conflict with parents, tribal leaders, and school officials. Directly and indirectly, school performance and home-community relationship commonly are Anglo affected, all too often with negative results.

(2) Even before birth, children are clobbered by fetal alcohol syndrome (FAS). Indian children have a high incidence of FAS and are part of the tragic FAS population which runs in the hundreds of thousands nationally. Alcoholism strikes directly at adults and youth, and creates crisis-proportion health and law enforcement problems. At the prenatal stage, FAS creates populations for special education classes and lifetime adult incapacity. Inadequate socialization, unresponsive education, and negative role modeling are major contributors to thE development of alcoholism. Apparently the use of alcoholic beverages puts Indians at risk since they seem to have less tolerance than other races have for alcohol.

(3) Anglo-oriented curricula, instructional materials, and teaching methods contribute to Indian school "failure." Such failure in the present and emerging world puts Indian youth at risk. Without formal education, their future options will be severely restricted, both on and off the reservation. "Failure" is very likely for the Indian youths who attend largely Anglo public schools. Even with good intentions, school staffs commonly have limited knowledge, attitudes, and skills needed to promote high-level Indian growth. Their low expectations too often commonly yield self-fulfilling prophecies: expect failure, communicate expectations directly and indirectly, and get failure. Open and subtle prejudice by Anglo students takes its toll on Indian youth's pride, dignity, and self-concept!

Schools operated by the U.S. Bureau of Indian Affairs have long been intrusive foreign institutions. No matter what the policies, BIA is ultimately Washington. Washington has meant oppression and insensitivity. BIA is an "apple" even with on-again-off-again honest efforts to make its schools more responsive and meaningful to Indians. Even with greater local Indian influence and involvement, BIA schools look red on the outside, too white on the inside. BIA schools should be fully transferred to Indian governments. Federal subsidies then will be needed to finance all the available productive approaches to undo the open and subtle negative influence of BIA schools and of White society.

Individual poverty amidst community economic underdevelopment creates a variety of crises. Tribal lands were often selected on the basis of their apparent undesirability for Whites. In a historic turn-around some reservations have created wealth from natural resources such as oil, hard-won legal rights such as water allocations, or economically desirable location near to Anglo communities (some locations desirable for shopping centers, golf courses, gambling casinos, and other developments).

Generally, individual poverty is a crisis. It commonly means recycling poverty from generation to generation. Poverty's homes usually have little or no stimulating reading or conversation, few good communications models, or strong motivation to extend schooling beyond the minimum. Little help with homework is available from parents or siblings. All too many Native American youth are at great risk. (Parenthetically, we note that there are many urban Indians with their own unique crises.)

African-Americans at Risk

Black/Negro/African-American long meant rural citizen. The great exodus to the cities several decades ago began to change the complexion of whole cities. Prolific birthrates speeded up the process of city coloration. In the 90's thinking Black to many means thinking urban. Often it means ignoring rural Black America.

Rural Blacks are in crisis even though (a) political reconstruction has yielded a great deal of power through voter registration and political action, (b) Black-friendly Congressional districts have been created, and (c) some unified economic actions to secure a fairer share of the economy have occurred.

Disproportionately, poverty grinds down individuals' dignity, sense of worth, self-respect, and motivation. Too few Afro role models demonstrate success to youth. Economic poverty often means learning poverty. It was a positive step when the nation adopted a policy to eliminate hunger and other blatant forms of deprivation. At the same time generation-after-generation social entitlements eventually produced family cycles of welfare dependency. Several generations of children became dependent on someone's providing minimal necessities, learned how to stay eligible, and ultimately were deprived of belief in self as capable of making choices and learning from consequences. Welfare tends to be the antithesis of confident, motivated, energetic, and autonomous behaviors. It tends to be self-perpetuating. A series of interrelated crises exists when huge proportions of the population have become dependent on debilitating welfare programs.

Many rural Blacks still reflect the past's societal inadequacies and crises. Too often, the youth are likely to lack the education, career skills, and social practices essential for survival. They are susceptible to the flourishing illegal economy of drugs, prostitution, and gambling. They also are susceptible to unscrupulous manipulation of self-serving politicians and entrepreneurs.

Throughout Black American history the family has been systematically broken up, degraded, and undermined. During slavery, real families existed at the permission of owners. Whimsically, in modern times a man in the house meant lowered welfare assistance. Males have been stereotyped as shuffling, shiftless, lazy, and incompetent. Educated in a system which does not seem relevant, even in recent years, Black males often collide with a White curriculum, White disciplinary standards, and seemingly hostile, insensitive Black and White teachers. They often are shoved out of classes by a system of suspensions and detentions, a system which further alienates them from an educational system which could and should provide upward mobility.

In a perceived hostile world, Blacks males often turn to the comforting and restrictive realm of gangs—which provides a security blanket of sorts and easy money long denied to their families. At an astounding rate, young Black males confront the legal system. They are detained, and they are on probation. Often they are being sought by legal authorities. Thrown together in detention centers by the justice system, they create a very effective educational setting—one in which each one often teaches others how to beat the system and how to improve illegal economic enterprises. It's a form of capitalism with a vengeance.

From a societal perspective, a major curse is child-like youth having children and thereby broadening poverty's cycles. Commonly under-educated and emotionally immature, youthful mothers are ill-equipped for parenting. The children-become-youth drift into a culture separate from adequate supervision by parent, community, church, police, and socializing agencies. The youth community too often is unsocial, asocial, and anti-social. They are a danger to each other, children, and adults.

Even at the pre-natal stage, babies of children are at risk. Too often, they do not get medical protection. Their mothers are improperly nourished and often addicted to drugs. Sexually transmitted diseases and smoking are also risk factors. Tragically, at birth many Afro-American babies begin life in crisis. For huge numbers, the crises are full blown by adolescence. The exploding crises are hard to slow down, much less to stop.

Hispanics at Risk

Spanish-speaking itinerant farm workers are a major force in the nation's food supply. They also produce many children whose children receive education in bits and pieces, state by state. Rotating crops rather than stable community determine where the family will be and what temporary friends will be nearby. A cross-section of citizens is not available to provide constructive role models.

Temporary living arrangements are not conducive to learning stable life patterns. Youth with problems are often not in one community long enough to get vital rehabilitative services. Transient youth may experience discrimination from teachers and from peers. With limited education and experiences in a normal community, youthful farm workers are at risk in terms of becoming fully functioning individuals and citizens.

Commonly, Spanish is the primary language. A controversial question is whether large-scale resistance to learning English qualifies as an at risk-factor. English is the language of education, commerce, and work in the U.S. — and much of the world. It provides access to the majority culture and effective interaction within it. Hispanics to a great extent communicate in Spanish and often are limited in or totally deficient in English. Youth from such homes are not immersed in English and do not gain other functional skills essential to school performance. As the Spanish-speaking peoples become America's largest minority group, the issues will become more crucial.

Even as the U.S. moves toward the time when non-Hispanic Caucasians will be only slightly more than half of the population, it is likely that English will continue to be the functional, unifying language. It is reasonable to claim that youth who lack English fluency are at least partially at risk in terms of being able to gain access to the society's range of opportunities.

The at-risk factors become greater for Hispanics who live in isolated, impoverished areas. Poverty and isolation are bad enough. Lacking the language of access to the benefits of the larger society further limits full membership in the American society.

The undocumented Hispanics, those who enter the U.S. illegally, are particularly problematical. Since they live in the shadows, their numbers are unknown. Not trusting the legal system and fearful of it, they are unlikely to seek protection when they are abused by the shady employers who hire them sometime and often exploit them. They do not have ready access to essential social and medical services. While they have rights to education, they often are fearful of being exposed if they go to school. If they attend classes, they find alien language, values, and content—sometimes an unfriendly environment.

In a school, they too often become gang members. Gangs provide immediate friendships, protection of sorts, a sense of belonging, and a means of getting money. There's a price for all this: conflict with school and police authorities. Often gang membership means danger, even life-threatening harm. Once in, gang members cannot easily get out. It is inherently an at-risk approach to life in a new country.

Asian and Pacific Islanders at Risk

Stereotypes of Asians in America depict life without risk to youth. They are pictured as obedient, hard-working, and successful—often an accurate picture. The family historically is closely knit, disciplined, committed to hard work and success, and absolutely dedicated to education. The young seek above all else to avoid shaming the family by failing in school or by behaving in nontraditional ways. To a great extent the positive stereotypes are real world, especially in first generation families. A fact to make the point: Asians have the lowest dropout rate of any racial group.

The car permits Asians, in common with all Americans, to escape the watchful eyes of family and family friends. Easily assimilated, at least superficially, Asian youth can gain access to the majority culture. That includes some non-Asian values, behaviors, and lifestyles.

Obviously, there is the lure of gangs. For many, the appeal for Asian youth is comparable to gang magnets for other youth. As Asians easily move in and out of American life, they can become entrapped by gangs and other forces which put them at risk.

Increasingly there are large members of Asian immigrants entering the U.S. Even with first-generation family affiliation, immigrant youth face some risks. They may wander from their values. They may lighten up on school work. They may be attracted to here-and-now fun and vices. They may neglect the deference which should be shown to school authorities and even to their families.

Nevertheless, the positive stereotypes may convince school personnel that most Asians will be motivated to do well, that they will be able to function well in the majority society. Asian students tend not to challenge or flaunt authority. Counselors and teachers may neglect Asians with problems, for they do not raise commonly recognized red flags of danger. Yet, Asians may have academic, social, emotional, and health needs which are ignored. The situation can increase in-crisis situations for Asian youth.

The greatest stereotype is that all Asians are alike! Within some Asian nationality groups and among others, there are great variations. Socio-economic differences exist. Length of residence in the U.S. is a major variable in determining the amount and kind of assimilation into the majority society which occurs. Lumping all Asian youth into one stereotype can put some at risk through neglect. There is no one model Asian any more than there is one model American.

Rural Asians are largely invisible nationwide. They are likely to be ignored. Their problems are likely to be ignored. Asian youths are unlikely to turn to non-Asian counselors and other professionals who could help them, often help which is needed. They need encouragement to seek help and open themselves to it.

Poor Whites at Risk

Since they are "white," Appalachians are not often thought of in terms of being either a minority or at risk. Geographically, Appalachians peoples live in the mountains and valleys that stretch from New York to Georgia. They are among the most easily identifiable whites at risk and illustrate that no one group is safe from risk.

Some of them are descendents of people who started West and never completed the journey. Maybe they liked what they saw in the mountains and stayed. Maybe they experienced trouble with wagons, horses, or illness that stopped them. Some were attracted by jobs in factories, in mines, or on the railroads. Some started to eke out a living on marginal farms.

Collectively they developed or maintained a distinctive speech pattern related to old English. Today, often it is characterized as a drawl. Even though they've learned to survive in an area that doesn't give up a livelihood freely, the Appalachians often are depicted as shiftless and lazy. Education levels may be minimal, and school learning sporadic. The stereotypes are encapsulated in the term "hillbilly." It is a derogatory term. Often hillbillies are the butt of jokes, such as jokes about moonshiners.

In school hillbilly youths stand out. With marginal learning backgrounds, with little help at home, they are at risk educationally. Poverty doesn't give them much hope. Poverty has had a strong hold for a long time. The closing of many coal mines hurt. Other large employers closed down and left many towns with few jobs. The economy that remained has not been a magnet for business, professional, and service replacements.

It's easy to ignore hillbillies in school. They're not rebels. They are not trouble-makers. They may be suspicious of authorities and avoid potential professional helpers. Teachers and counselors should search them out, to get them moving toward the main economic and social mainstream—if that is their goal. At least they should be helped to create options, to function well in the mainstream culture, or to remain by choice in the subsistence Appalachian economic areas.

Very clearly, they should be encouraged to develop their dignity, sense of worth, and self-respect. Their socioeconomic status often has scarred them. There are strengths and values which can be held with pride. Hillbillies can be taught to hold their heads high. They need help in counteracting violence, separated families, homelessness, and hunger —afflictions of America's poor whites and other minorities (Select Committee on Children, Youth, and Families, April 11, 1989).

At-risk Caucasians are not limited to the mountains and valleys by any means. They have migrated far and wide. They have developed locally. During the Great Depression, there were the Oakies. There are Oakie-like peoples today. The term "poor white trash" is related harsh terminology. Poverty-gripped whites are the largest group of the various peoples at-risk.

Not clearly recognized as a minority, at-risk group, poor whites— whatever they're called— are at risk and should be considered protected peoples. Perhaps the greatest risks faced by at-risk Caucasians is that they can easily be ignored or forced into by programs designed for other minorities.

An estimated 20 percent of the U.S. poor—whites and others—live in rural areas. As many as half of some rural areas people are poor. As long as people remain poor, they are likely to be a risk in terms of access to education and other ways to attain opportunities (Cooper and Ryan, 1993, p. 380).

PART III: CHARACTERISTICS OF RISK

In addition to whole populations with large numbers of at-risk youth, there are individuals at risk because of lifestyle, learning limitations, home situations, and other causes. The cited characteristics are not inevitable forces in becoming at risk. Added to the normal hazards of adolescence, they can become the forces which tip individuals from a precarious to an at-risk situation.

Rural Homeless at Risk

Millions of Americans are one paycheck from being homeless. Ideally our people would have savings to cushion them when jobs are lost. Ideally companies and agencies would provide severance pay and medical insurance to tide people over when they no longer are working. Ideally those who are fired would find new jobs. In less than an ideal world hundreds of thousands of Americans are economically vulnerable and can become homeless with shocking rapidity. The threatening consequences are economic, social, and emotional. No feeling and nothing in lifestyle are spared from the reach of homelessness.

The relatively few farmers of the nation can become homeless. Usually in debt for land, equipment, seeds, and fertilizers, small farmers lead precarious lives. Income can plummet as a result of changing economic conditions at home and abroad. Drought, floods, hard freezes, and other vagaries of nature may come in cycles; or they may wipe out income for several consecutive seasons. Farmers often do not have cushions to protect them from such jarring realities.

Homelessness when it comes does so with a jolt. Every aspect of life is shaken out of routines. Pride and self-respect may be wiped out within the total family. "What's the use" attitudes may take over. Youth may lose motivation to do well in school. Living in cars or parks, they cannot maintain normal appearances. They easily become subjects of ridicule and scorn. Teachers may feel uncomfortable being around them and their families. School attendance is likely to suffer. Lacking a place to do school work, homework is likely to be neglected.

Youth in homeless families are very much at risk. It's hard to stay in the same school. It's hard to hold on to motivation, to faith, and to trust. It's hard to get enough sleep, good nutrition, and medical treatment essential for well-being.

At a time when family unity is needed most, homeless families may not be able to stay together. Limited space in homeless shelters typically is reserved for mothers and young children. When shelters are available for males, space and privacy are not available for related females, children, or youth.

The ways out of homelessness are rough and difficult. Prospective employers may be suspicious of the unemployed. The unemployed may be marginally employable in term of skills and attitudes. They may have become unemployed when previous skills no longer were needed in the changing world of work. They may lack the motivation and the means to retread for a new job. Homeless youth usually have few constructive role models.

An escalation of homelessness comes when youth no longer stay with their families. Commonly, there is then no other good place for them. Typically they may drift from the home of various friends or relatives. The challenge is to find a way to survive locally. A common alternative is to drift into a city and join up with a band of homeless youth. Day-to-day existence rather than preparation for the future is their nebulous agenda. Too often days are spent mindlessly, without goals, or in efforts to get money through shady or criminal activity. Homelessness is a grim reaper.

Vast numbers of Americans are close to homelessness, according to Koegel of the RAND Corporation. He notes that one crisis, one major illness, or a layoff can push people into homelessness (Rohrlichs, 1993, p. B-1). Commendably, many make do under exceptionally challenging circumstances. Some adults work their way out of their homelessness. To do that, homeless youth require very sensitive and competent assistance.

The U.S. Department of Education estimates that some 220,000 children and youth are homeless. That's a lot of people in crisis!

Immigrants at Risk

Problems experienced by immigrants are numerous. They include culture shock, racism, language barriers, difficult standardized tests to determine mental and achievement levels, and lack of support services (Research and Policy Report, 1989, p. 89). Certain immigrants don't do well in their new country. Those from Haiti and Mexico often experience a hostile reception in the U.S. and have great difficulties in becoming assimilated. Others find open doors and are able to create many opportunities; Koreans and Cubans are examples of such peoples (Bock, 1993, p. 2-B).

Sexually-Transmitted Disease Risks

Adolescent sex continues to be a major source of risk. The United States has the highest rates among developed nations of teen pregnancy, abortion, and childbirth. Three million youths contract sexually transmitted diseases annually, according to the Guttmacher Institute (Scanlan, 1993, p. 26-A). While the AIDS crises have captured the nation's attention, a host of other sexually related problems create many crises for youth and challenges for those responsible for their wellbeing.

Youthful Homosexuals at Risk

Homosexuals in rural areas must lead a lonely life. Those who are out of the closet are few in number. They are subject to prejudice and discrimination. They may be isolated from normal social interactions. Those living the homosexual way in private may experience fears of discovery. They may feel uncertainty about their chosen way of dealing with their sexual preferences.

In either case, the at-risk factors are personal as well as social, physical, and emotional. The youth need understanding and sensitive professional attention and support to promote their maximum development as individuals and citizens.

Risks Associated with English Deficiencies

Youth with Limited English Proficiency (LEP) may be considered at risk if they are in a school district which does not properly serve them. If both the school district and student are deficient, in terms of teaching and learning,

LEP's are at risk academically and socially. They will be limited in their abilities to become acculturated, to become functionally literate, and to secure more than minimal paying jobs (if any at all). In a highly developed nation such as the U.S., the LEP's are likely to have a dismal future.

At least 5 percent of U.S. students, some 2 million, are LEP's (National Forum on Personnel Needs for Districts with Changing Demographics, 1990, p. 5). The numbers keep growing. Students from varied backgrounds keep spreading throughout the land. Their languages are very diverse. The challenges to school districts are great whether there are either few or many LEP's. The challenges are different, depending on the size of LEP student population. The problem in the former case is illustrated by the rural district that found itself responsible for educating a Chinese student. It could find no Chinese-speaking child to help the new student, and it could find no adult who could assist the child in the classroom. Fortunately the child's mother spoke excellent English and could help at home, and an English -only- speaking Chinese-American boy at school could serve as a buddy to assist in non-academic adjustments.

Nationwide there are some 100 languages spoken. Experts believe that speakers of these languages are spreading throughout the nation (National Forum, p.5). Triple goals for LEP's should include (a) maintenance of the native language and through it the culture, (b) transition into functional English, and (c) mastering English well enough to be fully functional in learning and later in moving into effective work and citizenship roles.

Truancy, Erratic Attendance, and Dropping Out as Risk

Truancy and erratic school attendance are both problems and indicators of problems in school and elsewhere. Truant students obviously can't succeed in school, and out of school they are subject to all sorts of temptations that thwart a good future life. Daytime crime is a youthful crime, with 85 percent of crime being committed by children and youth. Truancy is the single most common factor in adult criminal records, according to Levine (Levine, 1993, p. E-1). Dropping out of school too often is dropping out of further education and job training. It is possible to drop back in; with the passing the time, it gets more difficult.

Learning Disabilities as Risk

Inadequately assisted youth with learning disabilities are at great risk. They cannot fully manage their current lives; and they cannot prepare for autonomous, responsible adulthood. Westman (1988) identifies several disabilities which limit youths' maximum development: tempermental, cognitive, verbal language, written language, managerial, and self-system. There are many other classifications, all of which impact on full development and satisfying lifestyles. Schools without adequate staffing, materials, equipment, and facilities place students with disabilities at risk of becoming less than they could be.

Violence as Contributor to Risk

Youth have the right to attend schools and to live in neighborhoods which are safe, ones in which they can concentrate on learning and living. They should not fear mental, emotional, or physical harm. Increasingly the youth world is dangerous.

For many youth there are threats of violence and actual violence as a regular occurrence. The violence comes from gangs, weapons use, drug abuse, vandalism, racial and ethnic hatred, bullying, and sexual harassment (Lane, Richardson, and VanBerkum, 1993, p. 1). Kilpatrick estimates that there are 525,000 "attacks, shakedowns, and robberies in public high schools each month." The same author thinks that 135,000 students carry guns daily. Other weapons also are carried. For those who do not have them, weapons are readily available. Anderson says that there are 3 million crimes committed by youth each year (Anderson, 1993, p. 6-A). School consolidation has brought large numbers of youths together. In those large students bodies there are some violent ones. The risks are a result.

The Attorney General of California ruled that metal detectors in schools are constitutional under prevailing threats of violence. Critics charged that they are invasions of privacy (Lane, Richardson, and VanBerkum, p. 4). When young people have basis for fearing to go to school, clearly their learning and normal growth are at risk. Schools will unfortunately continue to reflect the all too prevalent violence in the larger society and to reflect as well the various social ills which contribute to violence.

Girls and women are especially vulnerable. Fear of rape and other violence leads to self-imposed restrictions on where they can go and when—and on what they can do to pursue educational, career, and social interests. That means that their potential for growth and development are at risk (Newborne, 1993, p. B-7). In many areas young males suffer from violence as a regular part of their lives; often the results are fatal. For the males the consequences are often the result of some choice, for example, joining a gang. For females the violence in their lives results from their gender; just being a female too often is a risk.

The Media as a Risk Factor

When the TV becomes babysitter for hours on end, children are placed in harm's way. The results extend into adolescence. Youth who stare at the tube for hours, mindlessly and nonproductively, are eating up time and potentiality. Their values and their minds are being controlled by the masters of marketing who determine what our youth see, hear, and experience— and to an alarming degree what they will become (if those raising our fear level about the media are correct). The bottom line is profit. The profit increases as the number of viewers is increased, at whatever the cost to the future of our children and youth. Cable has permitted the profit seeker to invade rural America.

The values of pop culture are often unrelated to the larger society—sometimes hostile to it, especially to authority figures such as teachers, parents, and law enforcement officials. Pop culture is communicated powerfully by experts in communication and behavior modification. Pop culture's "teaching" is commonly more powerful than that of parents, guardians, teachers, and religious leaders. Pop culture need only to attract the young in order to be successfully profitable. Youth are particularly susceptible to being attracted to the pop culture which targets them as a very important major market. Arcade games are in the same family of diversions. They lack redeeming characteristics.

Learning-impoverished Homes as Places of Risk

Youths in learning-impoverished homes are at risk. In a sense such youth are a new underclass. What characterizes such homes—indeed whole neighborhoods at times? First, they lack the positive social interactions which are centered around family interests, education, culture, and other aspects of life which are compatible with education and general development. Their TV watching is almost continuous and is devoid of mind-stretching and social/character building content. In too many cases the TV programs not only are limited in positive values, they are contemptuous of positive values such as learning. They may even glorify negative attitudes toward learning and culture. Music in impoverished homes is limited to only one or two types, neither of which is likely to be compatible with the music studied and practiced in schools.

A second major characteristic of impoverished homes is the absence of learning tools. Reading materials are limited to local papers—and sometimes even they are lacking. Magazines are those which focus on limited interests and hobbies. Few books are evident, and those are rarely educative in any sense of the word. Reading when undertaken is a diversion or escape; it is not used as an educational experience; it is not used to solve problems or assist in daily life. Educative publications such as encyclopedias, dictionaries, and other reference materials are lacking all together or are low in quality. Computers, calculators, and educational tools are not available. Enjoyable and growth-inducing games are not played by the family.

In barren home learning environments youth are at risk. They are receiving limiting inputs, and they are wasting their potentially productive hours. They are not involved in the kinds of thinking, experiencing, and role modeling which transfer positively into school and into other environments which promote desirable growth.

Gender As Risk

Sexism is alive in adolescence. Females may be viewed as sex objects. They may suffer much sexual harassment. They are counseled out of certain subjects and careers. Just being female results in being has treated a certain way or in being excluded from some opportunities. Great progress has been made in moving toward gender equity; much more is needed.

Endangerments to Health and Safety

Youth are inclined to experiment today with some of the common dangers to health and safety, much as their parents did before them! They put themselves at risk when they drink and drive. With abandon, they experiment with drugs. They smoke, and they use smokeless tobacco. They eat junk foods. They dive off high cliffs into unknown waters. They play "chicken" with their cars. They engage in "unsafe sex." They act as if they will live forever. They assume that being at-risk is normal. Surely readers can add to the list of ways in which youth put themselves at risk. Surely there must be some mystical protective shield around youths or not so many would survive the many endangerments to which they expose themselves— or to which many people and circumstances expose them. The ultimate risk is teen suicide, which takes thousands of youthful lives each year.

PART IV: FROM CRISES TO ACTIONS

Moving beyond the diagnosis of the crises to actions to remove them is an important priority for rural America. This action agenda is important for everyone, from the nation's capital to the smallest hamlet. A coordinated attack is needed by all rural institutions, agencies, organizations, enterprises and individuals. Those efforts should yield coordinated services and programs; they should eliminate gaps and redundancies. American can be rebuilt, one community, one life at a time!

Each effort can remove or minimize one problem at a time. Each effort joined with others can create a synergism of great power and effectiveness. No task is more important than the one to create an environment in which our youth attain their maximum potentiality for the good life today and for the rest of their lives— to the benefit of each individual and to the benefit of all!

Rural political subdivisions such as state and Congressional legislative districts commonly lack power compared to the ones which are urban or suburban. In political battles over spending the less powerful get less. The Supreme Court's ruling on one-person-one-vote legislative districts spread rural power rather thinly (a major change from the days when rural districts, with a pattern of re-electing representatives to powerful seniority-based positions, ruled legislative bodies). Another weakening action is the state and federal action mandate without essential financing to implement it. Such mandates actually undermine rural responsive initiatives to serve their unique needs. The external mandates eat up available local rural monies and often impose on rural areas weak imitations of programs designed for nonrural settings.

A major rural crisis management task is to secure equity and fairness for rural America. Then it can tool up to solve its individual and organizational crises. There are many, and they are daunting. Some of the historic strengths of rural America have been eroded. Rural "social captital" — parent and citizen involvement in their neighborhood schools, personal and neighborhood assistance in times of need, neighbors and relatives helping to oversee children and youth, and other positives of rural life. DeYoung says that "social capital" has been weakened by school consolidation, centralization, and urban models for education and human service programs. He claims that the erosions have put rural youth at risk (DeYoung, 1989).

Importantly, there are many opportunities for rural America's renascence waiting to burst forth once the crises are eliminated or pared down to controllable proportions! Averting crises and responding to challenges: that's a good way to build a bright future for our youth.

REFERENCES

Anderson, Jack. (Sept.1, 1993) Firearms become school epidemic. *Cumberland Times-News*, p.6-A.

Brodinsky, Ben. (1989, 1990). *Youth at Risk: Problems and Solutions*. Washington: American Association of School Administrators.

De Young, Alan. (spring 1989) The disappearance of "social capital" in rural America: Are all rural children "at risk"? *Rural Special Education Quarterly* 10, No. 1. pp. 38-45.

Helge, Doris (1991) *Rural, Exceptional, at Risk.* Reston, VA: Council for Exceptional Children, in *Research in Education,* April 1992. ED 339173.

Lane, Kenneth; Richardson, Michael; Van Berkum, Dennis. (1993) Safe schools: An analysis of the issues. A paper presented at the 1993 Annual Conference of the National Council of Professors of Educational Administration.

Levine, Bettijane. (Aug. 16, 1993) Tracking truants. *Los Angeles Times.* p. E-1.

National Forum on Personnel Needs for Districts with Changing Demographics (May, 1990) *Staffing the Multilingually Impacted Schools of the 1990's.* Washington: U.S. Department of Education.

Newborne, Helen. (Aug. 16, 1993) Mere talk won't make life safer for women. *Los Angeles Times.*

Research and Policy Report. 1989 *New Voices, Immigrant Students in U.S. Public Schools* (National Coalition of Advocates for Students), in *Educational Leadership,* 1989, 47(2).

Rohrlich, Ted. (Aug. 16, 1993) Cuts may double homelessness, experts say. *Los Angeles Times.*

Ryan, Kevin and Cooper, James. (1993) *Those Who Can, Teach.* Burlington, MA: Houghton Mifflin.

Scanlon, Christopher. (Sept. 5, 1993) U.S. to revise strategy on teen-age pregnancy. *The Baltimore Sun.*

Select Committee on Children, Youth and Families, U.S. House of Representatives. First Congress, First Session. *Working Families at the Margin: The Uncertain Future of America's Small Towns.*

Westman, Jack C. (1990) *Handbook of Learning Disabilities: A Multisystem Approach.* Des Moines, IA: Allyn-Bacon.

II

STUDENT PROBLEMS: UNDERSTANDING COMMUNICATION AND COPING

MICHAEL K. NEWMAN

6

Egalitocracy:
The Emancipation of Learners

Each year—without exception—Americans are given a respite from their normal routine (whether study, work, or leisurely pursuits) in order to celebrate the winning of their freedom from the mother country. July the fourth is symbolic of that fateful day when democracy became a way of life, and the bondage of a toxic political system no longer forced a people to yield to the whims of an incestuous bonding of church and state. Democracy, however, is a "system of representation" affording little or no direct, individual power.

An egalicratic system of government "empowers individuals" with equal social, political, and economic rights and privileges; individual differences and uniqueness are accorded the highest value, and the herd mentality is supplanted by cooperative team processing and decision making. This is the probable future of the global economy and, eventually, the world government—it could also be the answer to America's educational miscarriage.

"There are 83,248 public schools in the United States. Many of these schools are failing" (Pogrebin, 1991). The human casualties of this "apocalypse now" are the "27 percent, or one out of four students, who leave school before completing their high school diploma" (Carbo, 1993; Mitchell, 1991; Parnell, 1990, p. 21). If we combine the numbers of students who drop out with those who remain in school (at least for the present), but who are below grade level, the percentage for Whites is at the 74.8% level, Blacks at 48%, and Hispanics at almost the same level as Blacks—48.8% (Pearce, 1992).

At the rate of approximately 1 million each year (Carbo, 1993), academically ill-prepared students are being jettisoned into a beleaguered adult population of some 20 to 30 million Americans who cannot read or write. What is more alarming is that 20% of the high school students who remain in school until graduation are functionally illiterate (Mitchell, 1991), and only 4.8% of America's graduating class can work math on a high school level (Pearce, 1992).

Matters get worse when the focus is narrowed to Afro-Americans. Approximately 44% of Black men are high school dropouts, and are functionally illiterate (Radliffe II, 1991). The justice system in America sends more Black men to prison each year than to college, and prison costs four to five times more (Pogrebin, 1991). Even though Black males represent only 6% of the total population, 47% of prison inmates are Black males, and they constitute only 3% of the national college enrollment figure (Carbo, 1993).

If one were to wonder why this nation's prisons are overcrowded and why early release programs are common practice, one would need to look no farther than the local high school: 62% of prison inmates are high school dropouts (WYFF TV, 1991); add this number to the more than one in two welfare recipients who also leave school before graduation (WYFF TV, 1991) and the value of education, as a tax supported institution, can no longer be regarded by some in the agricultural community as a luxury for seasonal pursuit (migrant workers and others).

American students spend only about 9% of their time on school work, and approximately 22% watch television five hours or more each day. This gives American students in this category an undisputed first place out of the seven countries studied by the Education Testing Service (Routh, 1992). When compared with students in 14 other industrialized nations, American students ranked 13th in science and 14th in math scores (Pearce, 1992). The Educational Testing Service also studied the science performance of 13 year olds in seven different countries: American students scored 67% (5th place) and, yet, came in second (136 hours) as regards the average number of hours of instruction received each year (Routh, 1992). This may say something about how math is taught in American classrooms.

Leaders in the field of education, although their intentions were above reproach, in their over zealous attempt to open the doors of education to everyone, and to minimize the prospect of school failure, debased educational standards in America.

Today's average high school and college graduates are less educated—as measured by skills in a wide variety of subjects—than the American high school and college graduates of a generation ago (Kiplinger and Kiplinger, 1989, p. 150).

In the 1960s, 1 out of 10 college graduates had to accept a job that did not require a college degree. In the 1980s, 1 out of 5 did (NBC, 1992).

The educational leadership is not alone in this seemingly surreptitious demise of national educational achievement. Either concomitantly or superveniently various societal factors have come into play. This country has witnessed a growing and almost unmanageable lack of respect for authority; television has stolen a large portion of time that could be used for reading; parents are not as involved with their children; there is too much emphasis placed on sports, material possessions, and commercial entertainment; there is perpetual drug and alcohol abuse; as well as sexual promiscuity that leads, too often, to teen pregnancy (Kiplinger and Kiplinger, 1989).

According to the U.S. Department of Education's report entitled A Nation at Risk, "if an unfriendly foreign power had attempted to impose on America the mediocre education performance that exists today, we might well have viewed it as an act of war" (qtd. in Kiplinger and Kiplinger, 1989, p. 148). The mission of schools is to "teach academic skills that will enable [future workers] to earn a living and contribute to a vital nation" (qtd. in Kiplinger and Kiplinger, 1989, p.149).

Carl Rogers once said that "[t]he only man who is educated is the man who has learned to learn; the man who has learned how to adapt and change; the man who has realized that no knowledge is secure, that only the process of seeking knowledge gives a basis for security" (qtd. in Ellis, 1985, p. 9).

"[T]he teacher's ability to improve, motivate, and influence a [learner's] abilities and capabilities to be a [learner]" (Baker III, Roueche, & Gillett-Karam, 1990, p. 9) establishes the relationship between teaching and learning. The teacher's central task" is to enable the learner to perform the tasks of learning" (Baker III, Roueche, & Gillett-Karam, 1990, p. 10). When this mission is not accomplished, business and industry are forced to take up the slack, and consumers bear the brunt of these efforts as reflected in higher prices for products purchased.

"It is estimated that more than $30 billion is spent annually by U.S. public and private employers for employee education and training" (Parnell, 1990, p. 247). The trend is for this figure to increase, and for business and industry to enter into more partnerships with education, as well as, increase their own accredited, in-house academic programs (Johnston & Packer, 1987; Kiplinger & Kiplinger, 1989; Parnell, 1990)

According to Kiplinger and Kiplinger (1989, p. 155), approximately ten million employees are already taking courses every year, at a cost of $40 billion. By 2000, business will invest $80 billion to $100 billion a year in worker training and development, and nearly 10% of the work force will be in some sort of job training program.

Industry cannot afford to take over the role of the schools. Therefore, the educational system, industry, and government must work together to insure graduating students are prepared to perform the jobs required by our economy or we may see increasing numbers of functionally illiterate, unemployed, underemployed, or just plain dropped out (Bell, 1984).

According to the former Secretary of Education, T. H. Bell, this country needs educational reform and reform should focus on the goal of creating a

"Learning Society;" a commitment to life-long learning. Society needs to honor the belief that education is important not only because of what it contributes in material rewards, but also because of the value it adds to the general quality of one's life (Bell, 1984). Further, if the schools, in cooperation with government, industry, families and communities, do not work to make society a mirror image of what is taught in the schools, the outlook for quality education for all is bleak at best (Bowen, 1982).

The literature reveals that rapidly expanding technology, characteristic of the present service and information era, is demanding workers who are more capable of thinking, solving problems, and workers who can assume greater responsibility for their own learning—knowing "how to learn" (Kiplinger & Kiplinger, 1989). Today and tomorrow, higher levels of language, math, and reasoning skills are and will be sine qua non for employability (Johnston & Packer, 1987).

The National Research Council now estimates that the occupational half-life, the time it takes for one half of workers' skills to become obsolete, has declined from seven to fourteen years to three to five years. Workers at all levels of the workforce will need basic literacy and cognitive skills enabling them to be lifelong learners and adjust to new work situations (Parnell, 1990, p. 227).

In addition to the retraining demands placed on workers by the decreasing occupational half-life is the need to comprehend and synthesize the volume of information produced in this country that is doubling every two years (Kiplinger & Kiplinger, 1989). Without the knowledge and skills for "learning how to learn" the massive compounding of new information to be comprehended and, thus, necessity for perpetual retraining, workers may be unable to keep up with the ever changing requirements of their jobs (Kiplinger & Kiplinger, 1989). Therefore, students not only need to stay in school, but need to learn how they learn, and become skilled processors of information.

Although poverty is the undisputed and overwhelming demographic predictor of who will become our nation's dropouts (Paulu, 1987), ongoing research at over 80 universities across the country has and continues to reference the strong correlation between academic success and instruction that is congruent with students' learning preferences (Dunn & Dunn, 1993). Cafferty (1980) discovered that the closer the match between teaching style and learning style, the higher the student achievement. Therefore, teachers must consciously accommodate learning styles through provisioning or style flexing methods (Guild, 1980).

Marie Carbo (1980), who founded the National Reading Styles Institute and developed the Reading Styles Inventory (RSI), identified the perceptual strengths (auditory, visual, or tactual) of kindergartners. She taught 60 words to each child—20 through phonics (auditory), 210 through linguistics (visual) and 20 using a tactual approach. All 60 children achieved significantly higher scores on immediate recall ($p < .01$) and later recall ($p < .05$) when taught through their perceptual strength. Time of day or chronobiological preferences are equally important (Carbo, Dunn & Dunn, 1991).

"Whenever a class is in session, it is the wrong time of day for almost one third of its students . . . (Staff, 1992, p. 9). Murray (1980) compared learning styles of seventh and eighth grade, low-achievers. She discovered that many of the females preferred learning in the evening, whereas male counterparts preferred learning in the afternoon.

Andrews (1990) found that 55 of his underachieving elementary students were "morning birds," 70 were "night owls," 44 were late-morning preferents, and 100 were virtually non-functional in the morning, but came alive in the afternoon. After accommodating his individual students' chronobiological needs, their scores on the California Achievement Tests in reading and math went from the 30th percentile in 1986 to the 83rd percentile in 1989. Virostko (1983), among others, also discovered that matching elementary students' reading and mathematics instruction to their preferred time of day significantly ($p < .001$ increased their test scores over the scores they achieved when mismatched.

Gadwa and Giannitti's (Staff, 1988) study of junior and high school students' chronobiological preferents revealed that one-third of junior high and two-thirds of high school students learn best in the early morning. The majority of both groups prefer to learn during the hours of 11:00 a.m. and 3:30 in the afternoon. Approximately 13% prefer "late night." This would seem to place a greater emphasis on homework instead of classwork for these particular students, as well as point out a need for "shift-learning" (industry has offered "shift-work" for many years).

From a cultural perspective, Asian college students preferred early-morning learning much more often than their caucasian counterparts (Dunn & Griggs, 1990). Mexican-Americans shared an early-morning preference with Asians, but disliked afternoon learning (Lam-Phoon, 1986). Later in the day was preferred by Caucasians, African-Americans, and Greek elementary students (Jalali, 1989).

When a person is seated on a conventional classroom chair, approximately 75% of the body weight is supported on only four square inches of bone. This places a great deal of stress on the lower back and buttocks, and often causes fatigue, discomfort, and a need for frequent mobility (Branton, 1966). Teachers most often do not understand that children who are not sufficiently well-padded biologically, cannot sit on a hard seat for more than 10-12 minutes.

Many otherwise healthy, active students, whether global (right brain, deductive thought processors) or analytic (left brain, inductive thought processors), find it impossible to concentrate on new and difficult material when seated on wooden, plastic, or steel seats, but do earn statistically higher achievement test scores in relaxed, informal seating (Hodges, 1985; Nganwa-Baguman, 1986; Shea, 1983). Many of these students learn and retain more, and enjoy school better when they can be active learners, rather than passive (Dunn, et al., 1986).

Approximately 40% to 50% of adolescents find it difficult to sit in traditional classroom desks for more than 20 minutes, and the impact is greater on boys than girls. In fact, Lemmon (1985) and Griggs and Dunn (1988) reported statistically higher standardized test scores in reading and mathematics when students were permitted to sit comfortably during test-taking.

Just as important as matching learning and reading styles with instructional style, and accommodating time-of-day preferents (chronobiological needs) and formal vs informal classroom structure, is the need to permit students who require sound while learning to listen to easy-listening music with headphones so as not to distract others. DeGregoris (1986) discovered that some people think better while listening to soft music-without lyrics—than in quiet. Students in study groups achieved significantly better in the environment that responded to their learning style (whether quiet or allowing for music) (Pizzo, Dunn, & Dunn, 1990).

Another important consideration for the classroom, if achievement is vital, is an understanding of some students' need to snack while learning. MacMurren's (1985) study revealed that many students concentrate better while studying if allowed to eat, drink, or chew. This is a privilege that can be granted so long as students keep the classroom clean, and eat and drink healthy foods and beverages.

Research also indicates that lighting (whether dim or bright) affects 70% of students' achievement. Dunn, Krimsky, Murray, & Quinn (1985) reported that speed and accuracy, as well as achievement, increased merely when illumination was complimentary to individual preferences. These researchers also discovered that the amount of light with which analytics feel comfortable causes hyperactivity and nervousness among global students.

Given the above, certain strategies have been proposed to curb the dropout rate of an estimated 38,000 students each year: intervention before academic problems become chronic; provision for a nurturing rather than punitive school environment; espousal of high but realistic academic expectations; selection of teachers who can involve their students experientially in their learning; provision for a regular, ongoing inservice training for teachers that will provide them with state of the art instructional strategies and techniques, and continually refresh their spirit; provision for a variety of instructional programs; and, collaborative school-business-community programming (Paulu, 1987). All of the above strategies can become a reality, according to Dunn and Dunn (1993), if learning styles instruction is adopted by the school system.

In the existing traditional school system with its primary instructional method of lecture/textbook, paper/pencil approach to educating all students regardless of their learning preference, schools may be causing many of their own problems (Dunn & Dunn, 1993; Griggs, 1991). Three major studies have shown that the learning styles of school dropouts are significantly different from those of students who remained in school. Johnson (1984) compared 90 maryland school dropouts with 89 non-dropouts; Thrasher (1984) compared 130 at-risk sixth graders and 230 high school dropouts with equivalent samples of students in Florida; Gadwa and Griggs (1985) compared 103 high school dropouts with 214 students in an alternative high school and 213 students in traditional high schools.

These researchers discovered eight learning style differences that were statistically significant between high risk or dropout students compared to their counterparts who remained in school. Dropouts had learning preferences that were incongruent with traditional instruction and classroom environments (Dunn, 1989). Dropouts needed various accommodations in the classroom that are not found in traditional schools: to move around while learning (mobility), a variety of instructional resources, other than early morning classes, collegial rather than authoritative teachers, resources that accommodated their individual perceptual preferences and reinforced their learning through their secondary and tertiary preferences, an informal rather than formal seating arrangement, and soft as compared to bright illumination in the classroom—characteristics of global or right hemisphere learners (Dunn, 1989; Griggs & Dunn, 1988).

Other researchers investigated the learning styles of students at two different alternative high schools. One school offered a traditional approach to education: classroom is quiet (sound), has bright lights (illumination), fixed temperature for all students (warm vs cool), formal classroom design (compared to informal), learning is rigidly structured (no freedom of choice), students learn alone (no dyads, triads, etc.), teacher is authoritative (not personal), instruction is mostly lecture (auditory), no snacks allowed (intake), time for tests and other work is fixed for all (no allowance for chronobiological needs), no moving around the classroom (mobility), and instruction is analytical—sequential, inductive, left brain. The other high school afforded choices and experiential learning opportunities (Cooper, 1991).

The school that permitted choices and the opportunity for experiential learning had highly kinesthetic, teacher motivated students. The traditional, structured, alternative high school had students who "did not have a learning preference for structure" and, thus, their motivation for learning was significantly lower than students at the more open school (Cooper, 1991).

Dunn and Griggs (1987) encourage teachers: to allow at-risk (and other students) to redesign their classroom to respond to individual needs for informality and soft illumination; to show students how to translate textbooks into instructional materials that are a match with their learning styles (develop tactual and kinesthetic manipulatives for hands-on learning); to allow students the opportunity to move around while learning; and to be a coach or facilitator of learning (collegial) instead of using an authoritative approach—accommodating the global (right hemisphere) as well as the analytical (left hemisphere) learners (Dunn & Griggs, 1987).

Marshall (1992) conducted an informal study of over 9,000 teachers who attended teacher training workshops at the Center for Success in Learning in Dallas, Texas (Johns, 1992) over a five-year period. She reported that 85% - 90% of the teachers expressed a preference for learning new and difficult information visually, first (reading), and then reinforcing it auditorily (lecture). Teachers (90%) preferred to study alone, and this could account for their lack of use of "small group [and] cooperative learning teaching strategies" (Marshall, 1992, p. 7). A quiet classroom environment was preferred universally by the teachers surveyed. This unfortunately restricts their students who need sound while learning; and, generally neglects the learning preferences of global or non-traditional students.

Of the over 9,000 teachers polled, 50% preferred to move around and to sit in an informal learning environment—the reverse is also true for the other 50%. As many as 90% - 95% preferred assignments that required writing papers and reports, as well as written examinations (Marshall, 1992; Johns, 1992). The results of this informal survey indicate that teachers have a strong tendency to be a match with the traditional education instructional model in most areas of learning preference (Marshall, 1992; Johns, 1992).

There is ample evidence that we tend to be aware of our own learning style preferences and generalize these preferences to others. Teachers who are auditorily strong use auditory methods predominantly in the classroom; those who are analytic and use inductive reasoning in their approach to problem solving employ these strategies with students; teachers who equate quiet with learning impose those restrictions in the classroom and so on (Griggs, 1991, p. 94). Lenz, Ritchie, and Santana (Staff, 1992) in a limited study found a positive correlation between teaching style of the teacher and that of his or her favorite prior teacher. If teachers are instructing their students in the same ways that they would prefer to learn, (or in the same manner as their favorite teacher taught them, instead of the way in which they need to learn, as discovered by Lenz, Ritchie, and Santana [Staff, 1992]), they are creating a mismatch or an incongruence with the learning preference of many students, especially the at-risk and eventual dropout populations (Davis, 1989; Griggs, 1991; Johns, 1992).

Research indicates that only 30% of all students have auditory strengths (43% of dropouts have fair to poor auditory strengths). Visual learners comprise only 40% of the student population (53% of dropouts have fair to poor visual strengths). Only 15% of all students have tactile/kinesthetic strengths, however, 89% of dropouts have strong tactile abilities, and 99% have strong kinesthetic abilities (they have a strong need for hands-on, active learning) (Marshall, 1992).

Equally important to accommodating learning preferences in the classroom is the necessity for identifying those preferences, especially early on, before abatement of self-esteem and the establishment of a habitual pattern of academic inefficacy. Beaty's (1986) teachers in experimental and control groups were asked to identify their students' learning styles during their ongoing daily contacts through observations. They were able to identify only 4 of 19 student variables; self-motivation, teacher motivation, persistence, and light preferences. They were consistently unable to identify sound, structure, mobility, intake, seating, auditory and visual preferents, chronobiological preferents, variety vs. pattern, and authoritative vs. collegial teacher needs, nor could they identify which students would achieve well alone, in pairs, in a group, or with the teacher.

Beaty (1986) concluded that if teachers are going to implement a learning styles instructional approach, they need to use a commercially standardized test to identify their students' learning styles. The (LSI) Learning Styles Inventory and the (PEPS) Productivity Environmental Preference Survey (for adults) have been proven to have high reliability and validity (DeBello, 1990; LaMothe, et al., 1991), and are commercially available for purchase and scoring from Price Systems in Lawrence, Kansas (Price, Dunn & Dunn, 1991). The LSI and PEPS survey instruments, used to test children and adults, can be used at a relatively low cost as a beginning step toward implementing a learning styles instructional program that accommodates students' learning preferences (and teachers') and as a means to greater student academic success and retention.

Both practicing educators and those conducting research in education are convinced that almost all students can learn if they are given instruction that allows them the opportunity to stretch their minds in the areas where they are most intelligent and that also accommodate their learning strengths. Group paced learning that emphasizes competition against normative criteria (instead of criterion referenced), and that values only the linguistic and logical-mathematical domains of intelligence, will not bring forth the unique learning capabilities of all students (Gardner, 1985; Guilbault & Paul, 1993).

The factory assembly lines begun at the inception of the industrialized era no longer exist for the most part and, therefore, there is no further need for the 1950s educational model that requires students to restrain from eating, chewing, drinking, spitting, moving, lying down, teaching each other (used to be called cheating) and to sit quietly in straight-back, hard seats positioned in rows facing a lecturing teacher (Pearce, 1992). Today's workers need to know how to be active learners who can cooperate in problem solving teams with other workers. They need to be able to talk, eat or drink, and move around as needed to carry out the business of learning. This is the only way for students to discover their unique gifts and to latch onto the skills that they need to be competent learners (Dunn & Dunn, 1993; Guilbault & Paul, 1993).

Researchers have now discovered (Dunn & Dunn, 1993; Guilbault & Paul, 1993) that when students are given the opportunity to indulge or exercise their particular strengths, they are much more motivated to pay attention to various areas of instruction, they become more active learners in the classroom, their grades go up, and they feel better about themselves as achievers and as worthwhile individuals.

Recent research reveals that whenever a person focuses on new and/or difficult information with the intention to learn, that person literally grows more brain—increases the number of links or connective tissue between brain cells (also referred to as dendrites). The more the learner is challenged the more the brain produces new strans or dendrites (Guilbault & Paul, 1993); this process can occur even into old age, and this explains why almost anyone can learn.

Everyone has many different intelligences. Howard Gardner (1985), renowned psychologist who spent several years (with the financial backing of a grant) researching the roots of intelligence, believes that he has discovered seven kinds of intelligence: linguistic (verbal), logical-mathematical, musical, interpersonal, intrapersonal (introspective), spatial, and bodily-kinesthetic. The verbal and mathematical intelligences are usually the only two that are valued in school (Gardner, 1985).

Scientists believe that the more a person is given the opportunity (and uses it) to indulge his or her natural intelligence, the happier the person will be (Guilbault & Paul, 1993). If a person has a strong aptitude for something, he or she has to use it or face unhappiness. It is the reason some adults never advance in their work. Kids may become discipline problems or dropouts, bored or frustrated when what they are good at is not recognized (Guilbault & Paul, 1993).

The seven intelligences discovered by Howard Gardner need to be given equal time in school and equal importance. When they are attended to early in the day, students can more easily get through the rest of the day because when their particular strength has been given the exercise it is so eager for, the mind and body are energized and made ready to move on to other things.

Robert Sternburg, a psychologist who is known for his work on the subject of intelligence, believes that the I.Q. test causes many to think that they are inadequate. One reason for this, according to Sternburg, is that the intelligence quotient measures a person's knowledge in the areas of language and mathematics only. Therefore, if these areas are not the strengths of the person being tested, the resulting score becomes a distorted and fragmented view of his or her ability (Guilbault & Paul, 1993). Sternburg more appropriately defines intelligence as "the ability to organize your thoughts and coordinate them with your actions" (Guilbault & Paul, 1993).

Schools could become egalicratic by allowing their students equal social, political, and economic rights and privileges; by placing the highest value on individual differences and uniqueness, and by supplanting the herd mentality with cooperative processing and decision making that brings the learning system into the classroom—teachers, parents, business and industry, and government. This can be accomplished when the school system demonstrates to its students that they are valued consumers—evaluations or assessments are done to determine each student's strong attributes (intelligences), learning styles, and reading style, and instructional and environmentally-structured accommodations follow.

Students need to learn to think about their thinking (metacognition) in an environment where they feel safe, secure, loved, and respected (Chandler, 1991). Teachers need to have high expectations for students both academically and behaviorally. Not doing homework, being tardy, being absent, and not paying attention are unaccepted behaviors (Chandler, 1991).

The goals of education need to be about creating students who (1) know how to learn (2) communicate well with a variety of other people (3) concentrate well (4) can get whatever information they need (5) feel deeply, and (6) act wisely (Guilbault & Paul, 1993). Good schools are places that create opportunities for students to talk to teachers, to other students, and take information and do something with it; where teachers personalize themselves with students; where teachers may cover less content, but with more depth, more meaning, and more understanding; and where the theme of the learning process is, "How do people, events, and conditions influence change" (Pearce, 1992).

According to James Comer, author and child psychiatrist, the only place that we can make a difference to the child who has had a difficult family situation is in the schools—the first place and sometimes last place (Tait, 1992). Attitudes, values, and ways are transmitted from parents to offspring. As parents care for children an emotional attachment and bond develops between the child and parent in incidental ways as the child grows and lives with the parents. That is the beginning of the motivation for learning. When parents who already have a tie and a bond to their children are involved with the school and its teachers, that makes and seals the bond between school people and the children. Therefore, the parents help make the link from family to school by participating (Tait, 1992).

If schools, business and industry, government, and families can agree on a generic set of values (most people agree on traditional values such as honesty, integrity, consideration, courage, conviction, tolerance, justice, reliability, and a responsible life), this would relieve much of the anxiety on the parts of students who often are in a state of anomie (without values), and do not know what is expected of them (Guilbault & Paul, 1993). This would allow students to concentrate less on their insecurities and more on the process of education.

After all, education is how a society hands out its life chances, its options. And just like the proverbial man who has fallen into a hundred foot deep pit. His thousand thoughts are reduced to the single thought: "How can I get out of this pit" (Kapleau, 1979). This nation already knows how to get out of the pit, it just refuses to acknowledge the hole into which it dug itself; and surely the worst of all faults is to be aware of none.

REFERENCES

Andrews, R. H. (July/Sept., 1990). The development of a learning styles program in a low socioeconomic, underachieving, North Carolina elementary school. *Journal of Reading, Writing and Learning Disabilities International.* New York: Hemisphere Publishing, 6 (3), 307-314.

Baker III, G.A., Roueche, J.E. & Gillett-Karam, R. (1990). *Teaching as leading.* Washington, D. C.: American Association of Community and Junior Colleges.

Beaty, S. A. (1986). The effects of inservice training on the ability of teachers to observe learning styles of students. *Dissertation Abstracts International*, 47, 2530A.

Bell, T. H. (April 1984). Toward a learning society. *American Education.*

Bowen, H. R. (1982). Problems facing the nation. *The State of the Nation and the Agenda for Higher Education.* San Francisco: Jossey-Bass Publishers.

Branton, P. (1966). *The comfort of easy chairs.* (Tech. Rep. No. 22). Hartfordshire England: Furniture Industry Research Associates.

Cafferty, E. (1980). *An analysis of student performance based upon the degree of match between the educational cognitive style of the teachers and the educational cognitive style of the students.* Unpublished Doctoral Dissertation.

Carbo, M. (1980). An analysis of the relationship between the modality preferences of kindergartens and selected reading treatments as they affect the learning of a basic sight-word vocabulary. *Dissertation Abstracts International*, 45, 1282A.

Carbo, M. (1993). *Combining the power of reading styles with whole language.* Material presented at a one-day seminar sponsored by the National Reading Styles Institute, Roslyn Heights, NY.

Carbo, C., Dunn, R., & Dunn K. (1991). *Teaching students to read through their individual learning styles.* Boston: Allyn and Bacon.

Chandler, B. (Producer). (1991). *Learning in America: Schools that work.* Columbia, SC: SCETV.

Cooper, T. J. (1991). *An investigation of the learning styles of students at two contemporary alternative high schools in the District of Columbia.* Unpublished doctoral dissertation, George Washington University, Washington, D.C.

Curry, L. (1987). *Integrating concepts of cognitive learning style: A review with attention to psychometric standards.* Ottawa, Ontario, Canada: Canadian College of Health Science Executives.

Davis, B. S. (1989). *Relationship between cognitive style of teacher and cognitive style of child.* Unpublished manuscript, Francis Marion College, School of Education, Florence, SC.

DeBello, T. C. (1990). Comparison of eleven major learning styles models: Variables, appropriate populations, validity of instrumentation, and the research behind them. *Reading, Writing and Learning Disabilities*, 6, 203-222.

DeGregoris, C. N. (1986). Reading comprehension and the interaction of individual sound preferences and varied auditory distractions. *Dissertation Abstracts International, 47*, 3380A.

Dunn, R. (1989). Capitalizing on students' perceptual strengths to insure literacy while engaging in conventional lecture/discussion. *Reading Psychology, 9*, 431-453.

Dunn, R., Beaudry, J., & Klavas, A. (1989). Survey of research on learning styles. *Educational Leadership, 46*(6), 50-58.

Dunn, R., Della Valle, J., Dunn, K., Geisert, G., Sinatra, R., & Zenhausern, R. (1986). The effects of matching and mismatching students' mobility preferences on recognition and memory tables. *Journal of Educational Research. 79*(5), 267-272.

Dunn, R., & Dunn, K. (1993). *Teaching secondary students through their individual learning styles.* Boston: Allyn and Bacon.

Dunn, R., & Griggs, S. A. (1987). *Learning styles: Quiet revolution in American secondary schools.* Reston, VA: National Association of Secondary School Principals.

Dunn, R. & Griggs, S. A. (1990). Research on the learning style characteristics of selected racial and ethnic groups. *Journal of Reading, Writing, and Learning Disabilities.* Washington, D. C.: Hemisphere Press, 6(3), 621-627.

Dunn, R., Krimsky, J., Murray, J., & Quinn, P. (1985). Light up their lives: A review of research on the effects of lighting on children's achievement. *The Reading Teacher, 38*(9), 863-869.

Ellis, D. E. (1985). *Becoming a master student.* Rapid City: College Survival.

Gadwa, K., & Griggs, S. A. (1985). The school dropout: Implications for counselors. *School Counselor*, 33, 9-17.

Gardner, H. (1985). *Frames of mind.* Basic Books.

Griggs, S. A. (1991). *Learning styles counseling.* Ann Arbor, MI: School of Education, University of Michigan. (ERIC Counseling & Personnel Services Clearinghouse)

Griggs, S. A., & Dunn, R. (Sept./Oct., 1988). High school dropouts: Do they learn differently from those who remain in school? *The Principal, 34* (1), 1-8.

Guilbault, D., & Paul, G. (Producers). (1993). *Miracles: The new American revolution in learning.* [Film]. Denver: Journal Graphics.

Guild, P. O. (1980). Learning styles, knowledge, issues, and applications for classroom teachers. *Dissertation Abstracts International, 41*, 03A.

Hodges, H. (1985). An analysis of relationships among preferences for a formal/informal design, one element of learning style, academic achievement, and attitudes of seventh- and eighth-grade students in remedial mathematics classes in a New York City junior high school. *Dissertation Abstracts International, 45*, 2791A.

Jalali, F. A. (1989). A cross cultural comparative analysis of the learning styles and field dependence/independence characteristics of selected fourth-, fifth-, and sixth-grade students of Afro, Chinese, Greek, and Mexican American heritage (Doctoral dissertation, St. John's University, NY).

Johns, K. (June, 1992). *Trainer of teachers institute.* Material presented at the third annual CSL institute of the Center for Success in Learning, Dallas, TX. Unpublished manuscript.

Johnson, C. (1984). Identifying potential school dropouts. *Dissertation Abstracts International, 41*, 1389-04A.

Johnston, W. B., & Packer, A. H. (1987). *Workforce 2000.* Indianapolis: Hudson Institute.

Kapleau, R. P. (1979). *Zen dawn in the west.* Anchor Press/Doubleday.

Kiplinger, A. H., & Kiplinger, K. A. (1989). *America in the global '90s.* Washington, DC: The Kiplinger Washington Editors.

LaMothe, Billings, D. M., Belcher, A., Cobb, K., Nice, A., & Richardson, V. (1991). Reliability and validity of the productivity environmental preference survey (PEPS). *Nurse Educator, 15*,(4), 30-34.

Lam-Phoon, S. (1986). A comparative study of the learning styles of southeast Asian and American caucasian college students of two Seventh-Day Adventist campuses. (Doctoral dissertation, Andrews University, MI).

Lemmon, P. (1985). A school where learning styles make a difference. *Principal, 64*(4), 26-29.

MacMurren, H. (1985). A comparative study of the effects of matching and missmatching sixth-grade students with their learning style preferences for the physical element of intake and their subsequent reading speed and accuracy scores and attitudes. *Dissertation Abstracts International, 46*, 3247A.

Marshall, C. (Ed.). (June, 1992). *ABLE Insights*. (Available from The Center for Success in Learning, 1700 Preston Road, #400, Dallas, TX 75248).

Mitchell, P. (Producer). (1991). *Revolution at work.* [Film]. New York: ABC News.

Murray, C. A. (1980). The comparison of learning styles between low and high reading achievement subjects in the seventh and eighth grades in a public middle school. *Dissertation Abstracts International, 41*, 1005.

National Broadcasting Company (Producer). (1992). *NBC Nightly News*. New York: Author.

Nganwa-Baguman, M. J. (1986). Learning style: The effects of matching and mismatching pupils' design preferences on reading comprehension tests. (Bachelor's dissertation, University of Transkei, South Africa). Unpublished manuscript.

Parnell, D. (1990). *Dateline 2000.* Washington: Community College Press.

Paulu, N. (Nov., 1987). *Dealing with dropouts: The urban superintendent's call to action*. Washington, D.C.: Superintendent of Documents, U.S. Government Printing Office.

Pearce, J. (Producer). (1992). *America's schools . . . Pass or fail.* [Film]. New York: NBC.

Pogrebin, A. (Producer). (1991). *America's schools: Who gives a damn?* [Film]. New York: WNET.

Pizzo, J., Dunn, R., & Dunn, K. (July./Sept., 1990). A sound approach to reading: Responding to students' learning styles. *Journal of Reading, Writing, and Learning Disabilities, 6* (3), 249-260.

Price, G. E., Dunn, R., & Dunn, K. (1991). *Productivity environmental preference survey: An inventory for the identification of individual adult preferences in a working or learning environment*. Lawrence, KS: Price Systems.

Radliffe II, H. (Producer). (1991). *Project 2000.* [Film]. New York: CBS.

Routh, D. (Producer). (1992). *Southern solutions.* [Film]. Columbia, SC: SCETV.

Shea, T. C. (1983). An investigation of the relationships among preferences for the learning style element of design, selected instructional environments, and reading achievement with ninth-grade students to improve administrative determinations concerning effective educational facilities. *Dissertation Abstracts International, 44*, 204A.

Staff. (Autumn, 1988). St. John's University's center for the study of learning and teaching styles. *Learning Styles Network Newsletter, 9*(3), p. 3.

Staff. (Winter, 1992). St. John's University's center for the study of learning and teaching styles. *Learning Styles Network Newsletter, 12*(3), p. 3.

Thrasher, R. (1984). A study of the learning style preferences of at-risk sixth and ninth-grade students. Pompano Beach, FL: Florida Association of Alternative School Educators.

Tait, E. V. (Producer). (1992). *The legacy of Maggie's American dream.* [Film]. Columbia, SC: SCETV.

Virostko, J. (1983). An analysis of the relationships among academic achievement in mathematics and reading, assigned instructional schedules, and the learning style time preferences of third, fourth, fifth, and sixth grade students. *Dissertation Abstracts International, 44*, 1683A.

WYFF TV. (Producer). (1991). *Public Announcement.* [Film]. Greenville, SC: Author.

SANDY PRITZ
ALICE E. PRESSON

7

How To Make Evaluation Efforts In Dropout Prevention Work

The proportion of American youth between 16 and 24 years old who did not finish school has declined by only one percent since 1975. The impact of a 16 percent dropout rate to our society, to our economy, and to individual dropouts themselves is devastating. For example, the estimated average loss in federal and state income taxes is at least $58,930 per dropout during his or her lifetime. This amounts to $228.7 billion during the lifetime of the 3,881,000 dropouts between 16 and 24 years old in 1991.

Many things have historically impeded progress in reducing the dropout rate at the school building level; one has been the absence of routine efforts to evaluate progress in dropout prevention. The decision by school leaders to attack the dropout problem is not enough to insure success in reducing the dropout rate. The Southern Regional Education Board (SREB) and the Center on Education and Training for Employment (CETE) at The Ohio State University, who jointly administered a dropout prevention program for three years in six schools in six southern states, found that a major key to the success of efforts to see potential dropouts make academic progress and stay in school is the school's effort to keep track of its progress. The school that made the most progress in reducing its dropout rates wanted to know if what it was doing was working, how it could improve what did not work well, kept a current update on its dropout rate, and maintained a close watch on the academic progress and attendance of potential dropouts. *To effectively reduce the dropout rate and to see potential dropouts succeed academically requires that school leaders keep track of their efforts.*

Using an on-going evaluation system infused into the daily routine of dropout prevention efforts is an effective way to promote success. This article will describe typical pitfalls that school leaders face as they evaluate their dropout prevention efforts, what educators at all levels in a school system can do to assure that their work will succeed, the results they should expect, and how to recognize success in dropout prevention.

Evaluation's Pitfalls in Dropout Prevention

Evaluation of dropout prevention efforts often fall short by failing to provide critical information for decision-making at the school building or central office level. This occurs because such evaluations are fragmented, tacked onto an effort as an after-thought, focused mainly on overall annual dropout rates rather than on dropout prevention activities, and
required and developed by program administrators outside the school without involving school building leaders.

Evaluation of Fragments

The dropout problem is multifaceted. It is not amenable to single-or dual-faceted solutions. Students seldom drop out of high school for one reason alone. The various factors related to dropping out impinge upon each other integrally. For example, it is not reasonable to try to improve attendance monitoring without identifying the reasons why students might not want to attend school and determining what can encourage a student to attend school. Many evaluations, however, focus only upon activities designated as "dropout prevention" or are part of a "dropout prevention program." An evaluation that does not address all aspects of the dropout problem in a school will fail to provide important information. On the other hand, many school personnel who do see all the variables of dropping out hopelessly enmeshed with each other may tend to lose faith that they will see any clear picture emerge from evaluation efforts, and so they may lose motivation to proceed.

"Tacked on" Evaluations

In many cases, an evaluation process is added to a dropout prevention effort after the various dropout prevention activities were begun. This may occur for many reasons—the state department of education may require evaluation of current dropout prevention efforts before awarding funds or as part of a new state-wide accountability mandate; external evaluators may seek information of the school at the end of a dropout prevention project grant; the school board may want to know how effective a school's dropout prevention efforts are. Evaluations that are not built into a school-wide or district-wide dropout prevention effort from the beginning are unlikely to provide school leaders with information about progress of their efforts over time. If school leaders want to know how their dropout rate has changed over a five-year effort, but did not collect information on the dropout rate at the beginning, they will find it difficult to retrace their steps and determine a dropout rate if they must use a narrow definition of dropout. Grade point averages and numbers of days absent may be easier to acquire, but any further understanding of changes in academic achievement and attendance patterns would be impossible unless the need for such information was anticipated and thus collected. Furthermore, data collection—critical to an evaluation—seems to be a hassle that spawns resistance from those who have to add it to an already full list of responsibilities and who do not see it as a primary part of their job description. Might they also subconsciously fear that they themselves will be judged adversely if the data do not show dramatic gains, which they may judge to be highly improbable?

Bottom Line Evaluations

Too often evaluation of dropout prevention efforts focus only on bottom line results. Education leaders understandably want to see reduced dropout rates. Evaluations that are uniquely results-focused cannot reveal the reasons that could explain why the dropout rate may be what it is; they cannot explain the weaknesses or strengths in a dropout prevention effort; they cannot adequately offer recommendations for changing or refining a school's efforts. Evaluations that focus on both on the bottom line and the processes involved in reducing a school's dropout rate are the most helpful to school leaders in making decisions.

Evaluations Done With a "Project Mentality."

When a school dropout prevention effort occurs through a project and an evaluation is required as part of the project, unless school staff assist in developing the evaluation process, they are likely to regard it too as just another time consuming component of the project. They are unlikely to be involved personally in the evaluation processes—collecting information, analyzing the information, and disseminating the results. Unless they see dropout prevention as a long-term effort that involves the whole school staff, follow-up activities that respond to the findings of the evaluation will be unpopular in our quick-action society. Furthermore, those who were not part of the project are not apt to see themselves as part of the solution. Teachers and counselors thus need encouragement from administrators to make changes suggested through evaluations of their dropout prevention effort.

How to Make Evaluation Succeed in Dropout Prevention

Evaluation of dropout prevention efforts is a critical aspect in aspiring to reduce the dropout rate at all levels—school building, district, state, and national. It can enable educators to see where they have been and what they must do to reach a particular dropout rate. The evaluation plan must be sound, unbiased, and developed with the assistance of those whose activities will be evaluated and those who must respond to the results.

A single most important element in a successful dropout prevention program, and one that must be a focal point for any evaluation of a school's dropout prevention efforts, is the accurate identification of students who are most likely to leave school early if they do not receive special assistance. If identification procedures are not systematic and judgements too subjective, many potential dropouts will slip through the cracks without receiving essential help. Identifying students and placing them in a special program unto themselves, however can create negative effects from labeling. Any identification process must be guided by care and sensitivity. School staff should take care to place a student in an environment where he or she can develop a sense of belonging and make academic progress, without being stigmatized. Given that limited resources are available for addressing the dropout problem, any evaluation of a school's dropout program must determine whether or not students at greatest risk of dropping out are being identified and helped without lowering their self-esteem.

In planning evaluation of dropout prevention efforts, consider involving external evaluators to bring their expertise on evaluation, their objectivity, and a fresh perspective. They can greatly expedite the evaluation planning, help monitor the process, and compile and interpret data on the processes involved and the final outcomes. They can, for example, assist in designing evaluation instruments and conduct site visits to observe and interview those taking part in the program using methods structured for the selected objectives. These are tasks that cannot easily be assumed by those on site. They can say things in a final report that would be difficult, if not awkward, for local educators to say. However, involving them should not signal a transfer, physically or psychologically, of the locus of responsibility for the evaluation effort at the school site. Key factors in selecting external evaluators should be considerations such as their willingness to do the following.

- Facilitate actively the positive involvement of members of the site team in planning the evaluation effort and seeing it through, rather than adopt an attitude which says, "I'll take care of the whole thing because I know best how to do it."

- Explain evaluation options under consideration in clear, layperson terms, rather than make them seem so abstruse that only a wizard could understand. Respond to questions with a sincere desire to be sure that all concerns are discussed and resolved to everyone's satisfaction, so far as possible.
- Design an evaluation strategy and evaluation instruments that are customized to the specific goals and objects of your program, rather than take something "off the shelf."
- Design an evaluation strategy that is tied holistically to the needs assessment that should take place at the outset of program planning and can track progress in addressing the identified needs, so that evaluation is a natural part of the process from the beginning and not an after-the-fact event.

Administrators, teachers, and counselors can do much to improve the climate for dropout prevention evaluation and produce improved results.

Administrators:

- Communicate clearly the expectations regarding data collection and documentation; be willing to hear about difficulties and take a hand in resolving them.
- Articulate frequently the goals and objectives of the evaluation effort as well as the goals and objectives of the dropout prevention program.
- Support measures to make the data collection less tedious and less time-consuming, more hassle-free. These may include investigating how some data can be pulled from other record-keeping already going on rather than being double-entered, and how computer assistance can help.
- Promote evaluation as a team effort in which everyone shares a responsibility and benefit.
- Show an interest in the data—monitor it regularly and express appreciation to those who are diligently compiling them.
- Most important, take visible action based on the findings and make clear that the findings were important in determining what action to take. This is part of an overall philosophy that says, "It's worthwhile to learn by experience, our own and others, and we believe that action should be based on careful consideration of evidence rather than gut-level, seat-of-the-pants-impulse."

Teachers and Counselors:

- Take responsibility for getting a clear understanding of the evaluation plan and why it is important to the school, the students, and you.

- Don't ever slip behind in your documentation tasks or they will grow from molehills into mountains. They remain simple only if you capture what is happening while it is fresh in your mind.
- Plan and keep to a regular time for information collection tasks.
- Talk to other staff about the evaluation process in positive terms and share tips about what you find to be workable or time-saving.

Recognizing Success in Dropout Prevention

Successful dropout prevention efforts should, over time, reflect a decline in the dropout rate, an increase in daily attendance, and also noteworthy academic progress on the part of students at greatest risk of failing and dropping out. The following changes in how school works for potential dropouts should be reviewed also to determine what processes work well and what processes do not work well.

- Each school staff member not only recognizes the dropout problem and realizes that he or she shares responsibility for promoting meaningful academic success of potential dropouts, but acts on that realization.
- A whole school effort is designed to address the dropout problem, rather than developing another program for dealing with problem students by isolating them.
- A specific plan is laid out for teachers to give special attention, encouragement, and extra help to those students most at risk of dropping out.
- An individualized academic plan is developed and reviewed regularly for each student with basic skill deficiencies.
- Teachers and school leaders communicate to at-risk students that they hold high expectations for them and are willing to give them the extra help they need to meet those expectations.
- Teachers use instructional practices that address a variety of learning styles, rather than presenting their lessons in a single, traditional way that seems to work only for college-bound students.
- School leaders have eliminated the low level courses in math, science, and English that numb students' interest through repetitive drill work and content that is neither challenging, nor connected to the real world. Those courses have been replaced by others in which students must make an effort to master content that they will need for further learning on the job or in a postsecondary setting and which engage students actively in the learning process.
- A system for monitoring students' progress is in place to determine if those needing extra help and counseling have received it.

- Potential dropouts' desire to be in school is increased as evidenced by their attendance and degree of engagement in learning.
- Potential dropouts see the connection between school and their future and this is reflected in their plans, their schoolwork, and their activities.
- Potential dropouts realize that people at school care about them, their problems, and what happens to them in the future.

Of course, the above changes can occur only if schools have developed and implemented a plan for making such changes. Dropout prevention is a long-term effort and cannot be accomplished over night. It should be tied into the overall fabric of what school should be for our young people and must include a way to keep score on progress. When have we ever made progress as human beings without looking at ourselves to determine how to make improvements? Our coaches keep careful track of RBI's, Foul Shot Percentages, and Average Yards Gained in Rushing to help their team members perform better. Why don't we as educators do the same for our young people who are at risk of dropping out?

KARLA DRIEMEIER

8

Love, Sweat and Tears of Mentoring

This article will explain how one Junior High School mentoring program developed and led to a broader project considering a greater spectrum of children at a younger age. My discovery was how great the needs are at all levels.

My Jr. High reading program was started as a pull out class in which students came to my room two to five times a week. In this small group setting these students excelled. Unfortunately, when these same students returned to the normal classrooms, their grades remained at the "D" and "F" levels. About 75% of my students were Voluntary Transfer Students (VTS) from the inner-city. We worked in small groups in the areas of organizational strategies, study habits, and content reading and writing skills. I had taken several multi-cultural courses and one idea kept reoccurring; teachers' expectations are usually lower for Afro-American, inner-city students, but given the proper encouragement, these students could reach the same level of achievement as white, middle class students.

Frustration led me to try an intense intervention with two of these VTS students, Randall and Melvin, whom I considered the most at-risk of dropping out of school before graduation from high school.

I started by detaining Randall from lunch one day. I told of my frustration knowing he had good thinking skills and seeing him avoid using them in his other classes. He was very concerned that he would be 16 in the fall and was only starting the 8th grade. Nevertheless, he indicated that he would return to our school the following year. At the time, he was finishing his second year in seventh grade passing with D-'s. I knew from my work with him that he could make much better grades if he would complete and turn in all of his assignments and study for tests. He told me he wanted to do well in school but it was too hard to study and do homework with all the shootings and drug dealings going on around his home. I said it hurt me to watch him drown in his own potential. As he started to leave for his remaining 5 minutes of lunch he turned around to me and said, "Thank you, . . . for caring."

I had a similar meeting with Melvin, at which time he also indicated that he planned to return the next year. We discussed his many suspensions both on the school bus and in the school. He admitted whenever bothered by someone he would immediately react, not thinking about consequences. I told him it hurt me to watch him, with all of his potential, get into trouble, get suspended, and then see his grades plummet. He then confided he would rather face his mother than me when he got into trouble because he couldn't stand to see the hurt look on my face.

I had to try to do something to help these two young men. I was ready to make a commitment to find a new plan of action. I wanted to try to change Randall's study habits so he could experience success and feel better about himself. I also wanted to help Melvin improve his attendance and learn to think before he acted to eliminate his suspension problems, which in turn would help his grades improve, not to mention his future.

The following school year (1989-90) I decided to focus on high achievement for all of my students. At the same time I was also committed to finding a way to help Randall and Melvin become more successful students. At the beginning of our school year, my principal told the staff he would like each one of us to "adopt" one or two students for the year. He said we did not have to take them home with us but we could show special attention to them to see if we could help improve their self-esteem. At that point something clicked. I thought to myself, "Why not provide a home environment for Randall and Melvin which would promote positive study skills and homework completion?" I wondered if I could instill in them study habits that might benefit them for the rest of their academic careers.

Three weeks after school started I approached both young men with my idea. They seemed interested in trying this activity and I told them to discuss it with their moms. After it was discussed, I gave the mothers a call. I told them I would like to try to help their sons improve their study skills, grades and responsibility, and to expose them to some new experiences which would give more meaning to their learning. I planned to bring them home with me one or two evenings aweek and sometimes on weekends to prepare for major tests. The mothers were excited and completely in favor of this involvement. *Reality Therapy*, William Glasser (1965), reminded me that behavioral changes can occur when a student has a close and trusting relationship with a caring adult who has the resources to support him. Thus began my initiation into mentoring.

My project quickly mushroomed from two to five students and by the end of the first semester most of my city students were asking to come home with me. My five proteges had various problems, but there was a central element to success each one lacked, that of having a supportive adult who could offer assistance, i.e. a mentor. A mentor, as defined by Crockett and Smink (1991, p.3), is:

> *"a supportive relationship between a youth or young adult and someone who offers support, guidance and concrete assistance as the younger partner goes through a difficult period, enters a new area of experience, takes on important tasks or corrects an earlier problem.*
>
> *The relationship that develops (or doesn't) between adult mentors and their younger proteges defines the success or failure of any program. After all, program planners are trying to facilitate a relationship that generally evolves through a natural process of selection and mutual attraction."*

My mentoring program was one of natural selection. To understand the results of this program it is necessary to take a look at each student's background.

RANDALL

Randall lived in a six member, single parent family in a public housing area that had an extremely high crime and drug trafficking rate. Randall was the second oldest child and no family member had ever graduated from high school. He and his two brothers had witnessed murders, been shot at by unknown assailants, been beaten up with brass knuckles, and witnessed drug deals. Randall informed me he never had contact with his father but he knew he was wanted by the police. His mother dropped out of school in eleventh grade, then lived on welfare. She suffered through many years of depression. The mother's main concern was getting her five children through school so they would notlive the depressed life of welfare.

Randall was referred to me because his first year in seventh grade he made all F's. I started working with him at the beginning of his second year in seventh grade. I usually talked to him monthly about his grades and for about two weeks they would start to improve but then they would always drop back down because he would quit turning in work. Randall was very well mannered and rarely in trouble. He had never been suspended from school. As we discussed literature stories he seemed to have an uncanny amount of sensitivity for a young man his age. Randall rarely missed a day of school but was quiet in the classroom and kept mostly to himself. Eventually, I became closely involved with this entire family, including extended family members.

GOVERNORS STATE UNIVERSITY
UNIVERSITY PARK
IL 60466

MELVIN

Upon meeting Melvin, I was immediately impressed with his good manners and extended vocabulary. Whenever he heard a word he did not know he would ask what it meant and then try for several days to use it in context. He seemed to enjoy learning and was always eager to learn more. Melvin was referred to me because he was retained in seventh grade and was constantly in trouble. We started working together in 1987, his eighth grade year. After he joined my class, teachers commented on what a big change they saw in his interest in school. He reported daily to my class for extra credit work, but I was worried that he was doing more of my non-credit projects than assignments in his other subjects.

In the Spring of 1988 (in between Melvin's suspensions) my supervisor came to observe my class which included Melvin. We were working on comprehension activities associated with the book Durango Street by Frank Bonham. As usual Melvin had an upper level answer for each question I asked. In fact I had to hold him back to give otherstudents time to think. After observing the group, my supervisor asked why Melvin was in my remedial class, when he was obviously a gifted student. I told her I agreed with her assessment but because of low grades and suspensions he was placed with me. Even though he was only required to attend my class twice a week he usually chose to come in daily and sometimes twice a day. My supervisor looked at me and said, "If there is any way for you to save him, Karla, please do."

Melvin was starting ninth grade and lived with a single mother and a younger sister. Melvin's mother quit school when she became pregnant with him but went back to get her GED after her second child was born. She worked for awhile for a catering company but hurt her back and became dependent on welfare. Melvin was very affectionate with his mother and they seemed to have a close family relationship. Melvin was very outgoing and liked to joke. He seemed to enjoy people and philosophizing. Melvin's father lived in Detroit and even though he called him several times a year, their conversations centered around Melvin "being in any good fights lately."

THE PROJECT

At the beginning of the project I told Melvin and Randall I was going to push them to change their study habits and organizational skills and I knew if they cooperated (and didn't get suspended) they would see much improvement in their grades. The first evening we started they did not say a word on the way to my home. At dinner they answered direct questions but never initiated conversations. I was worried that they didn't feel comfortable, but within several weeks they were both out of their shells, interacting as part of my family.

Because of Randall's F on a history exam and D- on an English exam we concentrated on content subjects. As we covered each unit together, I checked his comprehension. When he missed something we went back to the material and I showed him how I discovered the answer. On this one to one level, in my home, he started to discover for himself how to analyze material and locate answers. I reviewed his assignment sheet every day and checked to see that he was taking the proper materials home. I acquired an extra set of text books he could keep at home and I emphasized immediately starting homework after dinner. In my home he would play around teasing and joking for about 15 minutes, then he would work for as long as two and one half hours.

Melvin and I discussed what prompted him to react in situations that led to suspensions. He started keeping track of when he wanted to react but didn't, knowing that he would have to report to me. We then discussed his feeling of power when he used self-control. I gave him a spiral notecard book for his new word a day, and, trying to improve his attendance, I bought him an alarm clock so he wouldn't have an excuse for missing the bus. We purchased a headset for music listening to be used during his 45 minute bus ride to and from school. We also requested that he sit immediately behind the bus driver so it would be clear that he was not causing trouble. Melvin's suspensions immediately stopped and I thought he was on the road to success.

Melvin and Randall were amazed my own two children did their homework without being reminded and that I would not allow radio, telephone or television until homework was completed. They found our discussions about current events, social situations and entertainment at the dinner table unusual and thought we "talked" funny. Soon they started to imitate us. I was amazed to hear them "talk" Shakespeare and other literary people. I saw that if they chose, they could speak standard English. When Randall and Melvin finally felt comfortable in my home we discussed the inequities of their environment, their many experiences with racism, and their family problems that were a result of living in low socio-economic conditions. Most middle class families were not aware of the magnitude of difficulties these families faced day to day.

As Melvin and Randall's grades improved other students said they wanted that same kind of help. Soon, several teachers asked if I could do something to help two other students, Korey and Devon. The two boys did not take school seriously and laughed at their F's. They also had repeated seventh grade and had experienced violence in their home environments. Teachers saw much untapped potential and were frustrated. The coach told me that Korey had more natural ability than any student he had ever seen but because of his attitude and lack of responsibility he would never be allowed on an athletic team. At Devon's request he joined our protege group. He started studying and became more responsible which resulted in his grades improving. I checked his assignment sheets daily and grades weekly. He sometimes joined us for dinner and study groups at my home. He started weight lifting with the coach after school and was soon allowed to participate on athletic teams. The coach said it was a shame that Korey was unworkable but it would take something short of a miracle to make Korey become more responsible. After Devon brought his grades up to honor role level, Korey asked if he couldn't please join us. Korey had similar results as Devon and soon the coach was calling me the "miracle worker."

In the classroom the teachers were very supportive of what I was doing. They gave me weekly reports on the progress of each of my students. When one started slipping they immediately notified me. I confronted the student and we discussed his short and long term goals. The first semester I read history and science tests aloud, pointing out test taking skills. By the second semester they no longer needed me to read aloud to them, although they still preferred taking the tests in my classroom.

Randall continued to need the most help for studying and was still easily distracted and unaccustomed to concentrating. He also had a much harder time with goal setting. For me to understand his situation better I contacted his mother weekly and visited his family on weekends twice a month. His mother decided to go back to school to get her GED and many times I helped her with English and math. She confided in me that her oldest son was becoming involved in a gang and not going to school regularly, and asked if I would talk to him. Randall also toldme he was worried about his brother who had been a sophomore for the last three years. One Sunday afternoon the uncle, mother, 3 sons, and I sat in their living room and talked about realistic goals and ambitions. The "unfairness" of their situation came up many times. We acknowledged it existed then discussed what they really wanted out of life and what they must do to achieve it. Many times I contacted our school counselor to find out how I could best help this family. Severe emergencies occurred and I was called for advise. They seemed to value my opinion and no matter how hopeless their situation appeared to me they always successfully handled their problems. I, in turn, discussed concerns I had with my own children, and I listened to their insights. We had a truly sharing exchange. I actually felt I was an extension of their family, and they, mine.

Randall started formulating goals, and as his self-esteem increased he began taking an active part in the classrooms. His grades greatly improved and I felt his self-esteem doubled. By the end of the first semester he still read slowly, but he could grasp the main idea, understand what questions were asking, formulate his answers for essay questions and not give up when he came to a question or problem that he could not immediately grasp. I watched him struggle with a math problem for 30 minutes, then finally arrive at the correct answer. I had suggested that he skip it, but he insisted on working it through.

CHARLES

In December Charles partially joined our group. He had been referred to me the previous year because of his limited vocabulary and poor grades. Charles was a friend of Randall's and seemed interested in what the proteges were accomplishing. When Charles enjoyed a course he was thorough in work completion and always well organized. I found out later that he had a mathematical mind and tremendous understanding of physical science. Charles was in ninth grade and said he planned to drop out the following year. He was extremely quiet, never smiled or joked in school, always had a serious look on his face, and never spoke unless he was directly asked a question. One weekend he called and said he was in some trouble and knew he was going to do the wrongthing. I asked if he wanted to come over and talk about it and he agreed. It took him two hours to get to my house on public transportation. Arriving around 8:00 P.M. he began by telling me that I really didn't know him and he was going to tell me some things that might shock me. I encouraged him to talk, which he did until 2:00 A.M. When he finished, the pain and torture of his past three years had been laid out and my mind was in turmoil trying to comprehend all he had said. I was drained from listening, he, exhausted from relieving his terrible burdens.

With Charles' permission I can reveal that he had fathered a child the previous year. The mother's new boyfriend had threatened to kill Charles' son because he "couldn't stand his face". Charles' life had also been threatened and he had been shot at several times and wounded, not to mention beaten up with a baseball bat. Charles worked at a part-time job to pay support for his son whom he visited weekly. Charles felt the threat to his son was real and he was extremely worried. The mother would not allow Charles to take his child, and the boyfriend said he would shoot Charles if he set foot in the house. In my naiavete I suggested he call the police which I found out he had done several times to no avail. My next suggestion was to find someone both parents trusted to care for Charles' son while this new boyfriend was around. The following week Charles talked to the young woman's aunt who agreed to take the child as long as Charles paid child support. This was only one of his problems brought forth that evening and I wondered how this young man with so many life threatening situations before him could come to school, concentrate, stay organized, complete assignments, and work at a part-time job. I now knew why I never saw a smile upon his face. Then I wondered how many kids had no adult that they could trust or with whom they could share their problems.

Several years later I asked Charles why he decided to share his problems with me on that cold December evening. He said I was only one of three adults he trusted. He knew his father and uncle would react violently, which might result in harm to his son, so he chose to trust me with the problem.

Serving as Charles' mentor was an emotionally exhausting yet successful experience. With Charles' permission I shared some of his concerns with our school counselor who helped guide me on how to help him. He didn't need academic help, but help with life, adult problems and encouragement. Throughout the next four years Charles called me when he knew he was going to make the wrong choice. We worked on goal setting using his son as a motivator. Charles decided to stay in school and I reread Reality Therapy. (Thank you William Glasser). I had never taken a counseling course, but counseling was what I had to do. Each time when Charles called and told me his new dilemma I asked him to remember his long term goals in life and what he wanted for his son. Then I would ask what short term goals would lead to his long term goals. Next I asked if he went ahead with his current decision, what would be the results and how would this effect his long and short term goals. I never knew when I hung up what he would do, but he never, to my knowledge, went ahead with his previous self-destructive decisions.

Our school counselor warned me that I must be prepared for something violent to happen to at least one of my five proteges since they all lived in such life threatening situations. I tried to keep that idea in the back of my head but I hoped and prayed they would all be safe. Remembering Glasser's theory (1965) that the adult must be willing to become involved if she is going to help make a change in the protege, I tried to keep my professional goals in mind, but I did not shy away from family or personal problems of my students.

At the end of the first semester all five of my proteges made C's, B's and A's. Randall even made the honor roll! I tried to use these five as role models and displayed their report cards in my classroom. All of my reading students were now much more concerned with grades and felt they too could bring them up. These five young men started receiving much more respect from their peers which lead to an increase in self-esteem. Their families were excited and proud. They started playing or excelling in sports with new confidence. No suspensions occurred and very few office referrals were made.

In the mid-semester the administration informed me that it did not "look proper" for me, a single parent, to take these youths to my home. I was told that I should work with student problems only during my 20 minute lunch period. I was informed that I could not take them to my home as long as I was a teacher and they were students in the district. Being an non-tenured teacher, the pain of reality stung. I felt like foster parents must feel when they are forced to give up children they love.

The young men interpreted this action as racially motivated and decided they would quit working to get even with the school administration. I was too shocked and hurt to understand what had actually happened.

As a team, we survived. The proteges could see my pain which seemed to strengthen our bonding. I was able to convince them to take higher level math and science courses for the following year. No one made the honor roll second semester but their grades were mainly B's and C's. Randall received his first suspension for fighting and his grades dropped the most. His mother asked the school if there was a paper she could sign to allow her son to continue visiting my home, but there was not. Charles was suspended for bringing a weapon to school. Melvin seemed the most angry and his attendance started dropping. Due to an increase in the need for elementary reading specialists, I was assigned to an elementary school for the following year.

You may be wondering what happened to my five proteges. For purposes of this presentation I shall leave my proteges until the conclusion of this article.

THE NEW PLAN

Returning to elementary school was extremely difficult for me. Ifelt I had discovered how to really make a difference in students'lives and now I was back to conducting 25 minute classes and simplyworking on reading problems. Meeting with my reading supervisor Ishared my frustrations. She suggested I create and submit a plan forworking with at-risk youth at the elementary level. She was touchedwith my previous years' work and said she would help me in anyway possible.

We met with elementary counselors and reading specialists andnoted the high absentee rate, low grades, low self-esteem, lack ofhomework completion and lack of parental involvement that accompaniedthose students who were not succeeding in school. Classroom teachers voiced concern for these students and indicated further that such students were very difficult to help in the classroom setting. In response to these findings, contact was made with other St. Louis County districts to determine what programs were being used to help the at-risk students. Meetings were held with principals, counselors, and reading teachers to see if they agreed on the need of a special program for at-risk students. They confirmed that the at-risk students were not having their needs addressed adequately. Telephone contact with a number of parents gave further support to the need for a special program to help these students overcome their difficulties in school before they became dropouts.

Next, I conducted a survey which identified possible at-risk students as those who had high absentee rates, below average grades, incomplete classwork, low motivation and low parental involvement. This group was then compared with the criteria that research indicates districts give as the major reasons for students dropping out of school (Barber and McClellan, 1987; Hahn, 1987). The results showed that:

(1) Of the students identified as at risk, 67% had significant absentee rates—the most frequently cited reason for dropouts according to Barber and McClellan (1987). Thus, it appeared critical for us to break this pattern of behavior before students reached sixteen;

(2) Classroom teacher records showed 83% had turned in less than 75% of their assigned classwork. Barber and McClellan (1987) listed lack of interest in school as the number two factor identifying dropouts. We felt that failure to hand in assigned work was indicative of this lack of interest;

(3) An analysis of the first semester grades for the 1989-90 school year showed 60% received two or more D's or F's on their final grade report. In addition, standardized test scores were compiled for the group. These showed that 83% were reading at or below the national 40th percentile on the Gates MacGinitie tests. Poor achievement is given as the number one reason for dropping out by Hahn (1987) and Barber and McClellan (1987) listed it as number three. Thus, it too was high on the list of risk factors;

(4) Teachers reported 78% of the 45 targeted students exhibited classroom behaviors which interfered with academic achievement. Negative behavior had to be changed to positive behavior if optimal learning was to take place. Research told us that behavioral changes occur when the student has a close and trusting relationship with one adult who has the resources to support him/her (Glasser, 1965);

(5) The survey for identifying at-risk students showed that 84% of the students were reported as having low self-esteem which correlates highly

with student dropout rate (McCarty, 1990). McCarty says further, the increasing of self-esteem requires daily attention: a once a week class in self-esteem makes little difference. He believes promoting self-esteem for at-risk students must be a priority in the educational system if the needs of these students are to be addressed.

It was found that all 45 of the candidates listed by the teachers and counselors as potentially high risk students did qualify on one or more of these critical factors. The need for special help for these severely at-risk students who would be in fourth, fifth and sixth grades in the 1990-91 school year was clearly indicated. Their special needs had to be met before they attended junior high school or they would unquestionably be at risk for dropping out of school before graduation.

Many of the targeted students were Voluntary Transfer Students who lived up to 40 miles away from school. Public buses did not travel from the city of St. Louis to Rockwood School District. Most of these single-parent families lived in poverty and did not own cars. They could not attend conferences due to lack of transportation. The parents reported having had negative school experiences when they were students and therefore felt reluctant to make school contact. In order to provide parent education and support, home visitations would be needed, according to Dryfoos (1990).

In response to these findings, objectives were developed. A mentor would work closely with students, parents, and professional school staff members. Students would then have an advocate who had the responsibility and resources to support them. Glasser (1965) indicated this model would improve academic achievement and raise students' expectations for themselves to a higher level. The results would be circular. Parental involvement along with school support would raise academic achievement. Improved academic achievement over time would raise self-esteem. Increasing self-esteem would, in turn, help students to set goals and improve motivation for further increases in academic achievement.

Implementation of this program required an additional half-time reading specialist whose time was devoted to:

(1) providing individual and small group instruction in the areas of study, organizational and content reading skills,
(2) making home contacts and visitations to gain parental support and to discuss parental concerns,
(3) communicating with teachers and counselors to keep them informed and to gain support and cooperation among professional staff,

(4) monitoring weekly the students' attendance and work completion,
(5) checking monthly on grades,
(6) locating and arranging visits by guest speakers, and
(7) providing self-esteem enhancing activities.

Classroom teachers enthusiastically agreed that this proposal would address the social and instructional needs of at-risk students. My supervisor and I filled out the many pages of paper work and I submitted my proposal to the state of Missouri for an Incentives for School Excellence (ISE) Grant. My grant was rated number one in its category and I received funding for the 1990-91 school year.

THE NEW PLAN IN ACTION

To begin the STAR program I created files on each participant, including addresses, phone numbers, previous grades, attendance and teacher concerns. Once identified, the STARs were randomly integrated into all fourth, fifth and sixth grade classrooms. All intermediate teachers automatically became STARs' teachers. On the second day of school, students were informed of the STAR program and given letters to explain the program. STAR classes and home visitations began the second week of school.

Parents, teachers, and students positively responded to the STAR program. Every parent welcomed me into their home and voiced appreciation for my concerns. Even the classroom teachers noted that students were excited and pleased to know I would be visiting their homes. A number of parents said they had felt alone with their child's "school program," and they were relieved to have me as a support person. At times they confided other problems in the home. By enlisting the help of the school counselor, faculty, and nurse, we were able to provide families with needed items such as furniture, clothing, food, glasses, eye operations, family counseling and family assistance. At one point, I found an eight-year-old child who was not going to school because of poor vision. We now have him enrolled in our school, and he is making great progress. One mother cried in my arms saying, "I have never seen a school who not only truly cares about my children, but cares about me, too." I served as a catalyst, but the faculty and staff worked cooperatively to make these changes.

Once I enlisted parent support, student attendance improved by leaps and bounds, but special cases required special assistance. Several times I contacted case workers and/or juvenile authorities who were also very supportive. I became familiar with the juvenile justice system and learned about the many social programs offered in both the city and county. As I spent more time with parents who needed my help, I began to see that the majority of my students with low self-esteem also had parents with severely low self-esteem. I made friendly calls and sent greeting cards to congratulate parents on the improvement that we saw with their children. I found something positive to say about each home or family. Many times this was difficult. Some homes had only a couch and a television. Many of my families did not have telephones or telephones were disconnected. One of the hardest parts of my job was dealing with the lack of home stimulation.

Student enthusiasm was unbelievable. Many non-qualifying students requested to be in STARS. My students overwhelmingly rated STARs as their favorite class because it gave them a sense of belonging and helped them raise their self-esteem. When asked why they were in STARs, they answered, "To help me be a better student," or "To help me get a better education."

One young lady who had been retained twice, sent to the principal's office an average of three times each week, and suspended numerous times for behavior problems both on the bus and at school, made a dramatic turn around. Her first year in STARs she was never sent to the office, suspended from school or bus, and had one of the highest work completion rates of any in STARs. Her grades went from mainly F's to all A's, B's, and C's. Her written self-description was:

> *"I am a girl. I like doing good work. I am good at dancing. My hair is black, I'm light skinned, and I have brown eyes. I am tall and lovely. What's special about myself is watching out for myself and taking care of me. I have a nice personality and a good friendship with people. Can you guess; who am I?"*

Lack of school suspensions and office referrals was an unanticipated outcome. Of my 32 students, only five were suspended from school. Previously the majority were suspended at least once, and many of them numerous times. It was also a rarity for a STAR to have an office referral and students took pride in that fact. I feel this is due to both increase in self-esteem and a desire to improve grades. This desire is so strong that many of my students gave up their recess at lunch to come to me for study help for tests, writing reports, and working on projects. At one point I had so many come in that I had to use a sign-up sheet. The amazing fact is these were students who previously looked forward only to recess. The previous year one student was suspended 8 times and missed 44 days of school. The first year of STARs he was never suspended and was absent only 8 days - a 500% improvement for a young man who was also the most frequent student in my room during recess time.

Overwhelming support of the teachers made the year highly successful. In the city of St. Louis, 100% of the STARs' teachers attended evening conferences, on their own time, and later commented to me how appreciative they were to have the opportunity to meet with city families "on their own turf." I was surprised to see how important this event was to the students. Dressed in their finest, families attended the Ice Cream Social and Parent Conference as a school activity; for many students this would be the only school activity their families would be able to attend. For the next week students discussed the event and seemed to really take pride in the fact that their families participated. Teachers began to open their eyes to some of the daily problems our city parents face; parents saw the teachers as approachable.

Teachers became such strong proponents that three of them "insisted" that I add three more students NOW, next year would be too late. They stated that the STAR program was the only thing that could help these young men. I added them second semester and they responded beautifully.

Comments from the teachers on the STAR program include:

"The kids have someone who really takes time out and cares for them."

"STARs helps keep kids on target and helps the teacher by giving additional parent contact and conferences."

"The STAR program is supportive, helpful and flexible, and by monitoring and adjusting, every student has the opportunity to succeed as a 'whole' person."

The three following objectives were met for the 1990-91 school year.

<u>Objective 1:</u> 81% of the targeted students missing 8 or more days in the 1989-90 school year, improved their attendance by at least 50% or more during the 1990-91 school year. Most of these students improved at a much higher rate than 50%.

<u>Objective 2:</u> 77% of the at-risk students turning in less than 75% of their homework assignments for the 1989-90 school year, improved their performance by turning in 85% or more during the 1990-91 school year.

<u>Objective 3:</u> 83% of the targeted students with two or more D's or F's in the content areas during the 1989-90 school year increased their

grades by one or more letter grades in two or more subjects by the end of the 1990-91 school year.

STARS CONTINUES

In the spring of 1991 I submitted my proposal to the state for an ISE Continuation Grant. Again it was accepted and I received funding.

In the new school year I reorganized STAR files, selected additional students, met with faculty and sent home letters with all participants. Once again all parents welcomed me into their homes. Several parents called saying, "I know you will be coming to visit us but I have a problem that I need help with now." One mother decided to help her son's self-esteem by allowing him to see his father, whom he had not seen since he was an infant. Another parent called for ideas on activities to help behavior problems at home. A non-custodial father started an academic schedule to help his son in math and science and it continued all year! One parent who had previously been belligerent with the school, became involved, helping out weekly. We again had several cases of needing eye glasses. Two mothers were on the verge of losing custody of their children, but with all of us working together they were able to keep their families intact.

Again student enthusiasm was very high. During testing week students insisted on having STARs class. One of the biggest successes was the one STAR student who had been retained the previous year. In the second year of STARs, she completed most of her work and passed all subjects. When asked on her "Pride Line" what she was proudest of in her life she wrote, "I brought my grades up." Another student who repeated fifth grade two years earlier because of all F's, described himself in a written paragraph as:

> *"I am proud of me because I am a positive thinker. I also look at myself as an optimist. I like to think the best of things. My favorite subject is science. When I get to college I plan to major in physics. I also love to play every sport, especially baseball and basketball. The reason I like basketball is because I'm a 5" ll 1/2" 6th grader. My parents also [say] I'm a big help around the house and all these things are why I'm proud of me!"*

My objectives continued the same as year one and we had almost identical results. Lack of school suspensions and office referrals also continued. Of the students in their second year of STARs only one was suspended from school. Several classes discussed how they had four or five suspensions before they were in STARs. They recognized the importance of changing their behavior.

Teacher support continued for STARs. Their comments included:

"I have found that the program raises the students' self-esteem! The students are proud to receive good grades and like to share that excitement. The one-to-one contact helps to keep them motivated. The assignment completion rate has increased greatly."

"The students' self-esteem seems to rise. Therefore, their school attitudes are better, and they are happier and more positive. It is amazing how trust in a friend and success can change a person!"

Overwhelming interest in the STARs program developed throughout the state. Many requests for information or observation were sent to me. STARs won a "Citicorp Innovator Success Award." I was invited to present my program to the National Dropout Prevention Conference in Pittsburgh, the State of Missouri IRA Conference, and the St. Louis Suburban IRA Conference.

The success of the STAR program was apparent:

(1) students maintained desire to learn and willingness to work as evidenced by improved attendance, work completion and grades;

(2) continued increase in student self-esteem as shown through self description;

(3) teacher acceptance and requests for assistance; and

(4) positive parent interaction with the school.

As a faculty we persisted in helping families become more functional. I was asked that year to be the United Way representative. After sharing the story of one home visit and how United Way had made a difference in that family, our faculty doubled it's pledges. As professionals we continue to be sensitive in our approach to teaching.

EPILOGUE

The good news is four of my five proteges have either graduated or are graduating this year. It has taken all of them only four years of high school to graduate. Charles graduated last year. He is in The Navy Hospital Corpsmen School and hopes to some day become a doctor. I hear from him monthly but now on a friendship level. He has learned how to make proper choices even though we struggled through some horrifying situations during his high school years. This Christmas he brought his son over for a visit. He now has custody and his mother is keeping his son while he is in training. We joke about how he would call me because he wanted someone to talk him out of his inappropriate solutions. He seems well disciplined and now laughs and smiles and jokes.

Devon and Korey are athletic stars. Their pictures and names are in the newspaper frequently. Korey became a track star his sophomore year. He also excels in basketball and is assured of a track scholarship. Devon excels in football, basketball, and track. He hopes to become a science teacher.

I hear from Randall about once a month and I still visit his family several times a year. I am currently working with his youngest sister who attends my school. Randall is proud to be on the honor roll his senior year. He is now 20 years old and plans to enroll in a junior college and work full-time after he gets his own apartment. All four young men are popular, well liked by the faculty and should have a bright future ahead of them.

It is amazing for me to think back to our "project year" and seehow far they have come. Other concerned adults assisted in their development along the way and I was very pleased to hear how open they were to receive help.

Melvin, however, is serving a 15 year sentence for murder. The last time I spoke to him on the phone he stated he is working on his GED and plans to get training for a profession while serving time. He says he thinks back to our times together as his favorite time. I, of course, was crushed when he and his mother informed me what had happened. I felt the loss of his potential as a personal death. I searched for what I might have done to have prevented this occurrence, but came to the conclusion that Melvin had to be responsible for his own decisions. I had offered what I thought was right, and he chose to ignore my repeated warnings and cries of concern. I still think back to Melvin's love of vocabulary and smile. One night, trying to broaden their cultural experiences, I served escargot for dinner. The young men were shocked that we would eat snails and refused to even try it. The next week in Melvin's geography class his teacher made a joke saying, "See the S car go." He was so excited that he "got" the joke that he came rushing down to my class to share the experience.

I have received more than I have given. I taught these young men what I learned in books. They taught me about the humaneness in life.

REFERENCES

Barber, L. W. and McClellan, M. C. (1987). Looking at America's Dropouts: Who Are They? *Phi Delta Kappan,* 69 (4), 264-267.

Crockett, L. and Smink, J. (1991). *The Mentoring Guidebook*. Clemson, SC: National Dropout Prevention Center.

Dryfoos, J. (1990). *The Achievement Train: High-Risk Children Get on Board.* Educational Letter published by the Harvard Graduate School in Association with Harvard University Press, Volume VI, (1), Jan/Feb.

Glasser, W. (1965). *Reality Therapy.* New York: Harper Row.

Hahn, A. (1987). Reaching Out to America's Dropouts: What to Do? *Phi Delta Kappan,* 69(4), 256-263.

McCarty, H. (1990). *Self Esteem: The Bottom Line with Students at Risk.* Speech presented at the Missouri State Conference for Students at Risk.

CINDY MOORE, JOSEPH ALLEN, KATHY HERRE
SUSAN PHILLIBER and GABRIEL KUPERMINC 9

Teen Outreach: *A Successful Program Preventing School Failure, School Dropout, and Teen Pregnancy*

HISTORY AND MISSION OF TEEN OUTREACH

Adolescents who leave school due to a pregnancy or for other reasons cost the nation billions of dollars for Federal assistance programs, and lost tax revenues and earnings (Loeber, & Dishion, 1983; National Research Council, 1987). This is in addition to the tremendous personal costs incurred by these adolescents over their lifetimes. Programs which use existing knowledge on adolescent development to help prevent these problems, and modify the pathways of adolescents already having difficulties, are desperately needed. Despite extensive interest in finding ways to reduce school dropout, and related problems such as teenage pregnancy (Cairns, Cairns, & Neckerman, 1989; Friedman, Glickman, & Utada, 1985; Michael, 1990; Scales, 1990), relatively few programs have actually documented success in reaching these goals. "Teen Outreach" is an example of such a program.

The Teen Outreach Program has attracted national attention for its role in preventing school dropout and teen pregnancy among junior and senior high school students. The report of the National Research Council's Panel on Adolescent Pregnancy and Childbearing, Risking the Future: Adolescent Sexuality, Pregnancy and Childbearing (1987), listed Teen Outreach as one of only three programs having documented effectiveness in reducing adolescent pregnancy. Extensive evaluations of the program's effects have shown that participants have a 33% lower rate of pregnancy, a 5% lower rate of course failure in school, an 18% lower rate of school suspension, and a 50% lower rate of school dropout, relative to comparison students. Given the magnitude and seriousness of the problems successfully addressed by the program, Teen Outreach is clearly an important intervention effort that could have a major impact on reducing school dropout and related problems as more schools and communities adopt it.

The Teen Outreach Program was conceived by a high school teacher in St. Louis in 1978. It initially attracted the support of the Danforth Foundation, and after 3 years was adopted by the Junior League of St. Louis. After several years of success at decreasing the rate of adolescent pregnancy and increasing the rate of high school graduation for at-risk teens, the Charles Stewart Mott Foundation funded a national replication effort in eight cities in 1984. Three years later, after rapid growth, the Teen Outreach Program was transitioned to the Association of Junior Leagues International (AJLI), which now supports the replication of the program.

As the success of the program in reducing dropout and pregnancy rates became increasingly well established, district-wide replication efforts began in 1991. In just 8 years, Teen Outreach expanded from having 9 classroom sites to 95 classroom sites (1992-3 school year). With enthusiasm for Teen Outreach still growing, AJLI is currently developing state and community models to institutionalize the program and to replicate it on a much wider basis. A state model of replication and dissemination is now being developed in California, and AJLI is working with sponsors in seven communities to develop a community - school partnership. Such a relationship will allow district-wide implementation of the program, and will help assure the continuation of funding for the program in areas where it has been set up.

The real mission of the Teen Outreach Program is to help teens to develop good judgment, a sense of responsibility, and cooperation, and to acquire life management competencies which will increase their chances of finishing school, and help them lead more productive lives outside the classroom. Documented benefits of this competency - based approach also include a reduction in problem behaviors, such as school drop-out, and unprotected sexual activity. In order to foster positive development in youth, the program seeks to provide participants with the opportunity to examine their values, and to try new roles. Creation of an environment that encourages risk-taking and sharing experiences is critical towards this end.

Components of the Teen Outreach Program

The Teen Outreach Program is comprised of two major components: a classroom curriculum, and a community service component. Both of these are critical to the program's success, and together give youth a sense of control and contribution. Students begin to see themselves as functioning effectively and being needed in the community, and learn to use the community resources to meet their own needs. In addition, the service learning component encourages shared responsibility between schools and communities for educational reform, and strengthens school - community relations.

Community Service

The community service component of Teen Outreach is one of its most unique features, and represents an important departure from more traditional models of education. For Teen Outreach students, the chance to expand their education "beyond the walls of the classroom" (Sarason, 1982) by performing meaningful volunteer work appears to enhance motivation and performance inside the classroom as well. For those students who find school least rewarding and interesting, real life settings, such as those provided by Teen Outreach, can be an alternative route to success. Yet, unlike paid employment, volunteer activities organized by Teen Outreach do not compete with school work, nor do they undermine parental influence by providing teens with early financial independence (Gottfredson, 1985).

Volunteerism has captured the interest of educators and policy-makers alike as a means of empowering young people (Allen, Philliber, & Hoggson, 1990b.; Rappaport, 1987). The helper-therapy principle suggests that empowerment results from being in a help-giving, rather than a help-seeking role (Riessman, 1965). Community service can further schools' mission of helping adolescents develop into competent adults by enhancing their reasoning skills, practical problem-solving abilities, capacities for abstract and hypothetical thought, and sense of social and personal responsibility (Kirby, 1989; Newmann, 1983).

One possible mechanism for some of these effects is that when teens succeed as volunteers, they come to believe that they can succeed at other attempts at competent behavior. This belief, in turn, may fuel a more persistent effort to perform competently in other endeavors (Bandura, 1977). The benefits to the volunteer may also occur in part because of the increased contact between teenagers and adult supervisors who serve as role models for them. By volunteering, adolescents may identify more with the prosocial values of adults. Such identification has been related to social competence and negatively related to problem behaviors (Allen, Leadbeater, & Aber, 1990a).

Also, research on youth's involvement in meaningful instrumental activity suggests that part of what makes volunteering a positive experience for students is that they are provided the opportunity of using skills they may not otherwise use, skills that are valued by both the student and the larger society. The use of such skills correlates with life satisfaction and self esteem (Maton, 1990). Together, these ideas suggest that the unprecedented success of the Teen Outreach approach is firmly grounded in our current knowledge of adolescent social, emotional and intellectual development.

In practice, there is substantial variation in the duration and quality of the volunteer experiences in which youth participate. That somewhat different implementations of the program are effective suggests the robustness of Teen Outreach. The program encourages teens to perform volunteer work that is meaningful to them, for an hour per week during the school year. Evaluation data collected to date indicate that the average Teen Outreach student performs more than 30 hours of volunteer work during the course of the program. A Teen Outreach coordinator, often a volunteer from the local Junior League, manages the service component of the program. These coordinators act as resources for the facilitators, provide transportation, mentor students, and organize field experiences.

Classroom Curriculum

The school-based curriculum, which emphasizes positive decision making skills, is the second component of the Teen Outreach Program which contributes to its success. A facilitator, often a teacher or guidance counselor, provides structure for the group and facilitates group and individual learning experiences. Generally, the facilitator uses group discussions and activities, rather than a lecture format, to present the material in each unit.

Over the course of the year, groups focus on a number of topics relevant to adolescent development. These include learning about their communities, self-esteem building, values clarification, capitalizing on diversity, communication, thoughtful decision-making, relationship building, human growth and development, and planning for the future. Of note is that although the Teen Outreach Program has been successful in reducing teen pregnancy rates, the materials on sex education comprise a relatively small part of the total curriculum.

The curriculum is written in the form of a teacher's guide for the facilitator, and includes a detailed outline for each unit, pertinent information, suggestions for structured experiences and activities, and lists of resource books and films. At the end of each session, the students make entries into journals; suggestions for journal topics are also included in the guide. The average participant in the program receives approximately 70 hours of classroom based discussion time (Allen, et al., 1990b).

Although the program was originally designed to be an after school elective program, it has now been offered by substantial numbers of schools as a regular part of the daily curriculum. Evaluation data suggest that the program is equally effective offered during or after school (Allen, et al., 1990b). Youth enter the program in a number of different ways. At some sites, students volunteer to participate in the program, while at others, Teen Outreach facilitators seek out students believed to be at high risk for leaving school or getting pregnant. The average group at one site consists of 15-20 females and males; 75% of the participants so far have been female (Philliber, & Allen, 1992). The program is offered to students at both the middle school and high school levels.

EVALUATION RESULTS

Effects on Participants

One of the most distinctive features of the Teen Outreach Program is that the effectiveness of the program has been carefully evaluated over the past eight years, using the most rigorous scientific evaluation methods. Thus, unlike many school-based interventions which claim to influence students' growth and development, Teen Outreach has produced eight consecutive years of hard evidence of its impact on students' behavior.

In addition, the program has recently gone beyond simple outcome evaluation, to focus carefully on examining why the program works, with whom it works, and under what conditions it is most effective. The evaluation strategy thus far has been to look separately at data from each consecutive year of the program. Questions are then generated which can be answered by data from the following year. In this manner, the information from the evaluation has become more focused over time. An additional strategy has been to aggregate the data from eight years, in order to gain an overall understanding of the program's effects upon the participants. Results from both sets of analyses are described below. Note that some of these results have been previously published in more detail; the reader is referred to Allen et al. (1990b), and Philliber and Allen (1992).

Over the first seven years of the evaluation period, data has been collected on 3986 Teen Outreach students and 4356 comparison students at 237 sites in both the United States and Canada. Comparison students were either chosen by school personnel who had selected the Teen Outreach students, and who matched them on the basis of socio-demographic backgrounds and levels of problem behaviors, or nominated by Teen Outreach students who thought they would fill out the questionnaire similar to the way the Teen Outreach student did. A strong effort has also been made to encourage sites to randomly assign students to the program vs. the control group, in order to help control for motivational differences existing in students that could contribute to greater improvements in the Teen Outreach students, independent of any programmatic effects. This allows conclusions about the effectiveness of the program to be drawn with much more certainty. Currently random assignment data have been collected on 472 Teen Outreach Program students and 496 control students.

The program has so far succeeded at serving youth from a wide range of backgrounds: participants have ranged in age from 11-21 years old, with an average age of 14.9 years. About 40% of the students are African-American, 40% are white, and 13% are Hispanic. Forty percent came from single parent families, and the parents of 20% of the students had less than a high school education.

The published evaluations of the program's effects on youth included information on 632 program participants and 855 comparison students from 35 sites at 30 schools across the United States (Allen, et al., 1990b). Teens indicated at the beginning and end of the program whether they had ever been pregnant or caused a pregnancy, failed a course, and been suspended. School dropout in the past year was also assessed at the end of the program. The number of problem behaviors was summed, and this number compared at the beginning and end of the program.

The number of hours students volunteered and spent in the classroom discussions was used in analyses assessing the relationship between participation in Teen Outreach and change in levels of problem behaviors. Results indicated that although the group of Teen Outreach students began the year with significantly higher levels of problem behaviors than the comparison group, by the end of the program they had significantly lower levels of suspension, school dropout and pregnancy. This relationship holds even when we account for any potential differences between Teen Outreach and comparison students in demographic characteristics.

Analyses of the first seven years of data show that, relative to comparison students, the Teen Outreach participants had a 5% lower rate of course failure in school, an 8% lower rate of school suspension, a 33% lower rate of pregnancy, and a 50% lower rate of school dropout. The differences in the rates of these problems between the two groups are statistically significant and remain so even after the student's race, gender, grade, mother's education, living arrangement and pre-program levels of these problem behaviors are controlled for. Again, the differences in rates of problem behaviors between the Teen Outreach group and the comparison group could not be explained by different makeups of the two groups. In other words, whether Teen Outreach was offered to students displaying high levels of initial problem behaviors or low levels, the program was effective in reducing those levels over the course of the school year.

The results from analyses of the subset of students who were randomly assigned to a group are consistent and also highly encouraging. In this group, Teen Outreach participants had a 32% lower rate of course failure in school, a 37% lower rate of school suspension, a 43% lower rate of pregnancy, and a 75% lower rate of school dropout, relative to the control group. As noted above, by randomly assigning students to a group, any differences in motivation between students prior to the beginning of the program will not affect the final comparisons in rates of problem behaviors. This provides more certainty that the program, not other unrelated factors, is responsible for their changes in behavior.

Facets of Implementation Related to Program's Success

After documenting the success of the Teen Outreach Program in improving outcomes for participants, efforts were made to better understand how the program works, and what facets were most clearly related to changes in behavior. For these analyses, comparisons have been made among different Teen Outreach sites. These analyses take advantage of the fact that different sites have implemented the program in slightly different ways. As a result, we can systematically examine these different implementations so as to identify the program features that are associated with the most successful Teen Outreach sites. These comparisons were based on information collected from 632 program participants and 855 comparison students. It is important to point out that at this point no causal relationships can be definitively demonstrated between program characteristics and student outcomes; we can only say that certain methods of implementation are consistently associated with greater program success.

After first accounting for factors such as student backgrounds, and school-wide demographic characteristics, several aspects of the Teen Outreach Program were identified as important predictors of its success across sites. First, the more volunteer hours a student worked, the fewer problems s/he had at the end of the program. This finding supports the idea that community service provides alternatives to other more problematic behaviors, and may allow teens to feel more competent. Second, students from higher grade levels tended to have significantly lower levels of problem behaviors at exit from program, compared to younger students. Thus, the program works better for older students. Third, a trend suggested that hours of participation in classroom discussions was related to fewer problems for younger students, although this trend only appeared among the middle-school aged students examined. However, the relatively consistent use of the curriculum across sites may have made it difficult to assess the impact of the curriculum, as there was no real way of comparing the effects of using the curriculum a great deal vs. very little (Allen, et al., 1990b).

Recently, by aggregating data across the first seven 7 years, more and more is being learned about factors associated with the program's success. Data were aggregated from September 1984 through June 1991, from 237 sites, involving 3986 students in Teen Outreach and 4356 matched comparison students. One very important question concerned whether the program worked as well with students from unique, difficult or problematic backgrounds as it did with students from more conventional backgrounds. Thus, comparisons were made between outcomes in adolescents from different ethnic and socio-economic backgrounds, and who had parents with different educational levels. In addition, changes in levels of problem behaviors in students already experiencing significant difficulties and students who were relatively better functioning at entry into the program were compared. Teen Outreach served all of these teens just as effectively, which is both an unusual and highly encouraging finding. The results document that the program promotes change in students from a wide range of backgrounds, with varying entry levels of problem behaviors. Thus the likelihood of successful future replications is great. Only two student characteristics were related to the program's success: Teen Outreach was slightly more effective when it served higher proportions of female students, and, as mentioned above, when it served high school vs. middle school age youth.

Because the number of hours of volunteer work is a crude measure of the overall experience, students were asked additional questions about the quality of their service experiences. Sites where students felt engaged by their volunteer work, and where they felt they had a choice in selecting the work, tended to be more successful. Further analyses clarified the relationship between number of hours students spent at community service, and program success: increasing from 0 - 20 hours of volunteering was related to the program's success, but more volunteering after that didn't necessarily lead to more successful programs. This is important because it indicates that students who volunteer less than 20 hours over the school year may not be realizing the full benefits of the program.

In looking at which aspects of the classroom component are most closely related to a reduction in problem behaviors, results indicated that facilitators of different ethnic backgrounds, gender, educational backgrounds, and ages were all equally successful in helping to reduce problem behaviors in the youth. Several aspects of the classroom experience did relate to the program's success, however. Particularly in middle schools, sites with classrooms in which students, rather than facilitators, did most of the talking, tended to be the most successful. For all ages, successful sites were ones where students felt the facilitator was sensitive to their feelings and needs, and where they felt the social environment of the program was emotionally supportive and safe.

Further, the most important aspect of facilitator sensitivity was whether students felt that s/he really liked them. When students felt that Teen Outreach dealt with their feelings, and that their facilitators tried to understand them and cared about whether they talked in class, they tended to show greater improvement. It was also important that students trusted that they wouldn't get laughed at if they talked about feeling lonely, and were able to talk about things that worried them in the classroom discussions. It did not seem to matter if students formed a strong bond with the facilitator on an individual level.

Slightly different structural implementations of the program were not uniformly associated with its success: the program fared equally well at urban and rural sites, and when it was offered for credit or no credit.

Because the finding that Teen Outreach is more effective with high school than middle school students was so consistent, it was important to identify factors related to this discrepancy in order to fine-tune the program for younger participants. One finding relevant to this difference was that the middle school sites were rated significantly lower than the high school sites on the two process measures that were most associated with program success: feeling understood and respected by the facilitator, and feeling that the Teen Outreach Program provided an emotionally supportive environment. It seems to be more difficult for facilitators to connect with the younger students, and this may in part account for the program's slightly reduced success with this age group. The program is currently developing a revised curriculum for middle school students in order to address their somewhat different needs.

SUMMARY

The Association of Junior Leagues International's Teen Outreach Program has shown clear and consistent success, over eight years of intensive evaluation, in reducing the incidence of course failure, school dropout, suspensions, and teenage pregnancies. Even more strikingly, it reduces pregnancy rates without focusing primarily upon sex education, contraceptive distribution, or other controversy-laden approaches. Rather, it promotes mature social development in youth by helping them take on useful, adult-like roles in their communities.

Future studies are planned to assess the Teen Outreach Program's ability to change outcomes which are more developmentally relevant for younger children, like skipping school. Also, long-term follow-up of Teen Outreach participants and comparison students will allow us to assess the stability of behavior changes after the students are no longer participating actively in the program. Follow-up, particularly with students beginning the program at younger ages, will also allow an assessment of the need for continued work with high-risk students.

The yearly evaluation of the Teen Outreach program has provided us with an unprecedented amount of information about the ingredients that are critical to its success. In the future, we look forward to building upon these early successes to expand this program into other schools, and school districts. Clearly, the need for successful preventive interventions in this area is pressing. Given this need, we find the evidence of the success for this particular intervention highly encouraging.

REFERENCES

Allen, J. P., Leadbeater, B. J., & Aber, J. L. (1990a). The relationship of adolescents' expectations and values to delinquency, hard drug use, and unprotected sexual intercourse. *Development and Psychopathology*, *2*, 85-98.

Allen, J. P., Philliber, S., & Hoggson, N. (1990b). School-based prevention of teenage pregnancy and school dropout: Process evaluation of the national replication of the Teen Outreach Program. *American Journal of Community Psychology*, *18*, 505-524.

Bandura, A. (1977). Self-efficacy: Toward a unifying theory of behavioral change. *Psychological Review*, *84*, 191-215.

Cairns, R.B., Cairns, B.D., & Neckerman, H.J. (1989). Early school dropout: Configurations and determinants. *Child Development*, *60*, 1437-1452.

Friedman, A.S., Glickman, N., & Utada, A. (1985). Does drug and alcohol use lead to failure to graduate from high school? *Journal of Drug Education*, *15*(4), 353-364.

Gottfredson, D. C. (1985). Youth employment, crime, and schooling: A longitudinal study of a national sample. *Developmental Psychology*, *21*, 419-432.

Kirby, K. (1989). *Community Service and Civic Education*. Washington, DC: Office of Educational Research and Improvement.

Loeber, R., & Dishion, T. (1983). Early predictors of male delinquency: A review. *Psychological Bulletin*, *94*(1), 68-99.

Maton, K. I. (1990). Meaningful involvement in instrumental activity and well-being: Studies of older adolescents and at-risk urban teenagers. *American Journal of Community Psychology*, *18*(2), 297-320.

Michael, N. (1990). Participants' views of a drop-out prevention program: Louisiana state youth opportunities unlimited. *The High School Journal*, *73*,(4), 200-212.

National Research Council. (1987). *Risking the future: Adolescent sexuality, pregnancy and child-bearing*. Washington, D.C.: National Academy Press.

Newmann, F. A. (1983). *Adolescents' Participation in Developmental Activity: A Method of Assessment*. Montreal, April 14, 1983.

Philliber, S., & Allen, J. P. (1992). Life options and community service: Teen Outreach Program. In B. C. Miller, J. J. Card, R. L. Paikoff, & J. L. Peterson (Eds.), *Preventing Adolescent Pregnancy: Model Programs and Evaluations* (pp. 139-155). Newbury Park: Sage.

Rappaport, J. (1987). Terms of empowerment/Exemplars of prevention: Toward a theory for community psychology. *American Journal of Community Psychology, 15*(2), 121-147.

Riessman, F. (1965). The helper-therapy principle. *Social Work, 10*, 27-32.

Sarason, S. B. (1982). *The culture of the school and the problem of change* (2nd ed.). Boston: Allyn and Bacon.

Scales, P. (1990). Developing capable young people: An alternative strategy for prevention programs. *Journal of Early Adolescence, 10*(4), 420-438.

MARIE CARBO

10

Sharply Increasing the Reading Ability of Potential Dropouts

Eric: And I'll tell you right now. I don't want anyone else to go through what I went through.

J.C.: It's hard. It's not fun.

Eric: It's real hard. It's boring. You get tired after you finish reading. You don't ever want to read again.

J.C.: As soon as you're out of school you don't read.

Eric: You go home and you watch T.V. and you lay down until it's time to do something else. That's how tired you are from reading.

J.C.: You want to forget about school.

Eric: Forget about everything in your life.

Just ask Eric and J.C. why they dislike reading. The list of complaints from these two middle-grade students has a familiar ring. Seldom were attempts made to discover their interests, much less how they learn. They say they were insulted by the low-level, uninteresting books; bored by the steady stream of mindless worksheets; embarrassed by their placement in special education classes and low reading groups; and devastated by retention.

A few years ago, Eric and J.C. were likely to become statistics- adding two more to the millions of American students who drop out of high school each year. Now their is more than just hope for potential dropouts. Strategies which have capitalized on the reading style strengths of at-risk students, have sharply accelerated their learning, often resulting in gains of five to twenty times former progress in reading, as well as large gains in language acquisition.

The purpose of this article, therefore, is to convince the reader that it is both imperative and extremely feasible to improve substantially the reading ability of potential dropouts, and to increase their chance of not just graduating from high school, but, more important, of deriving real benefit from the instruction leading to graduation.

With that end in mind, the next two sections of this article will link poor reading ability with dropping out of school, and will discuss the failure of current compensatory education programs in the classrooms reading practices to make even a dent in the enormous literacy problems facing the U.S.. The second half of this article will describe what we know about the reading styles (learning styles from reading) of at-risk students, and the strategies that have resulted in the highest reading gains in the shortest possible time.

Literacy and Dropouts

America's "most urgent educational needs" are to increase the gain scores of the lowest third of our students, and to increase high school and college graduation rates, especially for minority students, according to noted demographer Hodgkinson (1989). In this regard, Hodgkinson warns us that the educational reform movement has "flunked" the demographic agenda.

And it is highly unlikely that the U.S. will improve high school graduation rates, while maintaining adequate standards, unless the reading levels of most at-risk students are raised substantially. One of the major causes of students dropping out of high school is difficulties as early as second or third grade were found to be "the single most important factor in predicting which students would drop out of high school" (Griffin, 1987). Early reading failure was even a better prediction than poverty.

It's easy to understand why. Students who cannot read their text books have difficulty understanding their subjects or participating in class discussions. Each year they fall further behind in their school work until, finally, many give up. Current estimates from the National Assessment of Educational Progress (NAEP) indicate that about 40 percent of our seventh graders cannot read their texts with adequate ease and fluency to comprehend the materials. By twelfth grade the figure jumps to an alarming 60 percent (Foertsch, 1992).

Track Record of Compensatory Education Programs Is Poor

And what of the track record of the programs that are supposed to help youngsters with reading problems? Our poorest readers are likely to wallow in expensive remedial or special education programs for a decade or so and then drop out of school. Despite the huge amounts of money spent on compensatory and remedial programs, the students "often become lifers," because of the "poor quality of instruction they receive," according to Anderson and Pellicer (1990) who reported on programs designed to improve the achievement of economically deficient students.

Chapter 1 programs alone receive almost four billion dollars a year, or 20 percent of the U.S. Department of Education's budget. Yet, these programs, Anderson and Pellicer found, generally "fragment the curriculum," and are so "poorly coordinated with regular programs that student learning is actually impede."

Furthermore, the teachers in compensatory programs were reported to have low expectations, and consistently used unchallenging, low-level materials. Although students in compensatory and remedial programs are the very youngsters who need master teachers working with them, often teacher aides provide instruction, with students spending inordinate amounts of time working on low-level, pencil-and-paper tasks, alone at their desks. (Precisely the wrong approach for the most at-risk students who need high-interest, holistic, hands on approaches). Anderson and Pellicer recommended that remedial and compensatory students would "benefit greatly from increased expectations and demands."

Positive School Conditions For Reading Achievement a Rarity

Large amounts of data describing the reading habits of students in grades four, eight, and twelve, from the National Assessment of Educational Progress (NAEP), provide a clear picture of why American students, as a group, are not reading as much nor as well as they should (Foertsch, 1992). The very conditions for students that positively correlate to reading achievement apparently exist too rarely both in and outside our schools, namely:

- Large amounts of reading done in and outside school;
- Major deemphasis of workbook activities;
- Opportunities for connecting reading and writing;
- Reading a greater variety of texts (novels, poems, stories);
- Home support for literacy

Despite strong recommendations from the NAEP (Anrig & LaPointe, 1989; Langer, et al, 1990), few differences occurred between 1988 and 1990 regarding actual classroom instruction reading, and home support. Analyzing the 1990 data, the NAEP reported the following dismal findings:

- American students still read very little inside or outside of school;
- An overwhelming emphasis is still placed on workbook activities;
- American students have difficulty giving thoughtful responses when asked to "elaborate upon" what they have read;

- Most students still do not write about what they read on a weekly basis;
- Library use and access to reading materials in the home declined.

A particularly disturbing trend reported by the NAEP occurred between 1988 and 1990. Although there was a slight increase in the amount of reading students did in and outside of school, there was a sharp increase in the number of students who reported that they "never read for fun" (Foertsch, 1992). These data indicate that while students may be assigned more reading in school, they are enjoying reading less, and are growing to dislike reading more.

Basic Recommendations for Improving Reading Instruction

Eric and J.C.'s interview, which began this article, hit on one of the major causes of poor reading ability among our students. American students spend about three to five hours daily after school watching television, but only a few minutes per day reading (Rothman, 1992). As a group, U.S. students don't read well; in fact, they don't read much of anything.

To effect a dramatic change in the reading habits of American youngsters, especially those at risk of dropping out of school, our students must perceive the process of learning to read as something that is extremely pleasurable (Csikszentmihalyi, 1990). Learning to read, therefore, must become pleasure and quality oriented, rather than "skills" and stressed based, so that students associate reading with enjoyment and good books, and voluntarily spend large amounts of time reading- a crucial step toward becoming life-long readers.

Distilling Anderson and Pellicer's report on compensatory education programs, and the NAP report on prevalent reading instruction practices in grades four, eight and twelve, a number of important recommendations can be made. Compensatory education programs must be coordinated with both regular education programs and parent programs, so that professionals and parents are pulling together in the right direction for students. Low-level, pencil-andpaper tasks, and workbooks must be discarded, or, at the very least, used sparingly. In their place competent teachers need to use high interest, challenging reading materials, and give students time to write about what they read in a thoughtful manner.

I would add one important recommendation not in the aforementioned reports. Teachers need to use methods that enable students to read challenging materials with ease and fluency, such as special recorded books (see recommendation #4 at the end of this article).

High Gains in Reading Comprehension With Reading Style

Compared to the bleak picture painted by both the NAEP data and Anderson and Pellicer's report, educators working in the field of reading styles have achieved truly extraordinary results in short periods of time, with relatively small amounts of funding. The gain scores that follow are in reading comprehension on standardized achievement tests.

For example, Hodges, now Director of Research for the Association for Supervision and Curriculum Development (ASCD), directed a reading styles program for sixty, twice retained, seventh-graders in Harlem, New York City. At the program's inception, these students were reading on a preprimer to a fourth-grade reading level. Within ten months, the average gain reported by Hodges was 1.8 years, at least ten times the student's previous progress (Carbo, 1987).

In 1991 Queiruga's students broke all records, scoring a 26-month gain in only four months of using reading styles strategies. These youngsters were ninth and tenth graders, who had been in special education programs for most of their school careers, previously gaining only a few months in reading each year. Their gain scores were about twenty-four times their average achievement in previous school years (Queiruga, 1991).

Last, also in 1991, Genevieve Guerrero, principal of Margil Elementary in San Antonio I.S.D., reported that reading styles instruction had reduced the number of students who were at risk of school failure by 48%. In ten months the number of at-risk students had dropped from 302 students to 157. Within two years, Margil Elementary outdistanced most of the elementary schools in their district, moving from 62nd out of 65 school scholastically, to ninth place. These dramatic changes occurred in an inner-city school with a 98% Hispanic population (Profiles in Schools 1990-91...).

Reading Styles of Poor Readers

The extraordinary gain scores cited above could be more commonplace if there were a better understanding of students' reading styles—especially those of students at risk, and if instruction accommodated or "matched" those students' styles. Most of the thousands of poor readers that my colleagues and I have observed, interviewed and tested—regardless of grade level or type of school—have exhibited global, tactile, and kinesthetic reading styles. Their learning is often accelerated with holistic methods, an interdisciplinary curriculum, and highinterest, hands-on activities and materials that involve them emotionally (Carbo, Dunn & Dunn, 1986). Only rarely have they been exposed to instructional materials and procedures that motivate them and enable them to learn easily, but they usually make great strides in reading when the method of teaching accommodates their individual strengths.

Youngsters with global reading styles are whole-to-part learners. They require both high-interest reading materials that involve them emotionally (especially humor, mystery, and adventure), and holistic reading methods (e.g., choral reading, writing of stories, listening to tape recording of stories). To teach reading well to global learners, meaning is the key. Such youngsters recall words presented within the context of a well-written story more rapidly than they recall words presented in isolation or words presented in poorly conceived or poorly written stories. While all learners are helped by meaning, for the global students, high interest materials and emotional involvement is crucial.

Global learners also remember, dissimilar, high-interest words (e.g., monster, Charlie Brown, dinosaur) more easily than they remember the similar but low-interest words that appear in many beginning reading materials (e.g., bet, get, let). Global learners tend to rely heavily on visual cues; thus they often "draw" mental pictures to help them remember individual words. Understandably, such youngsters have trouble visualizing (and therefore learning) isolated letter sounds or words that have little meaning for them (Sinatra & StahlGemake, 1983; Oexle & Zenhausern, 1981).

As stated previously, poor readers tend to be strongly global, tactile, and kinesthetic. Tactile/kinesthetic learners have a better chance of understanding and remembering what they see and hear if they can touch, feel and experience what they are learning. To learn easily and well, students with a tactile/kinesthetic reading style must use a variety of hands-on resources (e.g., computers, games, typewriters); they also need a variety of kinesthetic materials and experiences (e.g., acting in plays, pantomiming, creating and using puppets for storytelling, reading directions and making a model).

How to Sharply Increase the Reading Ability of Potential Dropouts

Consistently, all of the reading styles programs that have achieved extraordinary reading gains, have used the following four important procedures. (See Note 1 to obtain more detailed information).

(1) Students' reading style strengths were identified, and that information was used to plan effective reading instruction, and discussed with other professionals, the students, and their parents. As a result all involved, including the students, had higher expectations for learning.

Reading styles can be identified using checklists, interviews, and questionnaires (Carbo, Dunn & Dunn, 1986). Particularly useful for this purpose is The Reading Style Inventory (RSI), which produces computerized reports. These RSI reports describe each student's reading style in detail, the methods, strategies, and materials that accommodate that style, and procedures for accommodating the reading style patterns of groups.

(2) Teachers emphasized strategies compatible with their students' reading styles. Among the most successful strategies used, were the following:

- Teachers used the reading methods and materials that were recommended on the students' Reading Style Inventory (see recommendation #1).
- Skillwork requiring a strongly analytic learning style was deemphasized. Instead, many examples and interesting materials were provided.
- Teachers experimented with different colored overlays. These were placed over a page of print for youngsters who experienced visual perception difficulties, such as letter reversals, or doubling letters. Often the correct colored overlay alleviated the problem substantially (Rickleman & Henk, 1990).
- Lessons were begun globally, with an overview in the form of a cartoon, filmstrip, visual aid, or an anecdote.
- Phonics was reserved for those youngsters who were sufficiently auditory to understand and process this type of information.
- The tactile and kinesthetic modalties of the learner were involved, and many visuals were included in each lesson. Whenever feasible, youngsters were allowed to work with peers, a friend, teachers, alone, and so on, depending on their sociological preference.
- Quiet working sections were established a sufficient distance from noisier areas.
- At least one special work area was created in each classroom. Teachers found that an informal reading section containing rugs, pillows, or soft chairs was particularly beneficial.

(3) Teachers found out about and discussed their students' reading interests, and provided reading materials based on those interests. Most students choose what they read (Carbo, 1983, Carbo, Dunn & Dunn, 1986; Queiruga, 1991). The older the student,the greater the need for a wide choice of reading materials. Teachers can find out through interviews and checklists, what the interests of their students are, and

then provide many well-written stories based on those interests. With the recorded book method described below, youngsters can often work with material well above their reading level.

(4) *Using special techniques for tape recording stories, teachers provided large amounts of high interest, challenging reading materials for their students, and students were able to read these materials fluently usually in a matter of minutes.*

In the mid seventies I used the method of recording described in this section, with eight learning disabled, elementary students reading two to five years below grade level. The group gained eight months in word recognition in six weeks (Carbo, 1978). Not only does this method improve reading fluency and comprehension, it also increases a student's language proficiency substantially.

To accelerate the process of learning to read, short amounts of high-interest material, somewhat above the student's reading level, should be recorded, using a slightly slow reading pace, short, natural phrases, and good expression. By placing a small amount of material on a tape side (as little as two minutes), even severely at-risk students can listen more than once to the recording, while following along in the book, without becoming bored or overwhelmed. After two or three listenings most students are able to read the passage fluently (Carbo, 1989; 1992).

A short story, for example, might require a few tape sides to complete, since only a few minutes are placed on each tape side. Students generally listen to the next tape side in the series each day, until they complete the story. Used daily, the recordings usually improve the language and writing of the youngsters as well as their reading fluency. Textbooks are generally the least desirable material to use initially. Only after students' reading levels have been raised, should they work extensively with textbooks.

Literacy levels in the United States are still ominously low, especially among those most ar risk of dropping out of high school. We know that dropouts tend disproportionately to be disabled readers. And we know that, even as reading ability in the U.S. is declining, rapid technological advances are making increasingly higher levels of reading essential. Unfortunately, the current practices in both compensatory education programs do not offer much hope for effecting the dramatic improvements that are needed in the literacy levels of many potential dropouts.

During the past decade, educators who have experimented with reading styles strategies, which capitalize upon the students' learning strengths and interests, have reported unusually high gains in reading and language acquisition in short periods of time. We do have both the ability and the knowledge to accelerate the process of learning to read and make that process pleasurable for students. In so doing, we can demonstrate to potential dropouts that they are able to learn rapidly and that they are indeed well worth saving.

Postscript

Here's a last excerpt from the same interview with Eric and J.C. that began this article. The two boys are discussing their reaction after listening to a book recording, while following along in the book and pedaling a stationary bike (to accommodate their need for kinesthetic movement while learning). The results speak for themselves.

> Eric: When you read on that thing, all the words just come out like that. I'm serious!
>
> J.C.: When I got up there, well when I started to read, I mean, I don't know, it was probably like a miracle. I started laughing because I couldn't help it because I was reading almost 100 percent better.

And what of Eric and J.C. now? They're doing just fine in high school.

REFERENCES

Anderson, L.W. & Peollicer, L.O. (1990). Synthesis of research on compensatory and remedial education. *Educational Leadership,* 10-16.

Anrig, G.R. & LaPointe, A.E. (1989). What we know about what students don't know. *Educational Leadership*, 4-9.

Carbo, M. (1978). Teaching reading with talking books. *The Reading Teacher, 32*, 267-273.

Carbo, M. (1983). Reading styles change from second to eighth grade. *Educational Leadership, 40* (5), 56-59.

Carbo, M. (1987). Reading styles research: What works isn't always phonics. *Phi Delta Kappan, 70*, 323-327.

Carbo, M. (1989). *How to Record Books For Maximum Reading Gains,* Roslyn Hgts, NY; National Reading Styles Institute.

Carbo, M. (1992). Eliminating the need for dumbed-down textbooks. *Educational Horizons*, 189-193.

Carbo, M., Dunn, R., and Dunn, K. (1986). *Teaching Students to Read Through Their Individual Learning Styles*. Englewood Cliffs, NJ; Prentice-Hall.

Csikszntmihalyi, M. (1990). "Enjoyment enhances learning." In the *Conference Preview* for the New Horizons for Learning International Summit on Lifespan Learning, pp. 7-8.

Carbo, M. (1992). Eliminating the need for dumbed-down textbooks. *Educational Horizons*, 189-193.

Carbo, M., Dunn, R., and Dunn, K. (1986). *Teaching Students to Read Through Their Individual Learning Styles*. Englewood Cliffs, NJ; Prentice-Hall.

Csikszntmihalyi, M. (1990). "Enjoyment enhances learning." In the *Conference Preview* for the New Horizons for Learning International Summit on Lifespan Learning, pp. 7-8.

Dunn, R. (1987). "Research on Instructional Environments: Implications for Student Achievement and Attitudes." *Professional School Psychology, 2* (1), 43-52.

Foertsch, M.A. (1992). *Reading In and Out of School: Factors influencing the literacy achievement of American students in grades 4, 8, and 12, in 1988 and 1990.* Washington, D.C.; Office of Educational Research and Improvement, U.S. Department of Education.

Griffin, J.L. (1987). Dropout rate tied to early failures. *Chicago Tribune*, July 31, 1.

Hodgkinson, H. (1989). *The same client: The demographics of education and service delivery systems*. Washington, D.C.: Institute for Educational Leadership, Inc./ Center for Demographic Policy.

Langer, J.A., Applebee, A.N., Mullis, I.V.S., & Foertsch, M.A. (1990). *Learning to Read in Our Nation's Schools: Instruction and Achievement in 1988 at grades 4, 8, and 12.* Princeton, NJ: National Assessment of Educational Progress, Education Testing Service.

Oexle, J.E. & Zenhausern, R. (1981). Differential hemispheric activation in good and poor readers. *International Journal of Neuroscience, 15*, 31-36.

Profiles of Schools, 1990-1991, San Antonio Independent School District (1991). San Antonio, TX: San Antonio I.S.D.

Queiruga, L. (1991). *A reading styles experiment with learning disabled, high school students*. Roslyn Hgts., NY: National Reading Styles.

Rickelman, R.J. & Henk, W.A. (1990). Colored overlays and tinted lens filters. *The Reading Teacher, 44*, 166-167.

Rothman, R. (1992). Reforms not widely incorporated, report concludes. *Education Week*, Feb. 5, 1992, 9.

Sinatra, R., & Stahl-Gemake, J. (1983). *Using the Right Brain in Language Arts*. Springfield, IL: Charles C. Thomas.

III

PROGRAMS THAT ARE MAKING A DIFFERENCE

JACK RAWLINSON
JOHN W. WILSON

11

Attend And Win: *A K-3 Dropout Prevention Program*

Today, with an alarming proportion of at risk students enrolled in public schools, the indication is that the future of dropout prevention is not in isolated programs that grow out of remediation courses. Rather the future is beginning services early and continuing them throughout school on an as needed basis. Typically, school officials have chosen to ignore warning signs and have waited until students have failed. Only then have attempts been made to remediate their problems. An emerging new consciousness about dropout prevention focuses on the schools and communities ability to identify and assist high risk students when the students need additional help, can benefit from the help, and before the problems become impossible to solve.

Research suggests that students do not suddenly turn into dropouts. School leaders must examine the educational experiences of the at risk students during the years prior to the legal age of dropping out to better understand the dropout problem. The decision to drop out of school is long term beginning with the child's first negative school experience. Because of this, dropout prevention must also be long term and must begin early in the student's educational career.

People often assume that dropping out of school is isolated to the secondary schools, because statistics commonly focus on how many ninth or tenth grade students fail to graduate from high school. While it is true that the greatest number of students leave school during the tenth to twelfth grade, the decision to quit is often made much earlier. Because of compulsory attendance laws, a casual observation of at risk students would suggest that students are not at risk of dropping out until they are in high school. Actually, many students should be considered at risk their first day of school.

Reports from many researchers (Cage, 1984; Pallas, 1986; Comer, 1988; Rumberger, 1986) indicate that most youth who drop out of school make the conscious decision long before the final act occurs. Some researchers suggest that once the decision is made to drop out it can be delayed but is seldom reversed. It is now widely accepted that dropping out for most students is only a visible sign of something that went wrong years before. It is with this understanding that elementary dropout prevention programs are built. Early detection of trouble and special services to meet the individual needs of at risk students are the keys to successful dropout prevention programs (National School Public Relations Association, 1972).

Literature on early school leaving describes a lack of success in school, alienation from classmates and teachers, and social exclusion, all of which are strong factors in the elementary school experiences of dropouts. Dropout prevention literature outlines successful elementary school program characteristics and ways of organizing school routines to enhance the student's probability of success. It is known that successful programs promote a sense of membership, identity and self-esteem. Successful programs also avoid the premature foreclosure of options for students.

A significant finding that has emerged from research about dropouts is the importance of the early identification of at risk students coupled with effectively designed prevention and intervention programs and strategies. Students drop out for many reasons. Every at risk child is an individual with an individual set of problems. Therefore, the structure and delivery of at risk programs must be responsive to individual personal and environmental needs of those students identified as at risk.

Intervention during a student's high school years or after he/she drops out is less effective and more costly than adequately designed prevention programs in elementary school (Cage 1984). Pallas (1986) asserted that, "the key to effective dropout prevention programs is the early identification of potential dropouts so services can be provided for at risk students prior to high school" (p. 2).

There are four primary areas of identification of at risk students in early elementary school: 1) attendance patterns, 2) academic achievement, 3) social behavior, and 4) grade retention(s) (Smith & Shepard, 1987; Barber & McClellan, 1987).

Children with poor attendance in elementary school are more likely to drop out of high school. Cage (1984) has supported this premise and has made a connection between high absenteeism and achievement. Barber & McClellan (1987) in a study of seventeen large school districts contends that attendance is the number one ranking predictor of dropping out and that negative attendance patterns begin as early as the primary grades. Attendance, therefore is one of the most critical elements in the early identification of potential dropouts.

Achievement or academic performance has also been identified as a predictor of future school failure. Forty-two percent of the dropouts in the

High School and Beyond study (Peng and Takai, 1983) had a "D" average in school. Cage (1984) stated that poor achievement in reading and basic skills is identifiable as early as the first grade. At risk students typically start school behind their peers and continue to fall further behind each school year.

Behavior is a critical variable identified in most dropout studies (Self, 1986). Inappropriate behavior patterns that begin in elementary school escalate as students become older. Improper or unacceptable behavior is a clear sign of other emotional or social problems with the student.

Retention is one of the most frequently observed precursors to dropping out. A student two grade levels behind his/her appropriate class has a 95% chance of dropping out.

Because dropping out of school is an individual decision and a symptom of deeper, underlying factors, there is no easily identifiable, single, dropout prevention strategy that will work for all students. No single plan of action can be designed to assure school success for every student. However, the greatest probability of success appears to be when services begin early, are individualized and address not only the educational but also the physical, social, and emotional needs of at risk children and their families.

BACKGOUND OF ATTEND AND WIN

In August, 1988 the Regional Superintendent of Schools for Gallatin, Hardin, Pope and Saline counties in Illinois received a Truant Alternative and Optional Education Program grant from the Illinois State Board of Education for the purpose of developing a dropout prevention program for the nine rural school districts in the region. The goal of the program was to identify and provide individualized services to at risk students in grades three, four and five. Using predictors of school failure (Vickers, 1988) and following extensive professional development, classroom teachers in the identified grades were asked to refer qualified students to the program. During the second semester of the 1988-89 school year students were identified, teacher referrals were made, and individualized services were started on a limited basis. With the beginning of the 1989-90 school year the Attend And Win Program was fully operational.

Classroom teachers were asked to identify students in their room who were:

- Behind grade placement in math
- Behind grade placement in reading
- Physically immature
- Mentally immature

- Troublesome socially
- Experiencing extreme family problems

Each teacher was asked to rank all students whom they referred according to the student's special needs. If a teacher referred five students to the program they were ranked 1-5. During the 1989-90 school year a total of 293 students were referred to the program and met the criteria to be accepted for special services. Home visits were made, the program explained to parent(s), and permission forms were signed by the parent(s) before any services were provided.

After the parent(s) granted permission for the student to be enrolled in the Attend And Win Program, project staff discussed perceived needs of each student with current and former classroom teachers, purged the student's permanent record for information, contacted the various social agencies involved for information, and discussed the student's needs. Only after all information was gathered were services started.

In the 1988-89 school year, 1145 students were enrolled in the third, fourth and fifth grades of the ten elementary schools in the region. The 293 who were referred represented 25.5% of the total enrollment. Most referrals were made by teachers but often parents would refer their own children. By the end of the school year parental permission had been obtained to serve 244 students. For various reasons, 49 parents, or 16.7% of those approached during the first year refused to allow their children to participate in the program. As the knowledge and reputation of the Attend And Win Program became established and parents became aware of the services available, the number of parents refusing permission has since diminished to near zero.

Of the 244 students served in the program during the first full year:

- 62% were male, 38% female.
- 60% were in the third grade, 24% in the fourth grade and 16% in the fifth grade.
- Nearly all (91%) were white (According to the School Report Cards, 98.5% of the elementary enrollment in the ten schools was white).
- 44% had repeated either one or two grades.
- The average school attendance rate was almost 95%.
- 51% lived with only one of their natural parents, 41% lived with both natural parents, and 8% lived with someone other than a natural parent (usually a grandparent).
- More than 72% were receiving other special services in school (e.g. special education, Chapter I).

- Approximately 50% were receiving services outside of the school from DCFS or Illinois Public Aid.

In October, 1988, three project counselor/social workers were employed as the project staff. A fourth counselor, a certified school psychologist, was added to the project staff in August, 1989. The three original counselor/social workers were highly motivated, certified elementary education teachers who were provided extensive professional development in counseling techniques and social services during the first three months of the project.

The project staff was responsible for developing an Individualized Educational Service Plan (I.E.S.P.) for each child served. Using the information gained from all participants associated with the child's education, project staff developed the Individual Educational Service Plan (I.E.S.P.) for each child, using a case management approach to the delivery of services.

In an attempt to determine the effectiveness of the Attend And Win Program, after three years of services a study (Rawlinson, 1992) was conducted to compare the reading and mathematics scores and attendance rates of the students who were referred and served to a control group consisting of those who were referred but not served. Reading and math scores and attendance rate data were gathered from the permanent records of all 293 students as data for making the comparison.

FINDINGS

The study was conducted to determine if the elementary dropout prevention program for students in Gallatin, Hardin, Pope, and Saline Counties in Illinois improved the educational achievement, attendance, and self esteem of the students served.

Specifically the study addressed the following questions:

(1) Was the school attendance rate of students served by the elementary dropout prevention program improved over a three year period of time?

(2) Were the reading achievement score of students served by the elementary dropout prevention program improved over a three year period of time?

(3) Were the mathematics achievement scores of students served by the elementary dropout prevention program improved over a three year period of time?

(4) Was the self concept of students served by the elementary dropout prevention program improved over a three year period of time?

The subjects of the study were at risk students who were enrolled in the third, fourth, and fifth grades during the 1988-89 school year and who were still enrolled at the end of the 1990-91 school year. The study examined the effects of a series of individualized special services and were measured by the Iowa Test of Basic Skills, the California Achievement Test, and the Rotter Incomplete Sentences Blank.

The study was designed to compare mathematics and reading achievement, attendance rates and measured self esteem. A comparison of reading and mathematics achievement (grade equivalency scores) and attendance rates were made for the year prior to the implementation of the program (1987-88) and for the same students after three years of additional individualized services (1990-91).

Measurement of self esteem consisted of a pretest in Fall 1988 and a posttest in Spring 1991. One-way analysis of variance and factorial analysis of variance procedures were used to determine if there were differences in achievement between the two groups after the two groups were treated statistically to control for the difference in baseline data.

Many parents who refused to allow their children to be served indicated that they felt their children did not need extra help. The raw data appeared to support this because the students not served scored significantly higher than those served. Raw data indicated that students who were provided special services gained in achievement scores when compared to those who were not served. In reading, students served by the program begin .4096 of a grade below those not served. During the three years served the margin was reduced to .1416 of a grade.

Math scores were similar. Students served started .5558 of a grade below the students not served and finished .2636 of a grade behind. In both reading and mathematics the gains were significant but not remarkable.

Attendance rates showed considerable improvement. Students served begin with .2372 fewer days absent than those not served and the difference grew to 2.881 days per year.

Self esteem scores also improved. The mean score of the Rotter Sentence Completion is 120.00 with a standard deviation of 14.1. During the three year program the student's mean score was improved by 3.5833 points.

When measured statistically the study yielded a significant difference between reading achievement of at risk students who were provided special individualized services over a period of three school years when compared to a similar group of at risk students who were provided no special services during the same time period.

The study also yielded significant differences between improvement of attendance rates of the group of at risk students who were served when compared to a group who were provided no special services over the same three year time period.

Similarly, there were differences between pretest and posttest self concept scores. However, although there were improvements in raw data there were no statistically significant differences between achievement scores of the two groups of at risk students in mathematics achievement.

CONCLUSIONS

This study supports findings of previous research (Mann, 1986; Wehlage and Rutter, 1986 a,b) indicating that many students enter school with skills and habits insufficient to succeed and that without special help will become school dropouts.

This study yielded significant differences between two groups of at risk students when a series of individualized special services were provided to one group of at risk elementary students and their reading achievement, attendance rates and self esteem were compared. Students were identified in the third, fourth, and fifth grades using predictors of school failure and were provided services during a three year period. Services were provided to students individually and determined by the student's primary identified reason for being at risk. The true test of the program will be seen as this group of students reaches their sixteenth birthday and dropout statistics are calculated.

REFERENCES

Barber, L. and McClellan, M. (1987, December). Looking at America's dropouts: Who are they? *Phi Delta Kappan*,256-262.

Cage, B. (1984, June). *Dropout prevention.* Bureau of Educational Research, The University of Mississippi. Division of Instruction, Mississippi State Department of Education.

Comer, J.P. (1988). Is parenting essential to good teaching? *NEA Today*, (January), 34-40.

Mann, D. (1986, Fall). Can we help dropouts: Thinking about the undoable. *Teachers College Record*, 87(3), 307-323.

National School Public Relations Association. (1972). *Dropouts: Prevention and rehabilitation; schools rescue potential failures.* Washington, DC: Author.

Pallas, A.M. (1986). *School dropouts in thc United States.* Department of Education, Center for Education Statistics (Publication No. 065-000-00276-1). Washington, DC: U.S. Government Printing Office.

Peng, S.S. and Takai, R.T. (1983). *High school dropouts: Descriptive information from high school and beyond.* National Center for Education Statistics Bulletin,

Rawlinson, J.E. (1992). *Effects of a dropout prevention program on at risk elementary students in grades three and four.* Doctoral dissertation. Southern Illinois University, Carbondale. Unpublished manuscript.

Rumberger, R.W. (1986, September). *High school dropouts: A problem for research, policy, and practices.* Stanford, CA: Stanford University Press.

Self, T.C. (1986). *Dropouts: A review of literature.* Washington, D.C.: Department of Education. (ERIC Document Reproduction Service No. ED 260307).

Smith, M.L. and Shepard, L.A. (1987). What doesn't work: Explaining policies of retention in the early grades. *Educational Leadership, 44*, 78-86.

Vickers, H.S. (1988). *Validation of identification procedures of children at risk for dropping out of school: A study of children and their families in grades 1-3.* (Doctoral dissertation, University of Delaware, 1988). Dissertation Abstracts International, 8914334.

Washington, DC: U.S. Department of Education. (ERIC Document Reproduction Service No. ED 236366).

Wehlage, G.G. and Rutter, R.A. (1986a, Fall). Dropping out: How much do schools contribute to the problem? *Teachers College Record, 87(3),* 374-392.

Wehlage, G.G. and Rutter, R.A. (1986b, April). *Evaluation of a model program for at-risk students.* Paper presented at the annual meeting of the American Educational Research Association, San Francisco, CA. Unpublished manuscript.

MARGAREE S. CROSBY
EMMA M. OWENS

12

Cooperative Learning: *An Alternative Educational Strategy to Tracking and Ability Grouping for World-Class Citizens*

INTRODUCTION

In-spite of numerous educational reforms over the past two decades, there continues to be numerous differences among students in the classrooms of this great nation. For over 100 years, a popular practice has been to group students into course sequences and classrooms on the basis of personal qualities, performances, or aspirations. This practice, known as tracking or ability grouping, is one of the most persistent practices in schools, especially secondary schools. Tracking/ability grouping is a harmful educational practice which results in several negative social effects, especially for racial and ethnic minorities.

Because students come to school from a wide range of differences in their readiness to learn, tracking appeared to make a lot of sense early on. The practice of tracking/ability grouping was developed and adopted with three general goals according to George (1988): (1) to raise the academic achievement of students beyond what it would be in mixed ability classes; (2) to help students feel better about school and themselves as learners; and (3) to help teachers be more effective and enjoy teaching with students grouped by ability between classes.

The effects of grouping have been argued by educators from the beginning. Since researchers and those who review research have been unable to reach a consensus regarding the advantages of ability grouping, the overriding message seems to be that nothing has been established with certainty. It is the purpose of this article to review the outmoded and ineffective practices of tracking/ability grouping and offer cooperative learning as an alternative that is more accountable to both what research identifies as an effective practice and to the students who need optimum preparation for the challenges of world-class citizenship in the twenty first century.

EDUCATIONAL RESEARCH ON ABILITY GROUPING

Within-class ability grouping is supported in the literature. In particular, Slavin (1986) found evidence that ability grouping is maximally effective when it is done for only one or two subjects and students are studying in heterogeneous classes for most of the day.

Strike (1983) reports that even thought there is debate concerning the effectiveness of ability grouping, most recently, the controversy concerns the fairness of it. Two major questions surface regarding tracking: (1) Is there a class bias involved? (2) Does tracking have any noteworthy impact on the educational outcomes?

Vanfossen, Jones, and Spade (1987) found that prior research indicated that the results of curriculum tracking fell into three categories. Specifically, one group of researchers (Breton, 1970; Schafer and Olexa, 1971; Rosenbaum, 1976; Alexander, Cook and McDill, 1978; Alexander and Eckland, 1980; Eder, 1981; and Oakes, 1982) presented evidence that tracking helps to maintain and perpetuate class status from one generation to another by sorting children from different backgrounds into different curricula programs where they are exposed to differential treatments and encounter different learning environments. Another group of researchers suggests that tracking plays a minimal role in status maintenance because students are placed into tracks more on the basis of ability and motivation than on the basis of class membership (Rehberg and Rosenthal, 1978; Davis and Haller, 1981; and Alexander and Cook, 1982). The third category of researchers implies that the debate may be irrelevant because tracking in high school does not have a significant impact upon achievement, values, and educational outcomes (Jencks et. al., 1972; Alexander and Cook, 1982; and Kulik and Kulik, 1982). Jenck et. al. (pp.34, 107) concluded that "neither track nor curriculum assignment seems to have an appreciable effect on students' cognitive development."

Vanfossen, Jones, and Spade (1987), addressed the role of tracking in the perpetuation of status advantage by focusing on three questions: (1) Does the pattern of recruitment of students into the different curricular programs reveal a class bias? (2) Does tracking at the high school level have any significant impact on achievement, values and educational outcomes? (3) Are there any concrete classroom or school experiences related to achievement that vary by track assignments?

Findings regarding these questions were as follows:

First, chances that a student will be in the top academic track are 53% if that student is in the top socioeconomic status (SES) quartile; and only 19% if he is in the bottom SES quartile. The chances that a student will be in a vocational track are 10% if he is in the top SES quartile and 30% if he is in the bottom SES quartile. Regardless of the reason for getting there, (prior academic performance, grades, teachers' recommendations, or educational aspirations, all of which are influenced by socioeconomic background), there are substantial differences among social classes in ultimate track destination. Secondly, the correlation coefficient was relatively small regarding the aforementioned question #2, but we should be aware that a small unique influence over a two-year period may signify a larger influence over the total period in which the students are enrolled in school. A number of authors have suggested that tracking begins as early as the first grade and that tracking decisions made at the higher levels may be based on tracking patterns established earlier. The cumulative impact may be substantial. Finally, findings of the Vanfossen study are consistent with other reports indicating that classes in the academic track are more serious, spend more time on task, spend less time handling discipline, and place a greater emphasis upon learning.

In view of these findings, the impact of tracking or ability grouping on minority students in a state-wide public school system was examined by Crosby and Owens (1991). Since principals are in a key position to enhance the development of a proper climate for upgrading schools, this study sought to determine the degree to which principals feel that ability grouping/tracking can contribute to the quality of education in their schools. It sought to determine if the principals in this state's public school system express attitudes toward ability grouping that are more supportive and facilitative. This group of principals did not express attitudes toward ability grouping that can be characterized as supportive and facilitative.

George (1988) has found a significant variance between educational research and common practices of school districts regarding ability grouping/tracking: eighty five percent (85%) of the research says no while eighty five percent (85%) of the schools say yes. It appears from his comprehensive review that tracking seems to make good common sense to many educators in spite of what the research says. It also appears to be supported most persistently by parents of high achievers who tend to credit ability grouping for their children's success. These parents often use their understanding of school district politics to influence decisions favoring tracking. In addition, tracking persists because tracking/ability grouping is more familiar and, therefore, appears to be easier for many teachers. This causes many career teachers to lobby against heterogeneous grouping strategies.

AN ALTERNATIVE TO TRACKING AND ABILITY GROUPING FOR THE WORLD-CLASS CITIZEN

Since most of the research on tracking/ability grouping indicates that tracking does not appear to do what it is expected to do with a majority of the students (George, 1988 and Slavin, 1991), it is considered to be one of the major unresolved issues in our educational system today. Furthermore, the practice of tracking/ability grouping may increase inequality in education since it accounts for and promotes one of the most undemocratic atmospheres in our schools (Nicholls, 1989 and Massachusetts Advocacy Center, 1990).

As we approach the twenty-first century, schools need to make reforms that will have the most positive effects upon children living in a complex world with significant anticipated mismatches between work place needs and work force capabilities. According to the National Alliance of Business (1986), the overall work force is predicted to decline while business's need for more and better trained workers will grow.

Throughout the nation, technology, international competition and population shifts are creating dramatic changes in the work force skills needed to maintain the competitive business edge for an overall healthy economy in America. At the same time, demographic shifts in the population foreshadow serious gaps in the supply of qualified labor.

Cooperative learning has been offered in recent years as a strategy to facilitate change in the daily experiences of students themselves. Cooperative learning builds upon the social instincts of children and adolescents as well as supplementing and replacing independent seat work with activities for small, mixed-ability groups. While tracking/ability grouping has been criticized for its impact on minorities, research reviewed by the Massachusetts Advocacy Center (1990) indicates that the variety of models of cooperative learning may have especially important benefits for African-American and Hispanic students.

The Massachusetts Advocacy Center (1990) also highlights research which shows that cooperative learning promotes higher productivity and achievement, more frequent use of higher level reasoning, greater retention of facts, better problem-solving skills, and improvement in conceptual skills. In addition, Slavin (1991) reviewed 67 studies and revealed that cooperative learning develops and enhances positive self-esteem, prosocial behavior, positive intergroup relations, improved attendance, improved classroom behavior, acceptance of academically handicapped children, and support for democratic values. He further notes that the particular methods used determines the effects of cooperative learning. However, the two necessary elements of all cooperative learning methods are group goals and individual accountability because this combination provides the critical motivation for students to take each other's learning seriously.

Since students are expected to work together toward the completion of a group task that benefits each member, most cooperative learning activities include both an academic and social skills objective. They all have students involved in team efforts designed to help one another master academic material.

Although small scale laboratory research on cooperation may be traced back to the late 1890s (Johnson, et. al.,1991), Slavin (1991) reveals that research on specific applications of cooperative learning to the classroom began in the early 1970s and continues to a great degree around the world.

COOPERATIVE EDUCATION MODELS WITH PROVEN BENEFITS TO STUDENTS

Some of the cooperative education models that have proved especially beneficial to students who have experienced little success in classes organized around traditional instructional approaches are described below as adapted from the Massachusetts Advocacy Center (1990, pp. 118-119):

Learning Together

Students work together in four-or-five member heterogeneous groups on assignments to produce a single group product. Students may be evaluated and rewarded on the basis of this single product or on a combination of their own performance and the overall performance of the group.

Group Investigation

Students work in small heterogeneous groups and assume substantial responsibility for deciding what information they will gather, how they will organize themselves to gather it, and how they will communicate what they have learned to their classmates. For example, a group might choose a subtopic within a class unit, break down this subtopic into individual tasks for each member of the group, and prepare a group report, presentation, or display for the whole class.

Jigsaw

A subject or topic to be learned is divided into sections or subtopics and each member of heterogeneous "home base" group is assigned responsibility for one section. Members of different home base groups who are working on the same section meet together in "expert groups" to discuss their topics. They then return to their home base groups and take turns teaching groupmates about their sections. Students are evaluated individually through quizzes, projects, or the like.

Jigsaw II

Similar to the original Jigsaw, all students are first provided common information. Students then break into expert groups to study their specific subtopics. There is team recognition based on team scores and often a newsletter recognizing team winners and individual high scorers, in addition to individual grades and scores.

Team-Games-Tournament (TGT)

Student work together in four-or five-member heterogeneous teams to help one another master material and prepare for competitions against members of other teams. For the competitions, each student is assigned to a three-person table with students from two other teams who are similar in skill level. In this way, all students have an equal chance to earn points to contribute to their team score.

Students Teams - Achievement Division (STAD)

In this variation of TGT, games and tournaments are replaced with a quiz. Thus while both TGT and STAD combine cooperative learning with team competition and group rewards for individual performance, STAD depersonalizes the competitive aspects of TGT. Quiz scores are translated into points based on how a student's individual score compares with the scores of other students of similar ability — whose identities are not disclosed by the teacher — or are based on individual improvement.

Team-Assisted Individualization (TAI)

Developed especially for math classes in grades three to six, TAI combines direct instruction by the teacher with follow-up practice using a team learning approach. Students work in heterogeneous teams on material appropriate to their individual skill level. Teammates help one another with problems and check on another's work. Meanwhile, the teacher calls forward students from the various teams who are working at the same level to instruct them as a group. In this way, TAI provides for both interactive peer learning and individualized instruction.

COOPERATIVE INTEGRATED READING AND COMPOSITION (CIRC)

This method is similar to TAI but is designed for instruction in reading, writing and language arts. Students work in mixed-ability teams on a series of reading activities or in writing in peer response groups using the "process writing" approach.

It would appear that cooperative learning provides all students with equal opportunity for success, gives students control over their learning, and develops communication, decision-making and interpersonal skills. Although there is great evidence of academic and social benefits that students receive from working in cooperative learning groups, students do not always conform to all expectations, and teachers may experience a few challenges. Since this is a subject of growing interest and the teacher's role in structuring cooperative learning situations is more than just structuring cooperation among students (Johnson et. al., 1984), there is a growing number of step-by-step guides to facilitating effective cooperative learning classroom practices (Johnson et. al., 1991; Topping, 1988; Calderon, 1990; Salvin 1991; and Ellis and Whaler, 1992). However, there is still a big need for greater professional cooperation and support at the classroom level from principals, teachers and other staff members to implement and/or facilitate highly effective cooperative learning processes at the school. There is also a great need for understanding and support by school board members, parents and other community members.

CONCLUSIONS AND RECOMMENDATIONS

There are several conclusions that may be drawn about grouping students. First, tracking/ability grouping continues to be practiced widely throughout this nation in spite of the significant amount of research which does not support it. Second, while tracking/ability grouping remains an unresolved issue, if not the single most controversial issue our schools' face, it contributes significantly to the school drop out problem and to the growth of an unproductive underclass in this country. Third, there are aspects of tracking/ability grouping which not all educators support. Fourth, there is a continuing transition in the attitudes of educators toward specific aspects of tracking/ability grouping.

Fifth, cooperative learning methods are more effective than traditional methods. Sixth, cooperative learning strategies teach the skills of the future needed for world-class citizens.

Finally, it may be concluded that educators have become sensitive and could continue to grow professionally by being exposed to the impact and fairness of ability grouping and other instructional practices. With the many different effective instructional approaches, ability grouping may not be needed. However, many educators would need professional support and assistance in moving to a higher level of teaching proficiency in the cooperative learning process. Also, sufficient funding for education in general is necessary to ensure the most manageable class sizes for optimum heterogeneous grouping. However, effective utilization of the students' peers in the cooperative learning process provides both great cost and instructional benefits.

REFERENCES

Alexander, K.L., and Cook, M.A. (1982). Curricula and Coursework: A Surprise Ending to a Familiar Story. *American Sociological Review*, 47, 626-40.

Alexander, K.L., Cook, M.A., and McDill, E.L. (1978). Curriculum Tracking and Educational Stratification: Some Further Evidence, *American Sociological Review*, 43, 47-66.

Alexander, K.L., and Eckland, B.U. (1980). The Explorations in Equality of Opportunity Survey of 1955 High School Sophomores. *Research in Sociology of Education and Socialization*, 1, 31-58.

Breton, R. (1970). Academic Stratification in Secondary Schools and the Educational Plans of Students. *Canadian Review of Sociology and Anthropology*, 7, 1.

Calderon, M. (1990). *Cooperative Learning for Limited English Proficient Students*. (Report 3). Baltimore, Maryland: John Hopkins University Center for Research on Effective Schooling for Disadvantaged Students.

Crosby, M.S. and and Owens, E.M. (1991). *An Assessment of Principal Attitudes Toward Ability in Grouping in the Public Schools of South Carolina*. Clemson, South Carolina: Clemson University Center for the Study of the Black Experience in Higher Education.

Davis, S.A., and Haller, E.T. (1981). Tracking Ability, and SES: Further Evidence on the Revisionist - Meritocratic Debate. *American Journal of Education*, 89, 283-304.

Eder, D. (1981). Ability Grouping As A Self-Fulfilling Prophecy: A Micro-Analysis of Teacher Student Interaction. *Sociology of Education*, 54, 151-62.

Ellis, S.E. and Whalen, S.F. (1992). Keys To Cooperative Learning. *Instructor*, 101, 34-37.

George, P.S. (1988). *What's the Truth About Tracking and Ability Grouping Really? An Explanation for Teachers and Parents*. Gainesville, Florida: University of Florida Teacher Education Resources.

Jencks, C., et. al, (1972). *Inequality, A Reassessment of the Effect of Family and School in America*. New York: Basic Books.

Johnson, D.W., et. al. (1991). *Cooperation In the Classroom* 5th ed. Minnesota: Interaction Book Company.

Kulik, C., and Kulik, J.A. (1982). Effects of Ability Grouping on Secondary School Students: A Meta-Analysis of Evaluation Findings. *American Education Research Journal,* 19, 415-28.

Massachusetts Advocacy Center (1990). *Locked In/Locked Out: Tracking and Placement Practices in Public Schools.* Boston: The Eusey Press, Inc.

Nicholls, J. (1989). *The Competitive Ethos and Democratic Education.* Cambridge: Harvard University Press.

Oakes, J. (1982). Classroom Social Relationships: Exploring the Bowles and Gintis Hypothesis. *Sociology of Education,* 55, 197-212.

Rehberg, R.A., and Rosenthal, T.R. (1978). *Class and Merit in the American High School.* New York: Longman.

Rosenbaum, J.E. (1976). *Making Inequality: The Hidden Curriculum of High School Tracking.* New York: Wiley.

Schafer, W., and Olexa, C. (1971). *Tracking and Opportunity.* Scranton, Pennsylvania: Chandler.

Salvin, R.E. (1986). *Ability Grouping and Student Achievement in Elementary Schools: A Best-Evidence Synthesis.* (Report 1). Baltimore, Maryland: Johns Hopkins University Center for Research on Elementary and Middle Schools.

Salvin, R.E. (1991). *Student Team Learning: A Practical Guide To Cooperative Learning* 3rd ed. Washington, D.C.: National Education Association.

Salvin, R.E. (1991). Synthesis of Research on Cooperative Learning. *Educational Leadership,* 48, 71-82.

Strike, M. (1983). Fairness and Ability Grouping. *Educational Theory,* 33, 125-134.

Topping, K. (1988). *The Peer Tutoring Handbook: Promoting Co-operative Learning.* Cambridge, Maryland: Brookline Books.

Vanfossen, B.E., Jones, J.D. and Spade, J.A. (1987). Curriculum and Tracking Status Maintenance. *Sociology of Education,* 104-122.

RHONDA ROWLAND
ELLEN SNOW

13

Positive Effects of a Demonstration Program for High School Students At Risk of Dropping Out of School

Every year nearly one million youth drop out of school (Smith & Lincoln, 1988). This prediction may be low, according to a report by the U.S. General Accounting Office that in 1985, 4.3 million young people dropped out of high school between the ages of 16 and 24 (Hahn, 1987). For one in four students in high school, dropping out helps eliminate problems of frustration and not belonging (Cavazos, 1989). These students are frequently older than their classmates, underachievers, and have other compounding problems related to drugs, pregnancy, and poverty (Barber & McClellan, 1987). For these youngsters, dropping out of school represents dropping out of society (Fennimore, 1988). At-risk students are often developmentally delayed (Glenn & Nelson, 1987), exhibiting behaviors at the high school level most often seen in a middle school child. At-risk children are still caught in the transition from childhood to young adulthood, and they struggle simultaneously for independence while, at the same time, trying to maintain child-like dependence due to the insecurity that independence brings them. They lack a socially competent self-image and their family relationships are often strained or very poor. They have strong identification with their peer group but lack important social skills such as verbalizing feelings and assertion.

Environmental changes have a great impact on the success or failure of children at school. Recognizing this, Sapone (1989) says that enhancing the entire life of the student will be productive for the at-risk child. School success follows a child's feeling of personal success.

The typical high school isolates students by not providing them with opportunities for success. Traditional high schools are "unlikely, even unable, to give at-risk students the quality of attention they need to succeed" (Wehlage, 1986, p. 23). In evaluating the results of successful schooling and at-risk students, Robledo (1990), reports that "feelings of isolation contribute to dropping out of school. Schools can help students develop a sense of belonging" (p. 6). Hamby (1989) states that at-risk students can be reached in two ways: "Make students competent learners and confirm them as worthy individuals by treating them with respect and acceptance" (p. 23).

The ideal high school for at-risk students gives them the quantity and quality of attention they need to succeed. It provides small class size and face-to-face communication with teachers who practice an extended role, responding to the whole student. "The school program should teach the personal, academic, and social skills that the at-risk student needs for school success" (Walker & Sylwester, 1991, p. 16). The school should enhance social competencies, including friendship-making skills, caring skills, assertiveness skills, and resistance skills (Benson, 1991). The following protective factors are seen as mediating the effects of risk factors: fewer stresses that are shorter in duration; positive school climate that provides students with opportunities for participation and gives them responsibilities and a sense of success at 'meaningful tasks; warm, close, personal relationship with an adult; and, planning as a coping skill Rutter (1979, 1984). Programs that offer a balanced curriculum recognize the multiple reasons for high-risk behavior, such as poor self-concept, anxiety, low social confidence, external locus of control, impulsivity, and low assertiveness skills (Botvin, 1986). Counseling is a major way to ensure that at-risk students maintain contact with the curriculum. It is the glue that holds the program together and allows students to stay connected to the school. It includes academic guidance, career awareness and planning, personal counseling, human service agency referral and coordination, and family support (Hamby, 1992). Counseling services that are responsive to and effective in overcoming the problems of at-risk students are extremely important. Guidance services focus on development needs of all individuals. Counseling is a process of working with students rather than doing something to or for them. It is important to assist students in developing self-awareness and self-acceptance to become aware of others, to establish healthy interpersonal relationships, and to improve upon decision-making related to the awareness of the world of work and life styles (Huisman, 1992).

PROGRAM ELEMENTS

The Strategies with Technology and Affective and Remedial Support Program (S.T.A.R.S.) is a demonstration program funded by the Center for Substance Abuse Prevention, Department of Health and Human Services. The program, beginning in the 1990-91 school year, is a five year grant and is designed to follow two cohorts of students through high school. There are four major components: 1) technology-based academics and remediation using a state-of-the-art computer lab; 2) regularly scheduled individual and group counseling sessions which focus on reducing the use of alcohol and other drugs, providing early intervention with youth already involved with alcohol and other drugs, and increasing students' positive self-perceptions concerning their ability to direct their lives; 3) parent involvement consisting of individual home visits by counselors and monthly group meetings on parenting issues; and 4) community mentors who provide students with adult friends to help them tie academics to careers. S.T.A.R.S. activities (computer lab and counseling) occur during one period of the school day. For the rest of the day, students are intermingled with other students in regular classes with traditional teachers.

As recommended by Botvin (1986), the program's support groups and training program include: a) problem-solving skills, b) cognitive skills for resisting peer pressure and media influences, c) skills for increasing self-control and self-discipline, d) skills for goal setting and goal accomplishment, e) coping strategies for relieving stress, f) general interpersonal skills such as initiating social interactions, g) assertiveness skills for making requests and saying "No", and h) skills for identifying, expressing, and coping with feelings. The teaching methods used in the support groups are broad in scope so as to appeal to the variety of learning types and/or learning differences of the students. Acknowledging that at-risk students often are kinesthetic learners with dominating right brain hemispheric orientation, counseling groups utilize experimental learning techniques such as role-playing, art, music, and games.

Process evaluation activities include ongoing monitoring and data gathering from all aspects of the program to provide information for decision-making, program intervention, and revision. The computer software generates diagnostic test results and prescriptions for appropriate lessons for students. Throughout the lessons, student progress is maintained by the networked computer program and reviewed by teachers to adjust levels and subjects as needed. Overall academic progress is monitored by S.T.A.R.S. teachers and counselors through conferences and joint planning meetings with other faculty. Counselors receive copies of failure reports for their students every three weeks and meet with the students to devise action plans to bring up their grades. Counselors receive daily printouts of student absences. If their students are absent two days in a row without an excuse counselors make phone calls or home visits to determine the cause of the absence. For discipline matters, counselors are notified when their students are sent to the office and they counsel with the students and frequently act as advocates for then in the referral process.

RESEARCH METHODS AND PROCEDURES

Research questions for this study are: 1) Would an affective/remedial program for at-risk high school students implemented for one class period result in attendance at school that legally allows students to receive credit for their courses? 2) Would an affective/remedial program for at-risk high school students implemented for one class period result in sufficient credits earned to allow students to progress to the next grade level? 3) Would an affective/remedial program for at-risk high school students implemented for one class period result in more positive attitudes? 4) Would an affective/remedial program for at-risk high school students implemented for one class period result in decreased discipline referrals? Data sources to answer these questions are: student and school records (attendance, credits earned, discipline referrals) and results of surveys designed to assess self-esteem, stress, peer relations, and family relations.

The population for the study includes 10th grade students identified by state and district qualifiers as being at-risk from two rural districts in the same county in central Texas. At-risk qualifiers include: being behind two or more grade levels in reading or mathematics, having been retained, having failed the state mandated test, or having failed at least two courses in one or two semesters and is not expected to graduate within four years of entry into 9th grade. Comparison groups were selected using the same characteristics. The make-up of the groups in the two school districts differ. In District A, students considered most at-risk of failing and dropping out were placed into the program and the comparison students, although as similar as possible, are not as seriously at-risk as program participants. In District B, an additional screen was placed on participating students to remove those with a history of flagrant attendance or discipline problems. The comparison group in District B includes some students who are more critically at-risk than those in the program. Due to the differences in the two populations, analyses are presented separately for the two districts.

RESULTS

Results are presented for one cohort of students in the program, those who began the program in 1990-91 as freshmen and were in the 10th grade in 1991-92.

ATTENDANCE

During 1990-91, in District A, the majority of S.T.A.R.S. students (90%) were in school the required number of days (13 allowed absences). All of the comparison students were in school as required. During 1991-92, 22 days absent were allowed. Most students that year were in school the required number of days (91% of 9th grade S.T.A.R.S. students and 98% of 9th grade comparisons; 93% of 10th grade S.T.A.R.S. students and 96% of 10th grade comparisons).

Percent Attendance
District A

	1990-91 9th Grade			1991-92 10th Grade	
Number Absences	S.T.A.R.S.	Comparison	Number Absences	S.T.A.R.S.	Comparison
0-13	90	100	0-22	93	96
14+	10	0	23+	7	4

In District B during 1990-91, 72% of S.T.A.R.S. students and 74% of comparison students were in school the required number of days. In 1991-92, 88% of S.T.A.R.S. 10th graders and 88% of S.T.A.R.S. 9th graders were in school the required number of days as compared to 81% of 10th grade comparisons and 72% of 9th grade comparisons.

Percent Attendance
District B

	1990-91 9th Grade			1991-92 10th Grade	
Number Absences	S.T.A.R.S.	Comparison	Number Absences	S.T.A.R.S.	Comparison
0-13	72	74	0-20	88	81
14+	28	26	21+	12	19

CREDITS

At the end of the first year (1990-91) in District A, 50% of S.T.A.R.S. 9th grade students earned sufficient credits (5) to become sophomores. An additional 13% of students earned 4 or 4.5 credits, allowing them to become sophomores if they took and passed courses during the summer. In District A (where the program comprised the most at-risk students), comparison students were more successful in earning credits, with 63% of students obtaining 5 or more credits. In 1991-92, of the continuing S.T.A.R.S. students from the previous year (1990-91 9th graders, now 1991-92 10th graders), 65% attained 4 or 5 credits. Comparison students attained more credits at both grade levels.

Percent of Students Earning Credits
District A 90-92
Number Credits Earned

		5 or more	4 or 4.5	Less than 4	*Number Students*
90-91	9th Grade S.T.A.R.S.	50	13	37	84
90-91	9th Grade Comparisons	62.5	12.5	25	32
91-92	10th Grade S.T.A.R.S.	46	19	35	74
91-92	10th Grade Comparisons	67	12	21	24

In District B, there are seven class periods each day and students can earn seven credits toward graduation each year. During 1990-91, 64% of the 9th grade S.T.A.R.S. students (who were screened for behavior and attendance problems) obtained 6 or 7 credits while only 33% of comparison students received that number.

Percent of Students Earning Credits
District B 90-92
Number of Credits Earned

		6 or 7	4 or 5	Less than 4	*Number Students*
90-91	9th Grade S.T.A.R.S.	64	24	12	63
90-91	9th Grade Comparisons	33	34	33	46
91-92	10th Grade S.T.A.R.S.	73	12	15	55
91-92	10th Grade Comparisons	67	18	5	21

In 1991-92, of the continuing S.T.A.R.S. students from the previous year (1990-91 9th graders, now 1991-92 10th graders), 73% attained 6 or 7 credits. Comparison students attained fewer credits at the 6 or 7 credit level at both grade levels.

Attitudes

The Hudson Scales (Self-Esteem, Stress, Peer Relations, and Family Relations) range from 0 to 100. A score of 30 indicates a potential problem; a score of 70 indicates distress. There are two tables for each district. One shows the average scores attained and the second one shows the percent of students in each group who scored at the cut score of 30 (indicating potential problems).

In District A, for 1991-92 S.T.A.R.S. 10th grade students, average scores exceeded the cut score of 30 on Family Relations, Self-Esteem, and Stress. A decrease in problems with Family Relations and Stress is noted in the second year for S.T.A.R.S. students. Comparison scores showed a decrease in problems the second year in Family Relations but Stress remains high. Self-esteem remained about the same over the two years.

Average Score
(Scale 0 - 100)
District A
10th Grade in 1991-92

	S.T.A.R.S.					Comparison				
	N	May 91	*N*	Oct. 91	May 92	*N*	May 91	*N*	Oct. 91	May 92
Index Family Relations	*64*	39	*37*	36	33	*31*	39	*19*	36	28
Index Self-Esteem	*68*	35	*38*	34	33	*32*	31	*20*	30	31
Index Stress	*64*	38	*33*	35	35	*31*	31	*20*	29	33
Index Peer Relations	*71*	25	*32*	24	27	*32*	22	*20*	22	27

Most students (S.T.A.R.S. and comparisons) demonstrated problems in family relations but the percent of students indicating problems decreased the second year. More than half of 10th grade students indicated potential problems in Self-Esteem and Stress.

Percent Students Scoring 30 or Above
District A
10th Grade in 1991-92

	S.T.A.R.S.					Comparison				
	N	May 91	*N*	Oct. 91	May 92	*N*	May 91	*N*	Oct. 91	May 92
Index Family Relations	*64*	80%	*37*	76%	43%	*31*	74%	*19*	68%	26%
Index Self-Esteem	*68*	59%	*38*	58%	55%	*32*	41%	*20*	35%	45%
Index Stress	*64*	61%	*33*	52%	52%	*31*	45%	*20*	40%	50%
Index Peer Relations	*71*	27%	*32*	16%	38%	*32*	19%	*20*	20%	25%

In District B, for 10th grade S.T.A.R.S. students who have been in the S.T.A.R.S. program for two years, average scores remained high in Self-Esteem and Stress. Average scores for the comparison group were at or exceeded the problem cut score on all measures in May 1992.

Average Score
(Scale 0 - 100)
District B
10th Grade in 1991-92

	S.T.A.R.S.					Comparison				
	N	May 91	*N*	Oct. 91	May 92	*N*	May 91	*N*	Oct. 91	May 92
Index Family Relations	*59*	36	*42*	37	27	*48*	38	*35*	35	33
Index Self-Esteem	59	31	*40*	32	36	*48*	37	*39*	39	38
Index Stress	*59*	32	*41*	32	35	*48*	39	*36*	36	37
Index Peer Relations	*59*	23	*41*	23	29	*48*	27	*28*	28	30

The percentage of 10th grade S.T.A.R.S. students who reported problems with Family Relations declined as it did for the comparison group. The largest number of students continued to have problems with Self-Esteem and Stress - both S.T.A.R.S. and comparison students.

Percent Students Scoring 30 or Above
District B
10th Grade in 1991-92

	S.T.A.R.S.					Comparison				
	N	May 91	*N*	Oct. 91	May 92	*N*	May 91	*N*	Oct. 91	May 92
Index Family Relations	*59*	68%	*42*	79%	38%	*48*	71%	*19*	74%	42%
Index Self-Esteem	*59*	53%	*40*	50%	65%	*48*	71%	*19*	74%	74%
Index Stress	*59*	54%	*41*	54%	54%	*48*	60%	*18*	61%	56%
Index Peer Relations	*59*	32%	*41*	29%	46%	*48*	44%	*19*	53%	53%

Discipline

Discipline referrals are categorized into types of infractions. In District A, for both years, the greatest number of offenses reported were tardies, failure to have supplies, disruptive behavior, and insubordination. In the second year, continuing students maintained their high occurrences of tardies but fewer students were disruptive, insubordinate, or failed to have supplies.

Percent Students Committing Offenses by Student Group
District A

	1990-91 (in 9th Grade)			1991-92 (in 10th Grade)		
Offense Description	STARS	Comparisons	All Others	STARS	Comparisons	All Others
Conference with student	*	*	*	*	*	*
Assault on student; fighting	15	16	7	15	6	7
Verbal abuse, threat personnel	0	0	0	19	0	1
Insubordination	39	25	24	19	8	7
Disruptive behavior	33	50	34	29	19	21
Theft	1	0	1	1	6	1
Vandalism	3	3	2	4	6	3
Profanity	16	6	10	20	11	9
Possession, use of drugs	1	0	0	0	0	0
Violation smoking rules	7	6	7	7	0	5
Tardy	52	38	41	55	31	50
Absent, truancy	21	9	8	32	19	29
Failure to have supplies	65	66	55	46	22	40
Other	12	6	5	9	6	5
Bus misconduct	5	6	2	6	6	2
Not attending detention	22	6	12	10	3	3
Leaving without permission	22	25	17	29	3	10

* Not a category in District A

In District B, the major infractions were failure to attend detention, multiple tardies, disruptive behavior, absence/truancy, and insubordination. During the first year, the largest percentage of students were disruptive and insubordinate in addition to not attending detention. In their second year, the percentage of students who were disruptive decreased slightly; fewer were insubordinate; more were absent or truant.

Percent Students Committing Offenses by Student Group District B

Offense Description	1990-91 (in 9th Grade) STARS	1990-91 (in 9th Grade) Comparisons	1990-91 (in 9th Grade) All Others	1991-92 (in 10th Grade) STARS	1991-92 (in 10th Grade) Comparisons	1991-92 (in 10th Grade) All Others
Conference with student	*	*	*	6	3	29
Assault on student; fighting	6	10	5	8	3	9
Verbal abuse, threat personnel	4	6	3	3	3	2
Insubordination	28	18	15	8	6	13
Disruptive behavior	29	22	16	25	3	30
Theft	4	2	2	2	0	1
Vandalism	3	2	1	0	0	3
Profanity	3	6	4	8	0	5
Possession, use of drugs	0	0	1	0	0	0
Violation smoking rules	0	0	2	3	0	3
Tardy	7	28	16	11	6	24
Absent, truancy	17	28	19	22	6	32
Failure to have supplies	3	2	1	0	0	3
Other	31	36	26	13	6	28
Bus misconduct	8	2	9	5	0	4
Not attending detention	38	32	27	22	12	43
Leaving without permission	1	6	2	8	3	4

* Category not used in 1990-91

Summary and Conclusions

The purpose of the school-based program is to meet the needs of at-risk high school students through an alternative academic program (computer lab) and intense counseling (weekly individual and group sessions). The focus of this paper is to present results of four research questions: Would an affective/remedial program for at-risk high school students implemented for one class period result in: 1) legally required attendance; 2) sufficient credits to allow students to progress to the next grade level; 3) improved attitudes toward themselves, their peers, their families, and reduced stress; and 4) decreased discipline referrals.

Attendance Absentee rates generally are high for at-risk students. Students must be in school to receive benefits of instruction and to receive credit for the courses they take. In both districts, attendance increased over the two years. In District A, the percentage of S.T.A.R.S. students attending school increased the second year. During their freshman year, 90% of S.T.A.R.S. students and 100% of comparison students were in school as required. During their sophomore year, 93% of S.T.A.R.S. students and 96% of comparison students were in school as required. In District B, attendance increased for both groups the second year. In 1990-91, freshmen S.T.A.R.S. demonstrated 72% attendance while comparison students showed 74% attendance. In 1991-92, S.T.A.R.S. attendance increased to 88% and comparison students to 81%.

Credits A focus of the counseling component of the program was on the encouragement of students to pass all of their courses, not only the computer lab. Counselors developed action plans with students who received failure notices every three weeks and they provided study space and tutorials for students. Over the two years, an increased number of students earned sufficient credits to progress to the next grade level. In District A, 50% of freshmen S.T.A.R.S. in 1990-91 earned their credits while in 1991-92, 63% of S.T.A.R.S. earned their credits. Of comparison students, 63% earned credits the first year; 73% the second year. In District B, the percentage increased from 64% to 73% for S.T.A.R.S. students and 33% to 67% for comparison students.

Attitudes The following personal/social characteristics are monitored: self-esteem, peer relations, family relations, and stress. In District A, second year S.T.A.R.S. students continued to manifest problem levels in self-esteem, stress, and family relations although the percent of students indicating problems with family relations and self-esteem decreased. Average problem levels for comparison students exceeded the cut score for stress and self-esteem. Comparison students indicated a decrease in problems with family relations and an increase with problems related to self-esteem and stress. In District B, scores for S.T.A.R.S. students remained above the cut score on self-esteem and stress, with an increased number of students indicating problems in self-esteem. For comparison students, the scores are above problem cut scores on all four (family relations, self-esteem, stress, and peer relations). Fewer comparison students indicated problems with family relations and stress the second year.

Discipline In District A, first year S.T.A.R.S. students demonstrated problems with failure to have supplies, tardies, insubordination, and disruptive behavior. The second year, high frequency of tardies remained but fewer students were disruptive, insubordinate, or failed to have supplies. Comparison students demonstrated the same behaviors, reducing all of them the second year. In District B, major infractions of S.T.A.R.S. students were failure to attend detention, multiple tardies, disruptive behavior, absence/truancy, and insubordination. The second year, fewer students were disruptive or insubordinate; however, more were absent or truant. Comparison students manifested problems in the same categories but the number of students with infractions reduced considerably the second year.

DISCUSSION

It is clear that a one-period a day program, rich in alternative academic approaches and intensive counseling, can make a positive impact on at-risk students. Positive effects have been demonstrated in attendance and credits received. Personal/social characteristics that remain problematic for students are stress and self-esteem. Remaining discipline problems center on tardies, disruptive behaviors, insubordination, and failure to attend detention. To provide a greater impact on student stress and self-esteem and behavior problems, there should be a consistent positive school climate for the students. The entire faculty should receive staff development on communicating with and encouraging students, classroom management of diverse students, teaching to various learning styles, and dealing with the problems and situations of at-risk students.

REFERENCES

Barber, L.W., & McClellan, M.C. (1987). America's dropouts: Who are they? *Phi Delta Kappan*, 69, 264-267.

Benson, P.L. (1991). *The troubled journey, a profile of American youth.* Minneapolis, MN: Search Institute.

Botvin, G.J. (1986). Substance abuse prevention research: Recent development and future directions. *Journal of School Health*, 56, 369-374.

Cavazos, L. (1989). *One on one: A guide for establishing mentor programs.* Washington, DC: U.S. Department of Education.

Fennimore, T.F. (1988). *A guide for dropout prevention.* Washington, D.: Office of Vocational and Adult Education.

Glenn, H.S., & Nelson, J. (1987). *Raising children for success.* Fair Oaks: Sunshine Press.

Hahn, A. (1987). Reaching out to America's dropouts: What to do? *Phi Delta Kappan*, 69, 256-263.

Hamby, J.V. (1989). How to get an "A" on your dropout prevention report card. *Educational Leadership*, 44, 21-28.

Hamby, J.V. (1992). *Vocational education for the 21st century.* Clemson, SC: National Dropout Prevention Center.

Hudson, Walter. (1990). *Index of Self-Esteem, Index of Peer Relations, Index of Stress, Index of Family Relations*. Tempe, AZ: Walmyr.5

Huisman, C. (1992). *Choices for educational opportunities*. Boone Community School District, Iowa.

Robledo, M.R. (1986). *Texas school dropout survey project.* San Antonio, TX: Intercultural Development Research Association.

Rutter, M. (1979). Protective factors and children's responses to stress and disadvantage. *Primary Prevention of Psychopathology,* (3) taken from: P*romoting social competence and coping in children.* M. Whalen-Dent, et. al., eds. Hanover, NH: University Press of New England, pp. 49-74.

Rutter, M. (1984). Resilient children. *Psychology Today*, pp. 57-65.

Sapone, C.V. (1989). *A mentorship model for students at-risk.* San Antonio, TX: Annual Conference of the National Council of States on Inservice Education. National Center for Research in Vocational Education. Unpublished manuscript.

Smith, R.C., & Lincoqln, C.A. (1988). *America's shame. America's hope: Twelve million youth at risk.* Chapel Hill, NC: MDC, Inc.

Walker, H., & Sylwester, R. (1991). Where is school along the path to prison.. *Educational Leadership,* 49, 14-17.

Wehlage, G.G., & Smith, G.A. (1986). *Program for at-risk students: A research agenda.* Madison, WI: Mimco. Unpublished manuscript.

LYLE C. JENSEN
EDWARD B. STRAUSER

14

The Utilization of Apprenticeship Experience in Alternative Education: *A Personalized Approach to Dropout Prevention*

The National Center for Health Statistics has noted that adolescent suicide and suicide attempts have nearly tripled in the past thirty years. American school children have been cited to have the highest rate of drug use of any industrialized nation. Over three million school children in the United States are presently alcohol dependent. The two-parent family with mother at home has become the exception rather than the norm; the concept of latchkey children no longer startles people. Exposure to countless hours of sex and violence on television during the formative years coupled with changing standards of morality adds to the confusion in a child's life. Approximately one in four students currently enrolled in school will drop out; up to one of every two students in urban-centered classrooms will not finish school. The percentage of females under fifteen who are sexually experienced has tripled in the past two decades. Clearly today's children are expected by peers and society to be self-sufficient and self-directed long before they are emotionally mature. Stressors are synergistic; it is obvious that at least some children will not cope. It is also obvious that educators must be increasingly attuned to the holistic development of the children they work with.

For many children, the behavioral and academic pattern established by the time they leave elementary school can lead to a prediction of continued failure. Add to this increased state mandated academic standards and the formula for disaster is in place for our "at-risk" student population.

Critics standing in judgment of education have demanded more for their taxpayer dollar and have assumed more subject oriented curricula is better. Many middle grades students often feel overwhelmed by the demands of the system and the end result is overt and inappropriate behavior and subsequent rejection. Frustrations are compounded for these students "at-risk." These individuals cannot handle increased academic requirements, yet in many schools emphasis on academic success has become the primary goal. Johnny is now expected not only to read, but he is expected to read in another language.

While alternative approaches in education have always been available for consideration, the stresses of our increasingly complex society are making the expanded availability of alternative education programs essential. No longer are traditional special education and vocational programs sufficiently responsive to the needs of the vast number of students encountering stress beyond their ability to cope.

Traditionally, school officials have considered stresses of childhood to be an "out-there" phenomenon. The mind set is that societal and parental factors are to blame for overwhelming the young, inexperienced minds of our children. We educators sympathize with our students but we are aware that we cannot mend broken marriages or cure alcoholic parents. We also feel that school is possibly the only safe haven for these children. We provide consistency and structures. We give positive feedback in the form of grades to those students who do well. Our students have an opportunity to spend the day in a warm building and have a hot lunch. This is all true but it is also true that within our academic structure we have a microcosm of society but with some major differences with the society at large. For instance, with the possible exception of special education for the severely learning disabled, the emotionally disturbed, and the mentally retarded, we do not have a social "safety net" in place. The downtrodden and disadvantaged must sink or swim. We tell the group that good grades are the key to success. Then we turn around and give these at-risk students D's and F's. This creates a very stressful situation where the students know they must succeed despite the fact that their skills may not be consistent with their peers. To make the situation even worse, we have an unfortunate tendency to give the good student the benefit of the doubt on a poorly written essay or mediocre term paper. The poorer student merely fails. With this type of treatment at school, is it any wonder that these children do not enjoy their academic experience? When the school, failure, and misery are all inextricably intertwined, traditional school based remediation programs fail to reach a considerable proportion of their target population.

A psychologically sound approach to deal with the problem of school being perceived as a place to fail would be to change the environment and learn from the real world. However, a background of exposure to subject oriented curricula is appropriately valued by society and school provides that exposure. For some children, a compromise can be effective.

One alternative program that has proven itself successful is a practical apprenticeship or exploratory work approach. One of the major advantages of this type of program (work study) is an environment which places greater emphasis on the individual student. Efforts are made to adapt instruction to the learning style or modality of the individual. Community based work experiences give the child an opportunity to learn and succeed without being hindered by reputation. The traditional approach wherein students are expected to keep pace with a prescribed curriculum does not occur. Because of this personalized approach, students who have encountered academic problems in the traditional school setting often come to realize concepts and ideas are within their grasp. These students are those individuals who have had that experience of being neglected within the traditional classroom setting because they have not kept pace with their peers. When instruction is adapted to individual differences, a true climate for education occurs.

Additional effort at stress reduction within the alternative setting is fostered through the development of positive peer relationships. In the alternative school, students readily recognize each individual has a special need. Because of this acceptance, there is less effort made to "prove oneself," less acting out. The program offers a structured approach, emphasizes basic skills, job relevant curricula, and career-oriented material coupled with vocational opportunities outside the classroom. Such a combination leads to a foundation for success and positive experiences minimize stress.

Students with underdeveloped social skills are often caught up in the circle of defeat within the traditional classroom setting. The child has often been labeled by family circumstances, reputation, the peers he associates with, and the clothes he wears. The acceptance of peers and society during transescence is particularly critical. School professionals working with the student at risk often have directly or indirectly made the child feel that he or she is: unintelligent, a troublemaker, always a problem in the classroom, and, in general, a student who will never succeed. With such low professional expectations, the Pygmaleon effect often results and the student internalizes the externally imposed concepts of the professionals into his own identity.

One of the major goals of the alternative apprenticeship or work study program is to interrupt the circle of defeat and provide the student with a supportive environment which minimizes negative stress while building confidence and emphasizing positive accomplishments.

Vocational apprenticeship assignments designed to accomodate students at-risk are especially responsive. In addition to academic demands, the apprenticeship alternative setting recognizes there are many stress-related factors facing students on a daily basis. Since alternative education students often have a history of behavioral problems, considerable effort is given to guide social development. Interaction with peers, conflict resolution, and on-going informal counselling can be a part of each school day. While the traditional fragmented schedule in most schools consists of forty to forty-five minute modules, alternative school models can have the flexibility afforded by block scheduling. Because of the unique nature of the program the teaching staff has the option to organize the schedule to accomodate a needs-centered curriculum. Students enrolled in such programs frequently exhibit stress and or stress-related crises which need immediate attention from the teaching staff. Student schedules in the alternative setting can be adjusted to accomodate discussion groups, rap sessions, or just unstructured time to air personal feelings and frustrations typical of adolescence. In a traditional school setting with a bell schedule, the likelihood of extending a class period would be unthinkable. However, the time devoted to such student concerns can prove invaluable and help students understand and cope with emotionally charged issues which are often part of their lives.

The emerging adolescent is subject to parental demands, academic requirements, and the most powerful influence, peer pressure. Since the "at-risk" student often does not conform to the prescribed and expected norm, he seeks attention through given behavioral patterns. This drive for attention often reaches explosive levels in the traditional classroom and results in isolation and possible suspension. Problems are often not solved, but rather compounded, and the child becomes caught up in a pattern leading to academic self destruction. The result is a low self-esteem and the child fully comprehends he does not fit, he is not liked, and school is not a pleasurable experience. Alternative education settings endeavor to accept and accomodate each student. These settings are able to cooperatively plan basic rules which are reviewed with the student during initial intake interviews with parent or guardian and home-school counselor. The staff makes a concentrated effort to communicate with the student and provides a positive-based curriculum plan which emphasizes success-oriented activities, including positive work-related attitudes. Students are often suspect of such non-traditional approaches but usually experience reasonable adjustments in a relatively short period of time. Many of these students have not been trusted, accepted or understood by their teachers at the traditional school. When the student realizes he has another chance at the alternative center, positive changes occur. Class size in such settings is small so teacher-student interaction is expected and guaranteed. Because it is recommended students be at the center on alternate weeks due to apprenticeship assignments, these students are quick to realize that the academic demands in the core areas must be satisfied or they may be retained in school during a work week. This is a rare occurrence in such alternative education settings as most students are particularly concerned and enthused about their job assignment.

On the job experience provides a sense of what the real world is about and builds commitment and responsibility. By definition, the student "at-risk" has had a history of academic failure, poor attendance patterns, a lack of essential work skills, and an internalized feeling of worthlessness. Because of the student's negative attitude and poor reputation at his home school, the likelihood of gainful employment opportunities within the community are limited. Participation in pull out apprenticeship programs offer the student an opportunity, a new beginning. Many of the students can be assigned work experience opportunities in small restaurants, garages, supermarkets, woodworking shops; they repair snowmobiles and lawnmowers, work in pet shops, print shops and do farm work, all the while gaining invaluable job-related skills. Of equal if not greater significance, are the positive relationships which are established between the student and his/her employer. Often students more than meet employer expectations and as a result are offered additional employment opportunities on their own time, weekends, and during holiday and summer vacations. When this occurs, the syndrome of failure the student has become accustomed to is supplanted by a positive sense of accomplishment. Students are quick to realize their efforts and contribution can make a difference, and the result is recognition and respect from not only their employers and the community, but their teachers, parents, and peers as well.

Alternative education with an apprenticeship focus provides a curriculum which is skill-oriented and career related. Emphasis is placed on the essentials of the ninth and tenth grade core subjects and students are prepared for the competency-based tests they will be required to pass when they return to their traditional school. Efforts are made on the part of the teaching staff to offer both relevant and significant activities which will assure academic growth and positive social development. A successful tool in social studies, for example, is the use of local newspapers. Secondary alternative education students are quick to review international and local news, sports events, store ads, classified listings, money news, and even Dear Abby. Rather than a forced activity, students enjoy the in-class interaction and learning becomes a pleasurable, non-threatening experience.

Efforts are made to include the students in planning as much as possible. Since flexible scheduling is often practiced in alternative school environments, students are able to meet in group settings, announcements for the day can be made, and the schedule is periodically reviewed. Time can be extended to discuss what happened on the job sites the previous week. Students are quick to share positive comments made by their employers on timesheets, and in some cases students have had positive experiences which are shared with the group. With such successes, faculty often have to remind themselves that for many of these students, these are initial work experiences which would not have been possible had the students not been enrolled in an alternative work-study program.

Since many alternative schools are housed in non- traditional environments, students have an additional opportunity to experience delegated assignments. The lunch program in many alternative schools, for example, is provided by a neighboring school district or vendor. Therefore, the opportunity of setting up for lunch and carrying in the hot and cold carts gives the student an opportunity to both contribute and participate directly in the school community. Most of these students would not have been selected for such a task at their traditional school.

Students respond well to these efforts to recognize their worth as individuals. In various interviews by regional newspapers, students, parents, employers and school administrators have given considerable praise to apprenticesip focused alternative high school programs. One fifteen year old boy enrolled in such a program who had failed every class the year previous found his name on the merit roll after the first semester and he surprised himself with nearly perfect attendance. A parent of a child whose mid-eighth grade performance guaranteed failure of that grade expected the transfer to the alternative school to be merely a delay tactic until her boy could be legally expelled. After a semester, she found herself to be one of the program's most ardent supporters. Many other parents have found themselves changed from skeptics to supporters of alternative education apprenticeship programs. It is recommended a parent advisory committee be formed which among other activities keeps local participating school districts and the community at large aware of the strengths of the program.

It is obviously unrealistic to expect any program of this nature to be totally without failure. However, the success rate in terms of measurable increases in academic and applied skills has gone well beyond initial expectations. Administrators from component school districts that subscribe to alternative high school programs are often pleased that expected attrition did not occur. Students enrolled in such work-study programs relate to the structural organization and particularly experience less stress due to the alternating school and work weeks. For most, school was no longer a place to continually remind them that they are academic failures with no chance to meet established and inflexible standards. A relevant curriculum has become so conducive to learning that most students often complete more skill work in their alternating weeks at school than they would have in the typical everyday attendance at their traditional school.

As districts consider such options to alleviate stress for their own "at risk" students they must realize that each alternative program has to be tailor-fit to the needs and resources of the district. Even at the initial proposal level it is crucial to consider curriculum planning from the stress reduction viewpoint.

Developing an alternative apprenticeship program is quite different than, for example, starting a new computer programming concentration where one would expect to attract motivated students who can handle typical classroom styles of instruction. Despite the individualization, this approach is not categorized as special education; mandated minimal competencies in academics must still be met. Research and experience has shown that this population of students respond best to a curricular presentation that emphasizes real life applications as much as possible. Teachers must be kept fully aware of the specifics of the jobsite environments so as to apply relevancy to each academic concentration. Furthermore, unrelenting effort must be given to directing positive attention to what individual students have been doing on the job. Although this type of approach is appropriate for virtually all middle and high school students, teachers must not forget that those students recommended for an alternative program are the individuals who have found school to be directly associated with reinforcing low self-concepts. Typically their established coping mechanisms for protecting what is left of their self-esteem are nearly always withdrawal ("I don't care") and/or negative means to attract attention and status from their peers.

Research in education indicates adolescent years can be a traumatic time of internal conflict which has a profound impact on the affective needs of today's youth. Educators, therefore, must recognize the negative implications of stress and endeavor to provide responsive alternative programs which will help our troubled youth "at-risk." These students must develop appropriate coping mechanisms and it is imperative that programs be established which will assure a sense of well-being and happiness which should be an intrinsic part of the adolescent years and the school experience. The alternative work study endeavors which are carefully designed and student-centered can alleviate school-imposed stress and insure the well-being of our most cherished resource, today's youth.

JOHN A. BUCCI
GRACE C. OSEDIACZ

15

The Human Services Mall:
A Model for Coordinated School-based Services for At-risk Students

NATIONAL POLICY ACTIVITY

There has been growing activity at the national level promoting the closer working relationship between schools and human service agencies. Described below are some important examples of this national activity.

The Family Support Act of 1988. This legislation aimed to strengthen families as part of the reform of the public welfare system. It encouraged a relationship between the educational and welfare communities as a key developmental partnership. (*New Partnerships*, 1989)

The Report of the Health/Education Symposium. A national symposium which explored ways to integrate and enhance the delivery of services to children in at-risk situations and their families resulted in the development of some national recommendations. Everett Koop, former United States Surgeon General and a participant in that symposium, cited the importance of developing "new organizational relationships at the family and community levels among schools, physicians, public health agencies and social service organizations." (*The Health/education Connection*, 1990, p. 7)

Joining Forces. This was an initiative cosponsored by the American Public Welfare Association and the Council of Chief State School Officers which operated between 1987-1992. Its purpose was to promote closer working relationships between schools and human service agencies so that the needs of children, especially those in at-risk situations, could be better met. (Levy & Copple,1989)

Policy Statement of the Council of Chief State School Officers. In a November 1992 policy statement titled Student Success through Collaboration this organization took the position that "Every community should develop a school linked support system for children and their families."(Council of Chief State School Officers, 1992, p. 11)

Educational Policy of the Clinton Administration. In an interpretation of "Putting People First," a policy statement of the Clinton administration,

Dunkle and Usdan (1993) of the Institute for Educational Leadership have argued that this must mean connecting education to other services. There are indications that the emphasis on coordinating health and social services for at-risk children will be on the agenda of Secretary of Education Richard W. Riley who provided leadership in this effort in his home state of South Carolina.

CHARITABLE FOUNDATION SUPPORT

The national interest in coordinating services to meet the needs of the whole child is reflected in the agendas of many major charitable organizations. In a variety of ways they are attempting to stimulate efforts by states and communities to implement collaboration. Some of the most visible of these foundation initiatives are described below.

Annie E. Casey Foundation - New Futures Initiatives. This foundation has funded projects in five cities across the United States to develop new strategies and resources for a variety of organizations that serve young people to prevent them from dropping out. 40 million dollars and a five year effort have been committed to changing the ways health services, social services, and employment programs are address the problems of disadvantaged youth in a coordinated way. (Center for the Study of Social Policy, 1989)

The Pew Foundation. This foundation has provided grants to states to reconfigure services offered by state agencies, local agencies and schools. Planning grants have been awarded to Kentucky, Florida, Minnesota, Georgia and Rhode Island. Three states will be funded for a nine year period during which they are expected to develop a universal contact system of inclusion and a broad-based prevention model.

Rockefeller Foundation . This prominent foundation provides grants to community foundations which in turn focus on issues affecting children and families. Its goal is to raise this issue to the top of the national agenda. The grants encourage partnerships among community agencies, businesses, and schools.

The Carnegie Foundation. Focusing especially on facilitating healthy adolescent development, this foundation has published the influential report, Turning Points (Carnegie Council on Adolescent Development, 1989) and has commissioned studies of interdisciplinary ways of addressing health problems. It has emphasized the intimate linkage of education and health in the schools.

STATE INITIATIVES

In recent years there have been numerous state efforts to enhance collaboration. Oregon, Utah, Rhode Island, Kentucky, South Carolina, and other states have passed legislation that mandates integrated social services in schools in order to address the needs of at-risk students. The various legislative packages include many elements including:

(1) Child Opportunity Zones with a full range of social services delivered at or near the school site.

(2) Integrated social services in the schools or located as close to the child and the family's community as possible

(3) Mandated health services at or near schools.

(4) Putting educational reform in the context of meeting all the needs of children.

(5) Establishing "Children's Cabinets" which encourage cooperation at the highest levels of all state bureaucratic offices with a mission to address the needs of children.

LOCAL INITIATIVES

In addition to the Newport, R.I. Human Services Mall which is described in this article, there are examples of other local efforts to implement school-based health and social service delivery. The list of such efforts is growing, but the following descriptions are representative of this growing movement in both large urban areas and small towns.

San Diego, California. The New Beginnings project is a large scale effort to develop interagency collaboration to serve needs of low income children, youth and families in San Diego. An experimental project at an elementary school utilizes portable classrooms to provide services to children adjacent to the school. The process of accomplishing collaboration and striving for long-term systemic change in the way services are delivered has been an illustrative case study. (Payzant, 1992)

Savannah, Georgia. With a grant from the Annie Casey Foundation, Savannah is attempting to integrate its human and educational services. Focusing primarily on four middle schools it has organized collaboratives, developed case management approaches, implemented mentoring programs and has developed a service delivery system that emphasizes a continuous flow of information.

Marshalltown, Iowa. Through its project, Caring Connection, this community with a population of 27,000 has organized a consortium of 22 local agencies which provide on-site services at the middle and high school levels. A variety of services are provided in many ways similar to the Newport Human Services Mall described in this paper.

Dade County, Florida. This county has implemented a system of co-located services on the school site or in portable offices adjacent to it. Child welfare, welfare, health services, mental health programs and substance abuse programs are offered to students and their families.

BENEFITS OF SCHOOL-BASED HUMAN SERVICES DELIVERY SYSTEMS

State and local governmental agencies and the school systems responsible for the education of children have come to realize that although children are in school during the day, this does not mean that schools should be solely responsible for providing for the "human" needs of students while they are in their care. They have come to realize that the whole community must share in delivering services which meet the human needs of these children. Schools and governmental agencies have also come to recognize that while families are not always able to connect with human service providers, their children are always required to be in school where they are available to receive services. This growing awareness and the evolving change in the way human services are delivered has caused many policy makers to recognize the potential benefits of school based human service delivery systems.

1. *Efficiency.* While there is much study to be done to calculate the specific benefits of coordinated human services, there is a growing feeling that the delivery of services to at-risk students will improve efficiency. With the child as the focus and the school as the locus, agencies and the school should avoid overlapping services as well as having students fall between the cracks. Since more children and families are likely to be served, the impact of the dollars spent should be greater.

2. *Access to students.* Since students are required by law to be in school, we know we can reach them with human services if those services are

delivered at the school. Social and health service agencies often struggle to find ways to reach children and their families who are in need of assistance.

3. *Coordination of Services.* Locating a variety of services at or near the school should result in better coordination. Working together to meet the needs of the same children should create a more efficient delivery system.

4. *Impacting the Learning Environment.* We know from experience that children have difficulty learning and may be disruptive to the educational process if their social and health needs are not met because of deficiencies in their environments outside of school. By directly addressing these needs in conjunction with their academic programs, their individual learning situations are improved as well as the general learning environment of the school.

5. *Ease of Referral.* Since agencies are represented at the school site, the process of referring students to these agencies is easier. There is a reduction of the bureaucratic obstacles that exist when agencies and schools operate as completely separate entities. The familiarity of the coordinator of a school-based center of human services with the various policies and procedures of various agencies increases the likelihood that the referral will be made in the best interests of the child.

6. *Improved Collaboration between Professionals.* Over time the various professions have developed separate cultures with different vocabularies, operating rules and approaches to serving the needs of children. It is expected that the close working relationships that will develop among professionals such as social workers, health professionals, counselors, psychologists, juvenile justice professionals and educators will break down the barriers that exist among them. By sharing the interest in focusing on the needs of the whole child, greater collaboration among the human services professionals and educators will result. This ultimately will benefit the children who have needs to be met.

7. *Increased Parent Involvement.* It is the hope and expectation of those involved in the coordinated delivery of human services in schools that parents will become more involved in all aspects of their children's lives. It will be easier for them to handle the logistics of dealing with the various agencies that can provide assistance to their children because those agencies will be located in one place.

THE HUMAN SERVICES MALL

The Human Services Mall located at Thompson Junior High School in Newport, R.I. serves as an excellent model and case study of a community's efforts to deliver human services to students in school. The establishment of the Mall was the result of planning by an informal task force consisting of the Newport School Department and local and state human services agencies. The goal of the collaboration was to meet the needs of the students and their parents at the school site, a logical focal point for the services which they provide.

The Mall's purpose is to provide a safe haven for junior high school students to receive mental health, substance abuse and health care services. These services include prevention and early intervention for serious mental health problems, health care, alcohol and substance abuse assessment and treatment, self-help groups, individual and group counseling, community service activities, job skills development, recreational activities and information resource and referral development.

ESTABLISHING THE HUMAN SERVICES MALL

Starting up the Human Services Mall required a lot of commitment to the idea along with much cooperation, hard work and leadership. While a complete case study is needed to adequately describe the complex process of establishing the Mall, a brief description of some of the steps may be a helpful guide to those who are considering starting similar programs.

The leadership provided by the Newport superintendent of schools, Donald Beaudette, was critical in getting the concept of the Human Services Mall started. Recognizing that a sizable portion of the student population lived in publicly subsidized housing and were in need of social and health services he brought together outside agencies and representatives from the community and the corporate sector to address their problems. Lengthy meetings extending over a period of eighteen months resulted in improved agency cooperation, a commitment to simultaneously address the needs of the whole child, and the establishment of the Interagency Collaborative of Newport (ICON).

With school/agency cooperation well established, the newly developed collaborative in Newport sought funding sources for the establishment of a service delivery system. Over time funds were secured from the Rhode Island Foundation, the Governor's Justice Commission, and the Administration for Children, Youth, and Families to supplement the commitments from the school department and the local agencies.

Recognizing the critical age of early adolescence the junior high school was selected as the site for the Mall. An unused classroom in the building was renovated and soundproofed to provide working offices for agency representatives who would meet with students. A new principal of the junior high school embraced the concept and was instrumental in providing leadership within the building. He created a climate of trust which resulted in support from the professional staff.

The position of Coordinator of the Human Services Mall was posted. The successful applicant had educational background and experience which encompassed both the fields of education and social services. This background gave her credibility both with the teachers and the human services professionals. With the coordinator on board, the work turned to the development of decision making mechanisms to connect the school and agency personnel with the children who had human service needs. This process of developing communications and mechanisms has continued to be refined through the years of the Mall's operation.

SERVICES PROVIDED IN THE HUMAN SERVICES MALL

The Mall provides an array of services to students including the following:

1. *Safe Haven.* The Human Services Mall serves as a neutral non-threatening environment for those students who are in crisis, need nurturing, or the support of caring adults. The Human Services Mall Coordinator, Executive Assistant or community agency staff provide this safe haven for students.
2. *Prevention/Early Intervention.* The primary focus of the Human Services Mall is to provide prevention services to educate and support children through the transitions of adolescence and the journey through the middle level school. By providing early interventions for those students who are facing difficulties, there is increased likelihood of retaining them in the school as well as in the home. It potentially prevents more serious problems for some students and their families.
3. *Crisis Management.* The Human Services Mall Coordinator works directly with the guidance personnel and administration to provide crisis intervention as needed. This intervention includes assessments, clinical consultation, and assistance in severe or trauma situations where key community services are necessary to resolve the crisis.
4. *Information/Resource Development.* On a daily basis the Human Services Mall Coordinator works with school personnel to connect students and their families to appropriate services. Should there be a gap in services within the community, the Coordinator is responsible for locating and recommending resources which will help resolve the problems presented by families, school personnel or community agencies.
5. *Referral.* The Human Services Mall Coordinator has the primary responsibility to provide appropriate referrals to community resources. She assists the guidance counselors and other pupil personnel services staff in locating services and making sure that referral information is timely and accurate.

6. *Case Management.* The Human Services Mall Coordinator is responsible to provide follow-up activities for students who are referred for outside assistance. This activity includes linkage to services which will assist in resolution of crises or other problems and monitoring services once the student/family is linked to a provider. Tracking service impact is the responsibility of the Coordinator in conjunction with school and agency personnel.

7. *Disciplinary Process.* As a member of the crisis management team, the Coordinator works closely with the administration of the middle school. This allows the student to receive important education and reorientation when an infraction of school rules occurs. In some instances in-school suspension is required; in other cases a "cooling off" period is part of the daily activity of students. This assistance creates an atmosphere of understanding for students who have traditionally been penalized for situations beyond their control.

8. *Counseling.* Counseling is available from community agencies and school personnel on both an individual and group basis. Counseling is provided in the areas of mental health, alcohol abuse and substance abuse. Assessment activities and self-help groups are also available on an as-needed basis.

9. *Job Skills Activities.* Students who are looking for job skills are connected with community resources to locate career and job skills programs. Students have been referred to a number of local programs which teach skills as well as encourage entrepreneurial enterprises in the community. Students have also been involved in assisting on a daily basis in the Human Service Mall as a way of learning office skills.

10. *Community Service Learning.* Since the Human Services Mall is staffed by community agency personnel, there was a built-in incentive to connect students to volunteer activities in the community. The Executive Assistant coordinates the activities of 14 students who are involved in volunteer activities. These activities include understanding homelessness and hunger, racial and ethnic prejudices, conducting food drives and working with elementary students to increase their reading skills. These activities have increased students' self-esteem and confidence as young adults.

KEY STAFF ROLES AND FUNCTIONS

The role of key staff in the circle of assistance which is provided in the on-site delivery of social and health services is defined by the activities and circumstances of each site. Within Thompson Junior High School the Guidance Counselors and the Mall Coordinator are responsible for the primary services which are delivered to students and their families. However, there are many players within the building and district who create the seamless web of services to students and their families.

Central Administration. The Superintendent provides the leadership to other executives in the community who are responsible for the service delivery systems. The Director of Pupil Personnel Services is the liaison to the Mall Coordinator and assists in troubleshooting activities.

Guidance. The guidance department is the first line of defense in the school environment. The school department has specific state and federal statutes which must be followed before activity moves to the Human Services Mall staff. The guidance counselors and the Coordinator are in daily contact and support each other on a constant basis in order to create a system of care for students and their families that is as seamless as possible.

Human Services Mall Coordinator. The major responsibility of the Coordinator is program development and maintenance. Creating new policies and assisting agency staff in understanding and working within the educational environment are also the role of the Coordinator.

School Administration. The Principal provides building management and support for the Human Services Mall staff and activities. On a daily basis the Assistant Principal is responsible for the coordination of faculty, students, guidance staff and Mall personnel to achieve the desired outcomes of the programming.

Faculty. The faculty receive training and information on a district level as well as on a building level in the areas of student development, community assistance and human needs. Interaction between agency staff and faculty is coordinated by guidance personnel and the assistant principal.

Agencies. Agency staff work directly with students and families and are shepherded through the school policies and procedures by the Human Services Mall Coordinator and guidance personnel.

Interagency Collaborative of Newport Executive Director and Executive Assistant. The Executive Assistant assists in coordinating schedules, community service learning activities and other daily tasks for the Human Services Mall. The Executive Director provides guidance, direction and supervision as well as trouble-shooting with the Coordinator on an as needed basis.

PROTOCOLS AND PROCEDURES

Through the years of operation, Mall personnel, school staff, and agency representatives have worked together to develop the protocols and procedures which serve as guidelines for the positive interaction of all of the participants on behalf of the children. Organizations and services that develop in some degree of isolation tend to establish rules and operating procedures that appear to be inscrutable, cumbersome and bureaucratic to the uninitiated. With healthy communication, hard work, and a commitment to reduce these obstacles to the delivery of services, protocols were developed which cut across the various organizational structures. These protocols are constantly subject to revision and improvement as rules and circumstances change. Protocols and procedures were developed to handle the following issues:

(1) Confidentiality Rules
(2) Referral of Students
(3) Suicide and Crisis Management
(4) Registration of Child Welfare Wards of the State
(5) Juvenile Offenders

BARRIERS TO THE ON-SITE DELIVERY OF HUMAN SERVICES

The efforts to establish a human service delivery system in schools is certain to encounter some obstacles in the form of institutional barriers. These barriers, which have been confronted in the Newport Human Services Mall can be clustered around the issues of trust, turf and tradition.

Building a Sense of Trust. Professionals who have been separated from each other and who are unfamiliar with each other's work need to overcome the barrier of mistrust if they are to work together collaboratively. School and agency personnel must learn to communicate, understand their respective professional goals and build a sense of trust around the common theme of helping the whole child. This issue of trust must also be extended to the parents or other adult guardians who are responsible for the children being served. It is often difficult to follow plans which affirm family autonomy and assist families to take steps to solve their own problems.

Turf Issues. Turf issues take many forms, but if they are not recognized and addressed they can present obstacles to a collaborative approach to human service delivery. An example of a turf issue is the question of who is responsible for the provision of service. This can result in children falling between the cracks or the unnecessary duplication of efforts. Turf protection also surfaces when it is not clear who is responsible for the payment of a service and when questions are raised about the qualifications of members of other professions or agencies. The issue of professional responsibility also rises when parents are asked to take responsibility for their children. Some human services professionals believe that, as the formally educated service providers, they should make the difficult decisions about children. As parental autonomy is affirmed, they are likely to respond that parents don't know what is best for their children.

Challenging Tradition. Traditional roles of professionals are difficult to change. The traditional role of the relationship of the school to the community is difficult to change. Yet, as we entertain new visions of the ways that organizations and institutions interact and serve the needs of at-risk children and families, tradition must be challenged. Professionals and members of the community need to take pause every time they find themselves restricted in their thinking because they think or say, "We've always done it this way."

THE FUTURE OF SCHOOL BASED HUMAN SERVICES

It is likely that the movement toward delivering human services on school sites is will continue and gain momentum. Programs like the Human Services Mall are likely to proliferate and to grow in popularity as a strategy for addressing the needs of communities where there is a concentration of at-risk families. The result of this development will be changes in the human services professions and in the way these services are organized. There may be an extension of the seamless web of service to include schools as well as agencies.

If this trend continues schools will also undergo some changes. School buildings in the future may be planned to accommodate offices for agency representatives. The school building will be used for longer hours and during summers to accommodate the needs of families who make use of these services. It is possible that our present concept of school as a place which focuses on academic learning will undergo revision so that it encompasses a wider range of human development. This trend bears watching and models like the Human Services Mall of Newport, R.I. should continue to draw our attention as a possible look into the future.

REFERENCES

Carnegie Council on Adolescent Development (1989). *Turning points: Preparing American youth for the 21st century.* New York: Carnegie Corporation of New York.

Center for the Study of Social Policy (1989). *New futures: Plans for assisting at-risk youth in five cities.* Washington, D. C.: The Center for the Study of Social Policy.

Cohen, D. (1989, March 15). Joining forces: An alliance of sectors envisioned to aid the most troubled young. *Education Week,* p. 6.

Council of Chief State School Officers (1992). *Student success through collaboration: A policy statement of the Council of Chief State School Officers.* Washington, D.C.: Council of Chief State School Officers.

Dunkle, M. & Usdan, M.D. (1993, March 3). Putting people first means connecting education to other services. *Education Week*, p. 44.

The health/education connection: Initiating dialogue on integrated services to children at risk and their families (1990). A report of a symposium sponsored by the American Association of Colleges for Teacher Education, the American Academy of Pediatrics, the Maternal and Child Health Bureau, and the U.S. Department of Health and Human Services. Unpublished manuscript.

Levy, J. E., & Copple, C. (1989). *Joining Forces: A report from the first year.* A report from the National Association of State Boards of Education.Unpublished manuscript.

New partnerships: Education's stake in the Family Support Act of 1988, (1989). A statement of the American Public Welfare Association, Center for Law and Social Policy, Center for the Study of Social Policy, Children's Educational Leadership, National Alliance of Business, National Association of State Boards of Education, National Governors' Association. Unpublished manuscript.

Payzant, T. W. (1992). New beginnings in San Diego: Developing a strategy for interagency collaboration. *Phi Delta Kappan*, 73, 139-146.

IV

NETWORKING ACTIVITIES AND RESOURCES

DOROTHY R. FIELDER

16

At Risk Grants for Elementary Schools

"Throwing money at it isn't going to solve the problem" is a familiar comment heard from many critics of American public education expressing skepticism at the notion that increasing educational funding might improve the system. One group of educators is seeking to dispel the myth, countering that it (increasing spending) has never been tried!

In the Fulton County (Georgia) School System, a committee of the Teacher Council decided that equal monetary resources to all schools are probably not equitable when the needs of at risk students remain unmet by existing funds. A recommendation to the Superintendent called for competitive grants to be awarded to schools which developed creative ideas for solving the problems and improving the achievement of their identified students at risk. Procedures for awarding the grants were also developed, with the following criteria for selection:

- Demonstrated educational need of student population
- Creativity/innovativeness of the approach
- Educational soundness of the project
- Degree to which the product is measurable
- Reasonableness of the budget presented
- Replicability of this project to other district schools
- Degree of parent/community/business partnership involvement
- Current availability of supplementary resources for at risk students
- Appropriateness of evaluation procedures

The Fulton County Board of Education went along with piloting the concept of competitive grants, approving a $100,000 line item in the operating budget for fiscal year 1993 to be earmarked for four $25,000 grants to elementary schools which best met the criteria as determined by a selection committee. The schools were promised that the funding would be extended for three years, as they showed progress in moving toward their goal of increasing achievement among the at risk youngsters.

The 31 elementary schools received an invitation to apply in the summer of 1992. Fifteen responded with written proposals which were given a paper screening by the seven-member selection committee, consisting of teachers and central office administrators. The committee held interviews with a three-person team from each of the seven highest scoring schools. Four were selected in mid-September for recommendation to the Superintendent, Dr. James H. Fox, Jr., who promptly approved them with orders to move ahead with implementation.

The following elementary proposals were approved for funding through at risk grants of $25,000 each in 1992-93: Brookview Elementary School's "Panda Read and Reap Club;" Hapeville Elementary School's "Project S.T.A.R." (Super Terrific At Reading, 'Riting, and 'Rithmetic); Mimosa Elementary School's "Project Boost;" and Spalding Drive Elementary School's "Spalding 2000." Brief descriptions of the project activities follow.

PANDA READ AND REAP CLUB

A giant panda, Brookview Elementary School's mascot, is the focus of the school's project, which serves over 150 students selected by each teacher in grades K - 5. These students are card-carrying members of the Panda Read and Reap Club and participate in all project activities. Principal Bobby Tuggle used the many talents of his staff and PTA president to organize plans to encourage independent reading at school and in the home. Goals are to build reading fluency, expand vocabulary, enrich language skills, and improve reading comprehension.

Each teacher has designated a Panda reading corner of the classroom, where the students can go for quiet reading, either silently or orally to a friendly, cuddly giant stuffed panda whose T-shirt conceals a tape recorder. Teachers are able to play back the recorded oral reading and give suggestions for improved fluency and expression. Word banks are formed for individual students from difficulties noted on the tapes. Other activities are performed in the inviting, functional panda centers such as writing on the typewriter or computer and playing word games. The centers are decorated with tropical plants, a floor lamp, student sized rocking chair, and a bean bag chair, and equipped with the typewriter, computer with printer, paper, pencils, dictionary, and thesaurus.

Parents are an important part of the Panda Read and Reap project. Workshops are held in the evenings to teach parenting skills and to encourage parents to become role models as readers with their children at home. Babysitting services are provided to parents by a storyteller. The parent role models are asked to verify that their children are reading at home by signing a daily reading card. Additional resources, including suggested books and topics, are shared with parents.

The Panda Read and Reap Club meets after school in the library once per month to share reading experiences and to hear guest authors and illustrators speak. They keep a journal of reactions to books read. Club members have written and performed a "reading rap" to celebrate their emphasis on reading.

Panda Pals are adults who volunteer as reading partners for each participating student, visiting with them for a minimum of twice a week. The Panda Pals represent the school certified and classified staff, parents, and business partners.

Brookview used a portion of its grant money to purchase a van which has been converted to a Panda library-on-wheels, complete with shelves and donated books and magazines. The brightly painted Panda Van visits nearby apartment complexes outside of school hours, with one of the school assistants driving and serving as librarian for the many students and parents who borrow books.

A culminating activity at the end of the school year is compilation of the children's writing and illustrations into an anthology, which will be published and bound for each participant. The anthology mirrors the emphasis in the district's language arts curriculum on the reading-writing connection.

PROJECT S.T.A.R.

With more than half of its students living in single parent homes, Hapeville Elementary School's project emphasizes parents as partners in education and the building of self esteem, as well as improving academic achievement among its 50 identified students. Those selected were targeted by standardized test scores below the 35th percentile, teacher recommendations, academic deficiencies, and low self esteem.

The primary activity of the project is an after school tutorial program staffed by certified teachers with a pupil-teacher ratio of about ten to one. The program meets two afternoons per week for 1 1/2 hours, with students having bus transportation provided.

During each month the first three weeks are devoted to tutoring in reading, mathematics, and writing. The low pupil-teacher ratio allows individual attention which is not possible during the regular school day. During all activities the value of responsibility and cooperation is taught and modeled.

Positive self esteem activities are the focus during the fourth week. School staff members and other experts are used to teach groups of the S.T.A.R.

participants about exploratory topics which interest them. Examples are photography, clowning, personal grooming, cooking, drama, ballet, horseback riding, and calligraphy. According to Cheryl Bogrow, principal of Hapeville Elementary School, a culminating activity for the group learning clown techniques is to visit a retirement home in the community and entertain the inhabitants by "clowning around."

Positive role models of older students from nearby middle and high schools provide PALS for each of the elementary students. They help in the tutoring sessions, encouraging their young partners to study and succeed.

Contracts with the parents of participants stress the importance of ensuring regular attendance during the school day and tutorial sessions and of insisting on the completion of homework, projects, and outside reading. Monthly parent workshops led by the counselor and instructional staff members concentrate on improving parenting skills, increasing school/home communication, and developing self esteem for parents and students.

PROJECT BOOST

Mimosa Elementary School is in the historic city of Roswell, which is about 20 miles north of Atlanta, a rapidly growing and changing community. Although the area has been considered affluent, pockets of poverty have developed and widened in the last decade. Much evidence of the change in demographics has surfaced at the school, with an increasing percent of students on the free and reduced price lunch program (21%) and a need for two Head Start classes for three- and four-year-olds. Problems youngsters are bringing to school with them include child abuse, hunger, and stress from homes where substance abuse exists. Apartments and single family homes in the area now house many immigrants from a number of foreign countries, whose children are struggling to learn the English language. Under the committed leadership of Principal Linda Markwell, the staff of Mimosa Elementary School wrote their at risk grant proposal with these many-faceted needs of their children in mind.

The main component of Project Boost is an afterschool tutorial program taught by teachers to students in small groups. The afternoon begins with a nutritious snack and then is broken into two segments, one hour of pure academics and a second hour of fun enrichment activities. The teachers take full advantage of the school's local area computer network which connects all classroom computers in the building to a fileserver. Special networked software in language arts and mathematics was selected and purchased with grant funds. The children alternately work with the teacher and the instructional software during the academic time. To meet the needs of the considerable Hispanic population, one of the tutors speaks Spanish. Their enrichment time is spent with other teachers who may do rhythm games with them in the music room, teach them weaving, or direct physical activities in the gym. Like Hapeville county school buses give transportation home to students whose parents cannot pick them up at 4:30.

Mimosa's program serves about 150 students in the afterschool program one day per week all year. The children were identified with multiple criteria: teacher survey, attendance records from the previous year, norm-referenced test scores, kindergarten screening assessment, and recommendations from the counselor. Factors considered were membership of single parent families, transiency, low socioeconomic status, low self esteem, disruptive behavior, social withdrawal.

As an incentive for good attendance during the regular school day and at the afterschool program, participants who have perfect attendance receive the privilege of special Saturday field trips to exciting events and places in the Atlanta area. Other special events include the appearance of guest speakers from the community during the afternoon sessions.

The school counselor helps to coordinate the activities which are designed to improve self esteem and confidence. She has organized volunteers from the staff by pairing each of them with individual Project Boost students in her PAL program. These volunteers take a special interest in their PAL each day, giving hugs, asking how they are doing in school and home, giving support and encouragement, and providing a positive adult role model.

Another major component of Project Boost is the continuation of the Family Assistance Support Team (FAST), chaired by the counselor and including teachers, assistant principal, school psychologist, social worker, and special education support teacher. The team works directly with outside agencies in the North Fulton community to connect families' needs with the appropriate agencies. It has set up support groups for at risk children with problems such as chemical dependency in the home, divorce, or death of a family member. A support group for teachers working with at risk children was led by a counselor from the Northside Mental Health Center. The same organization presented parenting workshops, where supper and babysitting were provided.

SPALDING 2000

Like Mimosa, Spalding Drive Elementary School has undergone changes in its student population in the past 15 years. It is located in a community called Sandy Springs, an unincorporated part of North Fulton County which is bordered by the Chattahoochee River on the north and the city of Atlanta on the south. The school's present diversity represents a change from one serving the children of mostly white, upper middle class professionals in single family homes during the mid-1970's to a school with 25% minority students and a wide range of socioeconomic and educational levels among its parents.

Spalding 2000 is an extension of the Greater North Fulton Education 2000 efforts to meet Goal 1 of the American education goals, "Every child will start to school ready to learn." The staff agreed with their principal, Rick White, that early intervention for students who are at risk will reap the greatest benefits and go farthest toward preventing school dropouts in later years. Language development was seen as the greatest gap among youngsters in grades K-2. To address these early childhood needs of at risk students a successful multifaceted grant proposal was developed.

A fully certified early childhood teacher was hired as an instructional assistant to go into each of the K-2 classes having at risk students twice per week and give small group instruction to the identified children, in cooperation with the classroom teacher. Techniques emphasize hands-on learning and language experience. Special computer software was added to the school's network for early childhood reading and mathematics.

One of Spalding Drive's most active parents volunteered to serve as the Spalding 2000 parent liaison for a small stipend. She provides community links to parents with needs, chairs the parent coordinating committee for the program, sets up parenting education workshops and meetings every three weeks, sends newsletters home, and encourages parental participation in the educational process. Transportation and sitters are provided for the parent meetings and theme parties. The school's counselor assists with the parent meetings by teaching parenting skills with the help of trained staff members. She works with individual families on their needs and holds support groups for students.

PAAWS (People At Work With Students) pairs an adult volunteer to read 30 minutes per day with students with below average reading skills. A nearby high school service club received a complementary grant to purchase materials to mentor and tutor kindergarten children as part of the Spalding 2000 plan.

SUMMARY

Each of the four Fulton County elementary at risk grants mirrors the talents of the staff and parents and addresses their particular community conditions. All have planned detailed evaluations which will measure the effects of their programs on achievement as well as related issues such as self concept, attendance, discipline, and parental involvement. The staffs look forward to finetuning their programs in the second and third years and sharing their successes with other Fulton County elementary schools.

The Superintendent plans to request the school board to budget for additional grants for at risk projects in the future. "Using a rifle instead of a shotgun," he says, might be the only way to target the students whose needs are greater than others'. Putting extra resources to work on their problems, with the creative ideas of the school staffs, appears to be working in these four elementary schools.

VANN PHILLIPS, LADEEN HOWARD
CAROLYN McKINLEY and MAGGIE BOWDEN

17

Off Campus Opportunities Program: *Collaboration at Work*

America has a problem. At a time when the job market requires a more highly educated work force than ever before, the high school drop-out rate and a high functional illiteracy rate are combining to create an ever-widening gap between job markets and the academic skills of employees. The Off Campus Opportunities Program (OCO) is a collaborative attempt between four agencies to reduce the drop-out rate by increasing basic skills of students and their confidence in their ability to finish high school.

As in many other communities throughout the country, Meriwether County leaders are looking for ways to address their educational concerns. Meriwether is a large, sparsely populated rural county with limited resources to bring to bear on its literacy and drop-out problems. It has a declining economy fueled in part by the cycle of poverty and illiteracy. It was against that the agencies came together to develop an intervention program.

BRINGING THE PARTNERS TOGETHER

Each of the partners in this program is commited to initiating programs that will restructure the traditional educational format of schools to better meet the needs of an ever-changing student population. The four key partners were the West Georgia Technical Institute, the Division of Rehabilitation Services (DRS)/Roosevelt Warm Springs Institute for Rehabilitation (RWSIR), the University of Georgia, and the Meriwether County School System.

RWSIR had recently expanded its Basic Education Program, designed for individuals with disabilities, to the community through the addition of the West Georgia Technical School's Community Based Literacy Program. This expansion added a complementary service to the existing Basic Education Program and enabled RWSIR to respond more directly to community educational needs. The success of the Basic Education Program coupled with the success of the Community Based Literacy Program fueled the desire to expand the scope of their contributions to the public school system. Existing curriculum and instructional methodology had a proven track record in dealing with students with multiple disabilities, and it was thought that this same curriculum and methodology might introduce a unique intervention within the public school system which would positively impact on high school retention.

The Meriwether County School System was very interested in reviewing this possibility and was willing to cooperatively identify a target population to initiate the program. There was a substantial number of students whom the school personnel deemed to be at great risk for drop-out and who needed an intervention geared specifically to their needs.

West Georgia Technical Institute, to demonstrate its community educational mission, agreed to secure funds to support the project and work cooperatively in developing a program description. The University of Georgia's primary role has been in the design and implementation of the research component continuing their long history of partnership and cooperation with various RWSIR and DRS initiatives.

After lengthy discussion, the partners concluded that an innovative educational intervention model could be developed based on the existing curriculum used by Basic Education teachers at the RWSIR and deliver that instruction to students identified as at-risk for dropping-out. A search of school records identified 156 students who fit the target profile of being sixteen or older and two or more years behind their peer group. Two project personnel met with the counselor and principal from each high school to ascertain which of these students were still registered and to discuss these students in terms of discipline, emotional stability, and attendance. Students who had been involved in drugs, were highly emotionally unstable, or whose attendance history indicated that they would be unlikely to attend any program consistently. were excluded. The rationale behind the first exclusion was that since the students would be in an off-campus setting, there would be additional freedoms which could be abused. Severely emotionally troubled youth were excluded because the OCO program was designed to assist those students not currently receiving other interventions. The last exclusion, attendance, was used as a screening tool to avoid wasting the limited number of slots available. Students with poor attendance were excluded only if the counselors or social worker considered their motivation to succeed was very low. This gross screening left a pool of 68 appropriate students. All were over sixteen and had been retained at least twice. Some of the girls were pregnant or had young children.

It was agreed that students would be transported from both high schools to the RWSIR campus for an intense academic remediation program involving reading, language, and math. The major areas to resolve included developing a research design, developing an orientation model which would encourage student participation, securing parental permission, evaluating the compatability of the basic education curriculum with public school standards, working out transportation arrangements, and discussing the involvement of other key players.

By focusing on a collective educational mission, each of these issues was resolved and the Off Campus Opportunities Program (OCO) was initiated. The following sections describe how each of the four partners approached the task of developing the program.

PROGRAM DEVELOPMENT AND APPLICATION

West Georgia Technical Institute

West Georgia Technical Institute has become increasingly concerned with community literacy needs and viewed the OCO Program as an opportunity to expand its community-based services while at the same time providing an opportunity for increased continuing education opportunities. They hoped that many of the OCO students would go on to take advantage of technical and vocational training offered by West Georgia Technical Institute.

The funding for this partnership project comes through the Georgia Department of Adult and Technical Education. West Georgia Technical Institute has been charged with the responsibility of administering these funds and the money has been used to provide one full time instructor, various consumable supplies, and limited equipment.

Roosevelt Warm Springs Institute for Rehabilitation (RWSIR)

RWSIR already had a Basic Education Program, so their task was to extend it to fit the needs of high school students, to check the curriculum against Georgia's Quality Core Curriculum (QCC) standards, and to design ways to interface with the school system.

The RWSIR Schoolhouse, designed and constructed in 1939, has large spacious rooms, high ceilings, many windows, wide halls, and excellent lighting. The routine is centered totally around the students, and is conducted in more relaxed and less regimented environment than is usual in traditional school settings. It was hypothesised that student anxiety would be reduced by the less crowded and more aesthetic atmosphere and that this would result in increased student gains.

It was soon discovered that the two populations, the high school students and the DSR clients, were more alike than different. The public school population may or may not be on a DRS caseload, i.e. enrolled in Special Education, but all are functioning below grade level. Residential patients and Independent

Living students have diagnosed disabilities and may or may not be public school drop-outs. All are in need of literacy instruction or academic skills remediation. The traditional students at RWSIR experience the same general learning difficulties as the public school students but have diagnosed disabilities that often compound their learning difficulties. In fact, the adaptive devices used to lessen these disabilities have been found to work quite effectively with the public school students.

The curriculum used in the OCO program is based on the Division of Rehabilitation's Cooperative Program concept. It is designed in an open-entry, educational literacy format which utilizes an eight-weeks progressive study period. The ninth week is allocated to the on-site instructors' evaluation and documentation of each students' subjective and objective performance. This documentation, in the form of progress reports, is sent to facility counselors and appropriate case managers for Roosevelt's residential patients and Independent Living students. This system fit well with the needs of the public schools. Reports for the high school students are sent to their counselors who incorporate them into the school's nine-weeks reporting procedures.

The curriculum emphasizes the attaining of skill competencies in reading, language, and math at each grade level rather than learning grade-level subject matter. The philosophy behind this approach is that a student, having developed competency in reading, language, and math at any grade level, will be able to study, understand, and learn any subject taught on that same grade level. Thus the students will become increasingly able to suceed in a regular high school program. A functional approach is used to teach skills using realistic life applications to the greatest extent possible. Each concept is studied and/or remediated until the student has attained competency, before moving to the next concept.

While the program instructor works exclusively with the public school students, the other three instructors also are able to help facilitate. With four instructors, no more than 7-9 students are assigned to an instructor at any given time. Work is graded daily and grades are refect functioning grade level progress.

The program encourages students to be responsible for their own learning by requiring them to set short and long term goals. They are also encouraged and reminded to prioritize their needs, time, and activities to get the maximum results from the work that is done. Students have some flexibility in their scheduled times for Reading, Language, and Math. While each student is allowed 50 minutes a day in each skill area, they may chose to spend more time in one area on a given day and make up the reduced time for the other subjects on the following day. Instructors monitor work to ascertain that all three areas are being studied, and that satisfactory progress is being made in each one.

Meriwether County

Like other high schools across the nation. Manchester and Greenville High Schools have recognized a need to restructure the learning environment. Instead of placing students in one or two main tracks, an attempt is being made to design small programs to fit the needs of small but different groups of students and to create programs flexible enough to change with changing student needs. Again, like other schools, they are also trying to find ways to provide students who are potential drop-outs with alternative educational experiences that will lead to academic success. It was with open arms, then, that the school system welcomed the partnership with the other three agencies and the OCO program was born.

In developing the OCO program, the school system was responsible for coordinating efforts in three major areas: students, curriculum, and program Iogistics. The majority of the work in all three areas was done prior to the program's inception, but modifications and adjustments had to be made throughout the year. particularly in the area of Iogistics.

The school social worker and a project teacher met for approximately an hour with each high school's student pool to explain the program and application procedures and students were given applications and information to take home to their parents for signatures. Of the total pool of 68 appropriate students, 29 returned signed applications which meant that additional screening was unnecessary. After the project started up, six more students returned forms and these were put on a waiting list. During the year, seven additional students were placed in the program through counselor referral. All of these later placements met the initial criteria for placement and had no drug, emotional, or inappropriate attendance problems.

At the same time that students were being identified and recruited, the curriculum was being assessed. Since one of the purposes of the program was to assist students to graduate from school, it was important that they earn credit for their work. The system's curriculum director cooperated with the project teacher in analysing the Basic Education curriculum that RWSIR had been using in its GED program against Georgia's Quality Core Curriculum (QCC). They discovered that it matched three state courses: Communication Skills, Basic Reading and Writing I, and General Mathematics I or II which meant that students could earn three Carnegie Units while attending the program. The matches were extremely close but additional objectives were identified to ensure an exact match. Contact was also made with the Georgia Department of Education and the Southern Association of Colleges and Schools (SACS) to ensure that the school would be in compliance with all standards.

The third area which had to addressed were the logistics of getting the students to and from the project and coordinating communcation between the project and the school. The two high schools begin the day and break for lunch at different times which meant that coordinating bus arrival times was difficult. It took several weeks and input from the transportation supervisor, project teachers, the school social worker, principals, assistant principals, and counselors before this was smoothed out.

There was no precedent for this type of program in the schools or RWSIR which meant that a system for moving information on attendance and grades had to be developed. This primarily involved the school counselors and the project teachers, although the school social worker needed to be involved in some attendance issues. Grading scales, progress reports, and grade reporting periods were discussed and forms for conveying this information were selected. After the project was underway, modifications were made until reporting ran smoothly.

A major part of the implementation of the OCO program from the system's standpoint has been the coordination of people. A large number of people with very different job responsibilities have had input into the program and it has taken all of their resourcefulness and commitment to make the project work.

The University of Georgia

The research component was a means to secure objective data to evaluate the project and to support the original hypotheses: that the project would increase student academic performance; contribute to high school retention and graduation or GED completion rates; and increase psychological well being on such factors as anxiety, stress and self esteem.

The original research design called for three population pools defined as follows:

(1) An experimental group which would bethe first thirty individuals determined at-risk who volunteered for the program.

(2) A control group made up of individuals determined to be at-risk and who volunteered for the program but who were precluded through lack of space.

(3) A comparison group made up of individuals determined to be at-risk but who did not volunteer to participate.

Time constraints and communication issues resulted in insufficient numbers for three groups therefore only a control group and a comparative group were identified. A comparative analysis will take place on those individuals who were determined to be at risk but did not volunteer to participate.

Academic pre- and post-testing and a battery of psychological tests were to be administered. In addition, attendance records were be kept and students tracked subsequent to the one year program to assess impact, if any, on the drop-out rate. General demographic data will also be captured. In addition, qualitative analyses will include interviews with high school teachers at both high schools, focus group discussions with parents of students involved in the program, focus group discussions with students participating in the program, and focus group discussions with teachers involved in the delivery of the program.

PRELIMINARY PROGRAM RESULTS

The OCO program was designed to be evaluated using data collected quantitatively through standardized pre-testing and post-testing of all participating students using the Test of Adult Basic Education (TABE) and a battery of psychological tests that included a Learning Styles Assessment, and qualitatively through interviews with teachers. At this point, only preliminary results are available but these are very encouraging.

The scores for the reading, math, and language series of the TABE indicated that the majority of students were at least 2-3 academic grades below their appropriate age placement. The mean reading score was 5.4 with a range of 2.2-10.0. The mean math score was 6.7 with a range of 2.0-9.0. The mean language score was 4.8 with a range of 1.9-9.5. These scores were used to develop an Individualized Prescribed Program (IPP) for each student. Once students were placed and began working at the pre-determined level, it was discovered that some students were not functioning at the level indicated by their test scores. Many students were actually functioning at levels 1-2 grades lower than indicated by their overall TABE test scores which made it necessary to re-evaluate each student's individual plan. Following the third grading period (week 27 of a 36 week year), functioning levels were compared with the original TABE scores. The mean reading functioning level was 8.5 for an increase of more than three grade levels over the original TABE score. The mean math functioning level was 8.6 or an increase of nearly two grade levels (1.9). The mean language functioning level was 7.3 or an increase of 2.5 grade levels. Only functioning levels are available at the present time since post-testing will be done at the end of the year.

Included with the pre-testing of academic skill areas was a battery of psychological tests, including a Learning Styles Assessment, given to reveal subjective areas of concern. This battery of tests, along with the TABE, enabled instructors to have a more complete data base on which to produce a more realistic IPP for each student.

The original intent of the OCO Program was not only to improve the academic success of the participants but also to decrease the drop-out rate of the students. Thirty students were originally enrolled in the program, and of these twelve are no longer in the program. Some of these students have been replaced with other students from a waiting list compiled by school counselors. A total of 37 students have been served by the OCO Program. Of the12 students no longer in the program, four were expelled from school making them ineligible for OCO participation, two were terminated by the OCO staff for inappropriate behavior, and one was withdrawn from the program at the request of school system officials. Of the 37 students who have been served, only five have dropped out of school giving the OCO program a retention rate of 68%. There were approximately 130 students originally qualified for the OCO program but only 30 were accepted. There were approximately 100 students who wanted to participate in the program. Nearly 70 % of those students are no longer actively enrolled in school.

Interviews with the regular classroom teachers of OCO students addressed academic performance, attitude, and behavior of these students before and after OCO enrollment. The greatest area of noted change was in attitude. The teachers reported that the students appeared to be more concerned about their classroom academic performance now than before they entered the OCO program. The teachers interviewed also reported that the OCO students appear to be more self-confident and have a greater degree of self-esteem. The data collected indicated that the teachers viewed the OCO program as a positive academic and social influence.

LESSONS LEARNED

Although all partners are pleased with the OCO project, there is always room for improvement and several lessons have been learned. The rapid implementation schedule was a basic limitation and contributed to some issues which could have been avoided by more detailed planning.

Early identification of student participants is important. Time did not permit students to start at the beginning of school which meant that schedules were disrupted. This will be avoided in future by identifying students at the end of the school year.

The research design would have been strengthened by having a control group, a comparative group, and a study group. Insufficient lead time made this impossible. In addition, the test battery should have been more carefully explained to students particularly to those participating in psychological evaluation for the first time. Again, more lead time would have enabled the team to make better use of the test results to plan for each student, to explain performance issues, and to assist in identifying intervention strategies.

Identifying the key players at the outset is essential when addressing inter-agency collaboration. It is necessary to involve those individuals who have both the interest in discussing innovative programs and the authority to act on them. Further, it is necessary to take the time necesary to build a trusting relationship with the second tier of players who may not be as initially commited to the program as its initiators. Although principals were aquainted with the program and endorsed it, if their input on specific issues had been sought earlier, their commitment could have been strengthened. Discipline was an issue which proved problematical and it has been decided that a student handbook will be produced which will describe the program and include policies and procedures. This handbook will be distributed to potential students, parents, school officials, and other individuals inquiring about the program. In particular, it will address those areas where behavioral norms and expectations may differ from the school setting.

Periodic reviews of the program and student progress were initiated during the year and these proved very helpful in forestalling problems. In future years these meetings will be a regular feature of the program.

FUTURE PLANS

The initiation of the OCO Program has enabled much communication and collaboration between different agencies to take place. In particular, it has strengthened the mutual commitment to address educational needs in the county and served as a forum to target other possibilities. Future plans include submission of a request for continuation of funding for year two with expansion recommendations for year three. We have discussed replicating the program within the school system and also cooperating with a Job Training Partnership Act (JTPA) program to offer a night class to those students who have already dropped out of school.

In addition, the inter-agency cooperation has provided an avenue to discuss other ways to share resources including using the public school classrooms and equipment to provide vocational training for DRS clients especially during the summer months when they are not being used by the school personnel. A long term idea calls for the formation of a community consortium which would address issues including health care, pscychologicsal services, social services, educational needs, and job skills.

It has been an exciting year for those involved in the OCO program. It has confirmed a belief that students can and will learn when the program is designed to fit the student rather than expecting the student to fit the program.

WENIFORT C. WASHINGTON

18

Linking School and Employment:
Achieving Success for All Students

Peter Drucker (1969) recommended two decades ago that the nation's economic stability and an educated work force would be directly related to the effectiveness of our schools. Yet, everyday more than 3,500 students, our most valuable natural resources, drop out of school, joining a larger unproductive segment of our people resources. The challenge facing educational leaders in this era of reform is achieving success for all students.

Reform is not a new concept in education, but few of our current efforts focus on the "forgotten half"—at-risk students whose specific education needs have been largely ignored, yet whose skills and competencies are essential to our nation's future competitiveness. As we face the challenges for the twenty-first century, we must not lose sight of those individuals with special challenges and barriers to participation.

We must especially focus improvement efforts on young people—in poverty, with disabilities, limited English proficiency, teen parents, African-American males, and potential dropouts—whose education and employment preparation needs may be greater, the barriers to success higher, and the need for targeted services and quality programs more acute (CCSSO, 1992).

Although these youth have been the target of many federal and categorically funded programs, there is no comprehensive school-to-employment transition strategy designed to assure them of education and employment success. Politics, budget priorities and lack of leadership vision provide barriers to prevent focus on this unique population. It is simply not "vogue" to focus on those destined for the lower rung of the economic ladder.

In our rhetoric and efforts, we profess a genuine desire to educate all children in a world class school environment. Yet, yearly, almost 700,000 students drop out of our nation's schools (Carnegie, 1988). Last year, another 800,000 graduated who could not read their diplomas.

Successful reform efforts will require strategies to combat the factors and forces impacting disadvantaged children. We cannot ignore the realities of the following statistics:

- Approximately 25% of all babies born in the country were born into families living in poverty which puts them into greater risk for disabilities related to malnutrition, inadequate health care, and other societal factors (NASDSE, 1992).
- The number of infants born drug exposed during the past five years has quadrupled; 11% of babies (or 375,000) are born exposed to illicit drugs (NASDSE, 1992).
- Approximately 85,000 children 6-15 years of age are in special education programs because of low birth rates.
- In 1989 2.4 million child abuse reports were filed, of which 400,000 were sexual abuse. Sixteen percent of children under age 3 are involved in child abuse and neglect (NASDSE, 1992).
- Twenty-five percent (25%) of all homeless people in the United States are children. On any given night, between 50,000 and 200,000 children have no home (Hodgkinson, September 1991).

Harold Hodgkinson reported in a recent study that 82% of all children now have working mothers. Fifteen million women are raising children without fathers present at an income level $400 over the poverty line. Hodgkinson further projected that "Sixty percent of all children will spend some time with a single parent before reaching age 18, making the single parent family the new typical American family" (Hodgkinson, 1991). These factors suggest that schools, business and government must respond rapidly to the changing family structure and increasing demand for custodial child services.

Another target population often overlooked in the reform agenda is African-American males. The national dropout rate averages between 17-19%—but escalates as high as 49.6% for black youth. The U.S. Department of Justice reported in 1991 that one in four black men are in jail, on trial, or on parole. While the U.S. population increased by 10% between 1980 and 1990, the prison population exploded by 139%. Prisoners cost taxpayers over $20,000 annually and 80% are dropouts (Hodgkinson, 1991). Clearly, it costs more to keep them in prison than to educate them!

The National Urban League found that the leading cause of death among 18 to 24 year old black men is murder by other black men. In addition, black and hispanic youth are suspended from schools at a rate three times that of their white counterparts.

Ronald Ferguson (1991) suggests the plight of African-American males is due primarily to poor learning outcomes and lack of employment opportunities. Over the past 40 years, unemployment rates for this population have been roughly twice those for their white counterparts. Ferguson's research of

African-American males concluded that math and social skills are critical for their economic outcome. Schools can make a difference.

Drucker, Hodgkinson and Ferguson agree there is a need to prioritize education for our nation's economic future. This priority includes improved services and educational outcomes for all children. In spite of these stats, schools can make a difference. Consider the fact that children on an average spend six hours a day in school. By the time they finish high school, they have an estimated 15,000 hours in school. We have the power, expertise, and presence to make a difference and motivate this unique population of children. However, to impact under-education and the dropout problem, we must first understand the complexity of factors surrounding the problem.

DEFINITION

There is often difficulty in defining "at risk" and "dropout population." What do we really mean? Comer (1987) defines "high risk" children as those who underachieve despite intellectual endowment and, as a result, will underachieve as adults. Slavin (1989) states that a student described as "at risk" is one who is in danger of failing to complete their education with an adequate level of skills. The term "at risk" is simply a new shine on an old pair of shoes.

Defining the "dropout population" is more complex. A major problem associated with the issue of dropouts is identifying a uniform definition and consistent reporting format. Numerous definitions appear in the literature but little agreement exists between school districts on what constitutes dropout status (Hahn, 1987). No two school systems, social service agencies, or government agencies use the same definition. In addition, school statistics are not always accurate and their methods of calculating the dropout rate varies from year to year and school to school making available figures unreliable.

Several major studies conducted by researchers in large urban school systems strongly support the need for a common definition. The Office of Educational Research and Improvement (OERI) Urban Superintendent Network (1987) suggests knowing whom we are talking about is a prerequisite to developing preventive programs. A definition commonly accepted by the urban superintendents was recommended by the task force of the Council of Chief State School Officers: "A pupil who leaves school, for any reason except death, before graduation or completion of a program of studies and without transferring to another school" (CCSSO, 1992, p. 11).

Some large districts found a need to specifically define dropouts to improve consistency of reporting (Halfer & Collins, 1987). For example, the New York City Board of Education defines a school dropout as: "Those students who left school during the 1985-86 school year without receiving a diploma, who did not enroll in another educational setting, and who have not been counted as dropouts in previous years" (p. 5).

Varying definitions of school dropouts in American schools lead to an inability to compare dropout rates across states and impedes development of preventive model programs for dropout prevention.

Another factor complicating the dropout problem is inconsistent calculations in data collection. Experts in the field point out that until a uniform and accurate system of calculating the dropout rate is developed by local school systems, dropout prevention efforts will continue to be directed toward a smaller number of "troubled teens," rather than toward the majority of at-risk students in some urban schools who will leave before graduation. In spite of varying definitions and inconsistent calculations in identification, dropouts tend to share many common characteristics.

CHARACTERISTICS/PROFILE

Throughout the literature, various characteristics emerge in association with school dropouts and at-risk students. Though some studies suggest demographic characteristics are not significant, others maintain a typical profile exists (Rhoda, 1986; Hodgkinson, 1985). Examination of major studies on the dropout problem suggests at-risk students who become dropouts share a number of common characteristics:

(1) Dropouts are usually from low income settings and often are from ethnic and minority cultures.

(2) They lack parental support, many come from single-parent environments, and tend to be adolescents who have extreme family or personal problems.

(3) Dropouts typically have been unsuccessful in school and tend to have low basic academic skills and low achievement levels. Truancy and poor attendance patterns are common characteristics found in this population, as well as discipline problems.

(4) Male students often drop out for economic reasons, whereas teen pregnancy is the most frequent reason for females not completing school. However, overall, more males drop out of school than females.

(5) Other common characteristics are low self-esteem, peer problems, teacher problems, and school transfers.

Demographic profiles of children and families give strong indication that many social factors interfere in the development and learning of children at an early age which set the stage for premature exit from school (Van Den Heubel, 1986). For example, the Children's Defense Fund (1985) identified key elements impacting early childhood development and learning.

Of the four- and five-year-olds in today's America, the potential students and workers in the year 2000:

- One in four is poor;
- One in three is nonwhite or Hispanic, of whom two in five are poor;
- One in five is at risk of becoming a teen parent;
- One in six has no health insurance;
- One in six lives in a family where neither parent has a job;
- One in two has a mother working outside the home, but only a minority receive quality child care; and
- One in seven is at risk of dropping out of school.

It is projected that about one-third of pre-school children are destined for school failure because of poverty, neglect, sickness, handicapped condition, and lack of adult protection and nurturance (Hodgkinson, September 1991).

Obviously many factors impact the dropout and at-risk problem. McDill, Natriello, and Pallo (1987) and Van Den Huebel (1988) found most factors can be grouped into three categories: school experiences, family circumstances and economic factors. Research suggests poor academic performance, truancy, discipline problems, and grade retainment are strong predictors of students dropping out of school. Secondly, the lack of family support systems, one parent families, dysfunctional families, and teen pregnancies are also identified as strong predictors of students dropping out of school. The third factor associated with students dropping out of school is economics. Male students, especially, report the reason for leaving school was to go to work.

These factors, though strong predictors of students dropping out of school, are further complicated by the school reform recommendations.

HIGHER STANDARDS AND SCHOOL REFORM

On the heels of an already crisis problem are the potential consequences of higher standards resulting from the reform movement. Research suggests, in general, students may benefit from higher standards but few reform agendas have addressed potentially unintended consequences for students already at risk of completing school.

Experts in the field suggest that the consequences of increased standards may also lead to greater academic stratification and less student choice (Natriello, 1986). Secondly, schools demanding more time may lead to increased conflict between demands placed on at-risk students. Finally, higher levels of achievement may lead to more students experiencing failure without apparent remedies. Ernest Boyer (1988) summarized the problem when he stated:

> *To require a failing student in an urban ghetto to take another unit of math or foreign language without offering a better environment or better teaching is like raising a hurdle for someone who has already stumbled without providing more coaching. (p. 4)*

The ultimate negative consequences of raising standards without additional help and support to students lies in the economic and cognitive cost of dropping out of school. But there is a hidden consequence of higher standards which may be even more pronounced for potential groups in the population. At-risk students unable to meet the new standards may force certain economic and ethnic groups to be pushed out of school in greater numbers. If we are to meet the needs of the 21st century, equal access to education for all students must be a primary goal for every policymaker, politician, and educational leader.

LINKING SCHOOL AND EMPLOYMENT

The challenge facing educational leaders and policymakers is not in raising standards, but an implementation of the new reform mandates through improved delivery of educational resources, and monitoring the impact of more challenging standards to assure both equity and excellence in education.

Secondly, the process goal for all educational institutions should be to support the development of a more systematic and orderly transition from school to employment for all young people. This transition should be viewed as a number of routes with a series of milestones (such as degrees and recognizable competencies) across and within sectors. "This transition must be viewed as a continuum of education, training and employment experiences supported by the health, social and family services that make it possible for young people with special challenges to access these opportunities, succeed in them, and attain the recognition and benefits of participation" (CCSSO Vision Statement, Denver, Colorado, October, 1992).

This transition must be based upon a strong elementary and secondary school experience in which all children and youth were successful. It should take students:

- From pre-school through to high school completion, into a range of post-secondary options,
- And beyond, to a continuous and life-long learning process.
- The system of transition must provide flexibility for looping back, stopping out, and reentering as personal conditions dictate.
- The system must contain mechanisms for participation by young people who lack a high school diploma or have special challenges to successful employment.
- The effort should result in high-wage, high-skill career opportunities.
- The effort must be a coordinated effort between schools, colleges, community-based organizations, social service agencies and the business community.

This mission must entail high performance expectations for all young people—no matter which route they take. The end result must be high expectations and high standards of performance.

In summary, there does not appear to be a single magical formula for successfully linking school and employment. Communities and students have varying needs and successful programs must be tailored to meet their unique needs. However, in reviewing effective programs, the following nine areas appear to be essential for most successful programs.

(1) COMMITMENT - Communicate Board commitment through development of district philosophy and policy to support academic and employment success for at-risk students.

(2) CLIMATE - Create a positive climate by hiring effective, visionary leadership who support sensitivity training and inservice development for faculty and staff, and an overall positive attitude toward the mission of dropout prevention.

(3) CASH - Establish a line item in the budget for appropriate resources, personnel, and materials to support transitional programs.

(4) CURRICULUM - Restructure curriculum to meet the needs of this special population with a broad range of instructional programs including alternative programs, individualized instruction, student centered activities, choice and program options, connection to work world, and a range of post-secondary options.

(5) COUNSELING - Develop counselors trained to meet the needs of at-risk students with skills for identification, monitoring of student progress, support, mentoring, and career planning.

(6) CARE - Establish high expectations for achievement, attendance, discipline, multicultural sensitivity, and human relations.

(7) COMPUTERS - Utilize technology for student needs inventory, student management, instructional support, evaluation and training.

(8) COLLABORATION/COALITION - Develop partnerships with parents and family, collaboration with community agencies (social service, chemical abuse, etc.), community organizations (churches, police, juvenile courts, etc.), and coalitions with business and industry.

(9) COORDINATION - Centralize program coordination and accountability for target populations with district-wide (total school) involvement and total staff participation.

In conclusion, schools must develop programs to prevent at-risk students from leaving school prematurely or under-educated. Strategies must be implemented to link school and employment and assure maximum utilization of all our people resources. As long as one student drops out of school each day, our nation's economic future is "at risk."

REFERENCES

Boyer, E. L. (1988). Early schooling and the nation's future,*Educational Leadership, 44*(6), 4-6.

Carnegie Foundation for the Advancement of Teaching (1998). *An Imperiled Generation: Saving Urban Schools*. Stanley O. Ikenberry, Chairman, Board of Trustees.

Children's Defense Fund (1987). *The Children's Time*. Washington, D.C.: Children's Defense Fund.

Comer, James (1987). New haven's community connection, *Educational Leadership, 44*(6), pg. 13-16.

Council of Chief State School Officials (CCSSO) (1992). Linking school and employment, *Resource Guide*, Denver, Colorado.

Drucker, P. (1969). *The Age of Discontinuity: Guidelines to Our Changing Society*. New York: Harper & Row.

Ferguson, Ronald (1991). *Social and Economic Prospects of African American Male*. Kellogg Foundation. Unpublished manuscript.

Hahn, A. (1987). Reaching out to america's dropouts: what to do? *Phi Delta Kappan, 69*(4), 256-263.

Halfar, L., & Collins, C. (1987). *The 1985-1986 Dropout Report.* (ERIC Document Reproduction Service No. ED 280 928). Brooklyn, NY: The New York Board of Education.

Hodgkinson, Harold (1991). Reform versus reality, *Phi Delta Kappan*, pg. 10.

Hodgkinson, H. L. (1985). *All in One System: Demographics of Education, Kindergarten through Graduate School.* Washington, D.C.: Institute for Educational Leadership.

McDill, E. L., Natriello, G., & Pallas, A. M. (1987). A population at risk: potential consequences of tougher school standards for student dropouts, In G. Natriello, (Ed.), *School Dropout Patterns and Policies*, (pp. 106-137). New York: Teachers College Press.

National Association of State Directors of Special Education (NASDSE), (1992). *Societal Pressures on the Educational System*, Alexandria, Virginia.

Natriello, G. (1986). *School Dropouts: Patterns and Policies.* New York, Teachers College Press.

OERI Urban Superintendents Network (1987). *Dealing with Dropouts: The Urban Superintendents Call to Actio*n. Washington, D.C.: Office of Educational Research and Improvement.

Rhoda, D. M. (1986). A meta-analysis of the effects of demographics, academic and non-academic factors on student retention. (Doctoral Dissertation, University of New Orleans). *Dissertation Abstracts International, 48,* 2A.

Slavin, Robert E. (1987). Making chapter 1 make a difference, *Phi Delta Kappan*, Vol. 69, Number 2, pg. 110-119.

Van Den Heuvel, D. (1988). *Children at Risk: An Old Reality with New Dimensions.* Madison, WI: Wisconsin Department of Public Instruction.

ELIZABETH PERNA

19

Networking to Dropout Prevention

Twenty percent of the babies born each year will be tough to teach. That means about one in five students in your building will be at-risk for dropping out (Hodgkinson, 1988). Most teachers and administrators are not prepared to deal with the range of children's current psychological and social needs.

Students' home lives are both blamed for low achievement in school and seen as salvation (Edwards & Young, 1992). In past times neighbors, parents, and teachers spoke in a "common voice." According to James Comer, a professor of child psychiatry at Yale University, his mother and teacher would meet at the local A & P to talk about his progress and behavior in school, sharing and reinforcing family and school values, naturally (Comer, 1990). Today, for many children, these types of communities and the ready relationships of relatives and neighbors have disappeared. Teachers rarely live in the economically depressed neighborhoods, where many of their students come from (Edwards & Young, 1992).

When homes and neighborhoods do not support attending and doing well in school, teachers with crowded classrooms often resent picking up the tab for extra time performing parenting and daycare responsibilities. Parents and other care providers do not understand why they pay taxes to a public entity, only to receive "no help." The result is angry teachers, parents and students. If only to let off pressure, dropping out of school becomes an increasingly viable alternative—especially when adults do not care about their children's success in school.

Chavez, Edwards and Oetting (1989) summarize national dropout data to indicate overall rate as declining. The short-term rate, especially for minority groups, is increasing. MexicanAmerican youths drop out more frequently than white Americans, but accurate rates are difficult to determine. In many areas ninth graders who leave school later are counted as dropouts; those who neglect to re-enroll or show up in the fall are not. Keeping in mind the struggle to achieve accurate dropout rates, the Mexican-American dropout rates are as high as 45%, and estimates for white American youths are as high as 30% in some areas.

There are many reasons why children drop out of school. Contributing factors include socioeconomic status, family-related education and occupational variables, school-related behaviors of dropouts, economic elements contributing to the dropouts' decisions to leave school, and a myriad of personal factors. Chavez, Oetting, and Edwards (1989) conclude new research efforts should focus on developing longitudinal, multivariate models, which are comprehensive with regard to the causes and consequences of dropping out.

In the mean time those of us who deal with the problem of at-risk students and dropouts in our districts and buildings need some answers right now. Here in Poudre R-1 School District, Fort Collins, Colorado, we reported a dropout rate of less than 3% for the past three years; and we track not only the ninth graders, but all secondary students, enrolled or not. This of course includes the "no shows."

Our district enjoys the benefits of a college town location, but we face the challenge of preventing dropouts in a growing student population lacking matching funds. as a school district of over 20,000 students, we experience negative repercussions from a substantial increase in local juvenile offenders. School-related crimes include truancy, robbery, aggravated harassment and menacing, drug sales and gun-related incidents. Situated between Denver, Colorado, and Cheyenne, Wyoming (locations with serious gang problems); we now grapple with at least six identified youth gang subpopulations. Consequently, we experience the challenge of keeping increasingly street-wise children in school—many of whom well understand the discrepancy involved with working for McDonald's at minimum wage and working for gang bosses for more money—including benefits such as free sex, liquor, and drugs.

There is no one to blame because what we experience is a societal problem. Agree or not, local communities in combination with local school buildings will have to contend with it. Since our district is low on funds for dropout prevention, we have been forced to seek help from a number of sources. Hence we have developed an office philosophy, a motto which has become the title of this article: "Networking to Dropout Prevention."

NETWORKING TO DROPOUT PREVENTION

We approach networking to dropout prevention in three ways:

- Continue to develop a good working relationship with local youth serving agencies, as overseen by Parallel Advocate Support System (PASS) personnel in the junior and senior high schools

- Installing "Jack Rabbit Class Assignment Hotline" into the elementaryschools
- Working to fund and implement the Home Visit Program in the elementary schools

Nurturing Working Relationships With Local Youth-Serving Agencies

For the past five years, we have been building a working relationship with local youthserving agencies. Some of the agencies we work with most directly are as follows:

- Department of Police Services
- Juvenile Justice System
- Department of Corrections
- Department of Social Services (DSS)
- Department Mental Health

A "working relationship" with a youth-serving agency is one by which we cut bureaucratic red tape to more quickly obtain services for district students and dropouts. Because office staffing is limited, these resources are crucial to us having any ability to help our children solve their problems. Our philosophy: If the caller needs help with personal problems, do what you can to assist, so that the child can get on with the business of going to school.

We start to develop working relationships with youth-serving agencies by first attending their meetings and getting to know contacts on a first-name basis. This tactic takes time because they all have large caseloads. A cheery, "Hello," plus taking the time to chat with secretaries will open many doors for you. This takes a certain willingness to introduce yourself to secretaries and other key personnel at the courts, inter-agency meetings, and other places where you can talk with the people who make decisions about your at-risk students and dropouts.

The ability to place agency leaders on your school district policy committees will pay off. We spearheaded placing key community leaders onto our district Gang Policy Committee (e.g., the juvenile director of the police force, the district attorney, and representatives from the Public Defenders' Office, DSS, and a citizen-based gang task force, among others). The results were better than expected. Not only did we design comprehensive policy, which was legally sound regarding weapons and gang activity in the school buildings; we were also able to develop a stronger working relationship with some powerful youth-serving agencies.

Another idea for expanding contacts is discreetly attending juvenile court. This tactic allows you to track your district's troubled children quickly, and you can eventually meet the DDS court intake person. Responsible for you school district's out-of-home placements, this person can offer a wealth of information regarding potential problem-children coming from outof-district.

Remember, your district is responsible for giving every school-aged resident a free education—even if the child is a criminal or an experienced product of Los Angeles gang scene. Perhaps you just had a "S.H.O.D.I." (Serious Habitual Offender—Directed Intervention) transfer into your district or building. That label means the student has amassed an extensive felony criminal record, which includes weapons use or aggravated harassment or menacing. As an administrator you have a potential hazard in your building.

We do not advocate you broadcast such sensitive information at the next staff meeting. However, in terms of eliminating the surprise element that often accompanies bad decisions, we have found information to be an important element in running district buildings more smoothly.

In many cases knowledge of a student's circumstances has really helped the various systems to deal more effectively with that student and his or her family. For example, our input at court has helped many children to better communicate their perspectives. Often, a child's improved school record has helped the magistrate to choose more successfully oriented options regarding staying in school and community service, as opposed to performing dead time in jail.

Our working relationship with agencies helps families in a variety of ways. For example, a family was experiencing some difficulty with their household furnace. We were alerted to the problem by an attendance clerk who was concerned about excessive absences on behalf of a PASS student. After some investigation, we discovered the family was physically struggling with the furnace fumes coming back into the home. They alerted the landlord, but he told them to,"wait a while and see." The PASS teacher helped the child make the right phone calls to a "friend" in the inspector's office. By afternoon, the furnace was running better, and the child was able to attend school with no problem the next day.

Perhaps you are uncomfortable, or time limited, during the primary stages of developing these relationships with your local, youth-serving agencies. Try spending a hundred dollars on coffee, cookies and space to hold an "Interagency Fair." Invite all the youth-serving agencies to set up a booth for sharing literature and information with your teaching, counseling, and special services staff. If possible, arrange to get college credit for school staff participants, and hold the fair in the fall—before major problems set in. It is much easier for staff to call the various agencies after they have sipped coffee, looked over pamphlets, and discussed questions with representatives.

As small part of Pupil Services, we in Dropout Prevention depend upon our support staff at the schools, too. Our PASS teachers in the junior and senior high schools work as advocates for at-risk students and dropouts. It is their job to know family situations, to stay abreast of local resources, and to teach at-risk students how to be more successful in school (See Appendix A). Acting as resource brokers for the PASS teachers, we visit their buildings at least every other week to provide updated information to share with their building staff, students and parents.

Since the district currently has no PASS teachers in the elementary schools, we are trying to implement a couple of programs to help the counselors deal with an increasing workload and to provide more ways for schools to network better with parents. These new programs are as follows:

- The Jack Rabbit Class Assignment Hotline
- The Home Visit Program

The Jack Rabbit Assignment Hotline

An elementary school principal has turned to a common tool, combining it with new technology to provide a means for improving children's school work: the telephone ("Phone System," 1993).

Taylor Elementary School Principal Reed Spencer predicts every school in the country having the new phone system in place within five years. Why? Because most parents want to know when their kids fall behind, but find it difficult to adjust their busy schedules to the schools. Now they can find out in their own time by using a sophisticated telephone system, which allows them to call 24 hours a day to get up-to-the minute messages on their children's homework—what is due, when it is due, and other announcements.

Parents can also leave messages for teachers and get automatic calls back. Children can check anytime on the week's lunch menu, or check what assignments are due that day. What Spencer calls a "phone phenomenon" is the Parent Link Telephone Audio Bulletin Board System.

We took the idea, used our own district-wide computer system and expertise to install and implement it at one of the elementaries. Considering a late introduction in the spring, what we called the "Jack Rabbit Class Assignment Hotline" was certainly successful. We plan to try it in the fall by adding another elementary school to service.

In terms of background, both the target elementary school teachers, as well as other district professionals, have been frustrated by the number of evening phone calls by students needing forgotten homework assignments. Parents, too, had expressed difficulty knowing what and when assignments are due.

The voice mail system offered the solutions to these problems as follows:

- The system provides students with an opportunity to take responsibility for getting information regarding forgotten or misplaced assignments without interrupting teachers at home.
- The system provides a convenient way for parents to check children's classroom assignments and other building information on a regular basis.

Many of the district schools are interesting in improving ways for parents to communicate more regularly with teachers. An opportunity to keep track of their children's daily assignments, plus other announcements and information, empowers parents with information necessary to help their children succeed in school. As with any proposed change that involves extra effort on behalf of teachers, parents, and students, however; a planned communication campaign would have been extremely helpful.

We plan to start by performing evaluative research. The first step involves sending preand-post test surveys out to parents, teachers, and students in the school newsletter (See questionnaire samples in Appendix B). Survey research uses questionnaires to interview large numbers of persons selected by scientific, probability-sampling methods and representative of target audiences. In this case we will survey the target elementary school teachers, students and parents. We hope to obtain statistical summaries of trends and specifically to measure interest and whether or not the class assignment hotline is being used successfully by the students, faculty, and parents.

The Home Visit Project

In conjunction with the Jack Rabbit Class Assignment Hotline (a telephone-based solution to the communication gap with parents) we need to reach out to parents of elementary students in a more personal way. As specified earlier when we described the problem, the fact that teachers do not always live in students' neighborhoods makes it tough for some parents to relate to schools at all.

We propose a program by which teachers are trained for all of their elementary-aged students, not just those identified as at-risk. When parents are comfortable with what their teachers and the schools are about, they will be more apt to support what the schools and teachers are trying to do. Of course this takes a certain amount of buy-in on behalf of the staff. We think monetary reimbursement, time for visits, and proper training will help.

A successful home visit may only be taking tome for a cup of coffee with the parent. At least the parent would be able to place a face with the voice at the end of the class assignment hotline. In addition, if problems arise in the classroom, the teacher already knows the parent, and consequently, support for behavior or discipline choices may be less difficult to procure. Perhaps the parents want to volunteer, but they are not sure how to help. The teacher might offer a list of jobs to choose from. Having the teacher hand the list of up-and-coming activities or information about using the class assignment hotline is more powerful, and personal, communication tool than any newsletter. Finally, there may be important things about the family or student the teacher would discover immediately. Any clues to the homelife of students is certainly a key to that child's success in school.

CONCLUSION

Poudre R-1 School District in Fort Collins has a low dropout rate, but holding that steady takes a cooperative effort on behalf of many people in a variety of agencies. Each school district is different. Actually, with increased site-based management, each building handles its students and family population with a special flavor. The three strategies we discussed have the capabilities to work separately in buildings with district-wide supervision to help with updating resources and technological aspects.

The programs are not inexpensive. Perhaps you can mold these programs to piggy-back onto other, existing situations. For example, if your district attendance works off a main computer for student information and attendance, you can talk with an expert about writing and installing a class assignment and information hotline. Computerized student information will help you track truancy, not to mention dangerous juvenile offenders. If you can give truancy reports the Probation Department, they may be able to help you with truancy issues.

The key to the success in implementing any of these programs is buy-in on behalf of your staff, the district administration, and the parents. It takes time to implement ideas. So, until the ideas start to manifest results, keep talking to and reassuring the people you work with. Once they know, for example, that you have information they cannot or do not have time to get, they will seek you out.

Manifesting results takes research. That is you must be able to show before-and-after data, and you must be able to interpret the results as related, somehow, to your idea. Read over any application for federal grant, and you will see examples of questions related to showing measurable results from the dropout prevention program ideas you choose to implement.

REFERENCES

Chavez, E., Edwards, R., & Oetting, E. R. Mexican-American and white American school dropout's drug use, health status, and involvement in violence. *Public Health Reports,* 104. (6) 594-604.

Comer, J. P. (1990). Home, school, and academic learning, in John I. Goodlad and Pamela Keating eds. *Access to Knowledge: an Agenda for Our Nation's Schools.* (New York: College Entrance Examination Board, p. 23).

Edwards, P. A., and Young, S. (1992). Beyond parents: Family, community, and school involvement. *Phi Delta Kappan, 74,* (1) 72-81.

Hodgkinson, Harold L. (1988). Facing the future: Demographics and statistics to manage today's schools for tomorrow's children. *School Administrator 8,* (45) 25-31.

Phone system keeps parents abreast of kid's schoolwork. (1993, February). *The Denver Post.* p. 15.

Teaching Youth At Risk: Teaching Framework. (1989). *USA TODAY,* Educational Services Department, Gannett Co., Inc.

APPENDIX

According to curriculum designer Pam Sysum, PASS is unique because it's a cognitivebased approach with curriculum geared to serve needs of high risk students. How? By a concentrated effort on behalf of the school and a variety of community resources.

A team of regular teachers, the principal and the PASS teacher identify high-risk students who qualify for PASS. In addition to regular class time, they attend PASS class as an elective for 45 minutes, five days a week.

Among various characteristics, youth at risk often have trouble dealing with traditional classrooms, exhibit behavioral problems and poor self-esteem and become bored quickly by lack of variety in the classroom (U.S.A. TODAY Educational Services Department, 1989). PASS class teaches high risk kids to cope with regular classes.

The PASS instructors also teach life skills and work as advocates for their students with other teachers, administration, parents and community resources such as Social Services or the Food Distribution Center among others.

When a student has trouble in a regular class, the PASS teacher helps by facilitating communication between the student, the regular teacher and the principal.

Principals don't have to deal with situations involving problem students immediately. Unlike programs with volunteers, principals and other building staff can rely on the PASS teacher to have consistent, professional skills for handling difficult students first.

As commonly found in other dropout prevention programs, the PASS teacher can develop a mentor relationship with students. But PASS staff are paid professionals who also work with other teachers and administrators by identifying at-risk students and heading off trouble before it gets to the office in the infamous action/reaction cycle.

Another unique characteristic: It's not a pull-out program like Self-Contained Special Education where difficult students are separated from the mainstream. Instead, PASS kids get to see healthy role models for their age groups too.

DENNIS N. JACKSON

20

Moving From Reactive to Proactive Planning for Students At-Risk: *Indiana's Story*

Evidence exists that over the past forty years the American economy has been on the decline with regard to competing in foreign markets. As a nation we are in the midst of profound economic change. This reality has prompted many diverse sectors of our society to scrutinize our system of public education. We are not successfully reaching the majority of the youth in schools. It appears that we are not successfully teaching the basic skills, problem solving techniques or motivating the youth to learn these vital skills.

The economic change began to appear with the 1950 U.S. Census, for the first time, more Americans were employed in the service sector than in the production sector in our nation's economy. During the past forty years employment in the production sector has continued to decline, while growth in the service sector has out paced all other types of employment. These newly created service jobs offer a much lower pay than do the manufacturing job they are replacing. By 1990 manufacturing jobs accounted for 19% of the earning the United States. It is presently estimated that by the year 2000, the decline of manufacturing share of earning will have further been eroded to about 18% (Lilly Endowment, 1993).

The Hudson Institute put it very succinctly when they said; "If every child who reaches the age of 17 between now and the year 2000 could read sophisticated materials, write clearly, speak articulately, and solve complex problems requiring algebra and statistics, the American economy could easily approach or exceed this 4% growth of the boom scenario. Boosted by the productivity of a well-qualified work force, U.S. based companies would reassert historic American leadership in old and new industries and the American workers would enjoy the rising standards of living they enjoyed in the 1950's and 1960's" (Mott Foundation, 1988, page 3).

However, as David T. Kearns, Chairman and Chief Executive Officer of Xerox, speaking for many American businessmen pointed out that the implication for many of the children and youth entering our educational system the end results will be tragic. He further predicts that the basic skills

GOVERNORS STATE UNIVERSITY
UNIVERSITY PARK
IL. 60466

presently in our work force, particularly at the entry level, are simply not good enough for the United States to compete in a world economy (Mott Foundation, 1988, pg.40).

Educational scrutiny began in earnest to gain a deeper understanding of the educational system. The 1983 publication, *A Nation At-Risk: The Imperative for Educational Reform* by the National Commission on Excellence in Education was the first mayor review of the educational system. The now familiar statement that jarred the reality of the educational community and legislative policy makers states:

"If an unfriendly foreign power had attempted to impose on an American the mediocre educational performance that exists today, we might well have viewed it as an act of war. As it stands, we have allowed this to happen to ourselves. We have even squandered the gains in student achievement made in the wake of the Sputnik challenge. Moreover, we have dismantled essential support systems which helped make those gains possible. We have, in effect, been committing [sic] an act of unthinking, unilateral educational disarmament" (Education Week, 1983).

This shocking perspective of the state of education nationally spurred educators, administrators, policy experts, and legislators to find new and different ways to reform and restructure the educational process and delivery system.

One of the most comprehensive policy studies was *Children in Need: Investment Strategies for the Educationally Disadvantaged,* (1987) compiled by the Committee for Economic Development (CED), an independent, nonprofit, research and education organization composed of approximately 250 U.S. business executives and educators. Their report advocated both restructuring the public schools to better serve the disadvantaged and formulating programs tailored to students who have dropped out or are at risk of dropping out. They further stressed that by improving the prospects for disadvantaged children, this effort should not be viewed as an expense but as an excellent investment, one that can be postponed only at much greater cost to society.

The CED's report recommended a three-part strategy for improving the educational prospect for disadvantaged children. The strategy included: 1) prevention through early intervention programs for children from birth to age five nd for teenagers; 2) restructuring the foundations of education - school organization, staffing, management, and financing; and 3) retention and re-entry programs for students still in school and for dropouts. The CED's report further indicated that we are creating a permanent under class of youth who have grown up in a poverty environment. Presently, these youth cannot hold a job because they lack literacy skills and appropriate work habits. These youth cannot enter the mainstream of society feeling trapped in a web of dependency and failure (NSBA, 1989).

Efforts that had been directed toward the educationally disadvantaged or educationally at-risk students were demonstration projects or part of the diminishing federal program overlay; they were not directed at providing services to the vast majority of at-risk youth. Combining the efforts of these federal programs and projects, they provide less than 7% of the money for public elementary and secondary education. On the other hand the states provide over half (53.2%) of the public funding for elementary and secondary education and are in a position to exercise leadership on behalf of at-risk children and youth.(NSBA, 1989). Despite the commitment put forth by the federal government to improve the educational status of disadvantaged and at-risk youth, state government has always had the primary responsibility for public education.

The Charles Stewart Mott Foundation was concerned with how states government were progressing toward addressing the at-risk youth problem. It was their desire to learn about state and local programs to determine at-risk students needs and the extent to whom those needs were being met. The Charles Stewart Mott Foundation (1988) surveyed all 50 states governments in an effort to determine how each state was serving the needs of at-risk youth. In determining the degree of services being provided to these youth, the foundation established a four phase progression of developmental services. The first of the four progressive phases was 1) preawareness/awareness of the problem and continuing on to the 2) action phase, 3) consolidation and the final phase 4) full implementation of policy, legislation and programming in support of the at-risk youth (Mott Foundation, 1988 p. 25).

Based on numerous studies from 1980-1985, meager efforts directed toward assisting at-risk school age youth were indicated. A few progressive states had begun to make some progress in this area; however, a far greater number of states remained unaware of the significance of the problem. As stated in the Foundations report, "the big majority of the states, based on this continuum, have not progressed beyond Phase I. We place 36 of the states in this stage, some of them so newly come to their awareness that not all of the descriptors apply to them" (Mott Foundation, 1988, p. 26).

During the same time frame, the Foundation identified 14 states which could describe their progress with at-risk youth as being in the second phase of this continuum. In order to be placed in the second phase those states had to have 1) awareness of the problem, 2) some policy developed, 3) legislation and, 4) program development. The 14 states that were able to meet the criteria were: California, Connecticut, Florida, Illinois, Maryland, Massachusetts, Minnesota,

New York, Oregon, Pennsylvania, Rhode Island, Texas, Washington and Wisconsin. At this time Indiana was identified as one of the 11 states that was showing enough progress with their at-risk youth efforts in Phase I to merit mention as a state that could move quickly into Phase II. The other 10 states identified were Arkansas, Colorado, Delaware, Kentucky, Maine, New Hampshire, New Jersey, North Carolina, Ohio and South Carolina (Mott Foundation, 1988, p. 26).

During the mid 1980's Indiana's Governor, key legislators and educators began to focus their attention on the relationship between the schools and the shape of the future for all of us. This implied that students in our classrooms today would shape public policy tomorrow. Kindergarten pupils enrolled in the fall of 1987 will be members of the class of 2000. These students will form the primary work force in the early decade of the next century. Our best forecast about jobs and occupations indicate that these young people will engage in as many as five careers in their lifetime, that they must be prepared for frequent retraining, and that today's schooling must develop their skills for a lifetime of learning.

Was Indiana up to the challenge? In the 1987 Annual Progress Report to the Citizens of Indiana, the Department of Education pointed out that data from the U.S. Census indicated that one-third of adult Hoosiers hold no high school diploma, that Indiana ranks 46th in the U.S. in years of schooling completed by its residents of age 25 or older, and that Indiana is 47th among the states in the percentage of its population with four years of college. Our state college officials tell us that one in four graduates of Indiana high schools require remedial English and mathematics courses when entering college.

Professor C. Lawrence Beymer at Indiana State University, (1987), also found that when Indiana is ranked among the 15 largest states, it has the fifth highest percentage of adults who dropped out of school. In metropolitan areas, the percentage of drop-outs is nearly double the percentage in rural areas. Dr. Beymer projects that Indiana's graduation rate may fall to 70 percent by the end of the century, and the U.S. rate to 60 percent (Indiana, D.O.E., 1989, p.1).

Thus, in 1987 the Governor signed into law a comprehensive package of educational reform legislation designed to respond to Indiana's realities. The legislative initiatives were drafted by task forces of interested citizens, educators, parents and business leaders from across the state working with the Indiana Department of Education. The eight legislative initiatives which became known as the A+ Program were: a) longer school year, b) performance-based accreditation system, c) performance-based awards program, d) beginning teacher internship program, e) staff performance evaluation, f) Indiana state-wide testing for educational progress program (ISTEP), g) achievement standards and promotion program (extended learning or summer school), and h) educational opportunity program for at-risk students.

Specifically, these initiatives were designed as strategies to achieve six goals included in the reform legislation.

(1) Performance by Indiana students on a nationally normed standardized achievement test at a defined percentile level that is above the national average for every grade level in which the test is administered on a state-wide basis.

(2) A targeted reduction of the percentage of Indiana students requiring remedial instruction.

(3) A targeted increase in student participation in post-secondary education.

(4) A targeted increase in student attendance rate.

(5) A targeted increase in the secondary school graduation rate.

(6) A targeted increase in parental involvement in education.

The Indiana General Assembly set aside nearly 20 million dollars annually as part of the A+ Reform Package for the Educational Opportunity Program for At-Risk Students. This program was identified for "students at risk of failure...at-risk of dropping out of school...at a time when the nation itself is at-risk of being overtaken in commerce, industry, science and technological innovations by competitors with better training and a more competitive work force". The sentiment of the legislators at this time was that every dollar spent today on education and/or innovative programs that addresses Indiana's "at-risk" student population will reduce public spending tomorrow. Their interest appeared to be focused primarily on reducing public spending in the form of remediation and retraining programs, social services, unemployment compensation, incarceration, and for crime related rehabilitation programs.

When the legislature began to look at the relationship between education and crime, they became very much aware of the burden placed on taxpayers for providing services to those individuals who have dropped out of school. With regard to the area of education and crime, Harold Hodgkinson (1991) in a recent article pointed out that more than 80% of America's one million prisoners have dropped out of our public schools. Furthermore 63% of those inmates released will be returned back to jail for a serious crime within three years. This does not appear to be a very good investment of taxpayers dollars.

The estimated cost to taxpayers to incarcerate an individual in prison for one year is approximately 20 thousand dollars per year. At the same time it is estimated that the cost to taxpayers for supporting a college student for one year is approximately $3,300 per year. This would appear to be a very profitable investment for all those individuals involved. The data regarding early intervention programs such as Head Start indicate that for every dollar spent on a child in that program, taxpayers will save $7.00 in later services that the child will not need (Hodgkinson, 1991). The more of those children who attended a high quality day care/preschool, the greater the probability that they will complete high school, job training program, college, and hold jobs and support themselves.

The At-Risk Student legislation grew out of the realization that in Indiana there are a number of students who are difficult to keep in school and even more difficult to educate following the traditional education model. The learning needs of these atrisk children indicate that alternative approaches were needed in the techniques of instruction, the establishment of a responsive learning environments, and alternative curriculum designs. It was also assumed that these students need additional help and support if they are to succeed in school and become productive members of their respective communities.

The next question for every school corporation became "who are Indiana's at-risk students?" The new legislation had given local school corporations the responsibility of locally defining the at-risk students to be served. This approach allowed local schools to focus on those students whom they believe are most in need of services. While statute left the definition for "at-risk students" to local school corporations, the legislation did direct the Department of Education to "develop a formula that provided each school corporation with an allocation of funds for at-risk students".

An at-risk formula subcommittee, made up of Department of Education staff and state fiscal analyst, was convened to develop an equitable funding formula. The formula required that consideration must be given to three census factors of the school and community as determined by the most recent U.S. Census. These factors are generally linked to poor school attendance and poor academic performance. When all three factors are present in a students home, that student runs a high risk of not being able to compete successfully with other students. The three factors

(1) The percentage of families in the school corporation with children less than eighteen (18) years of age that have a family income at or below the poverty level (POV);

(2) The percentage of noninstitutionalized children in the school corporation whose parents do not live together with the household (FAM);

(3) The percentage of the population in the school corporation that is at least nineteen (19) years of age and not graduated from high school (EDL).

The law further stipulates that no one factor may be weighted more than fifty percent (50%) in the funding formula (Indiana D.O.E., 1989).

After careful deliberation, the at-risk formula subcommittee decided to weight each of the given "at-risk factors" against an "academic failure factor" defined by the absentee (ABSRATE), dropout (DROPRATE), and "failure" (FAILRATE) rate experienced by each of Indiana's 304 school corporations. The logic of this methodology was predicated on the assumption that equitable "At-Risk" weights should be validated against demonstrable academic failure. These variables were defined as follows:

ABSRATE=	Percentage of school days missed by the average student
DROPRATE=	Total dropouts (grades 7-12) / Total corporation enrollments in these grades (AY 85-86)
FAILRATE=	Number of students in grades 3, 6, and 8 falling below the IBCST* cut score/Total enrollment in these grades (AY 86-87) (*Indiana Basic Competency Skills Test)

DATA ANALYSIS

The purpose of the data analysis was to derive a formula to equitably distribute funds to local educational agencies. In an effort to obtain an appropriate weighing system to assure equitable distribution, the following questions were investigated:

(1) What is the nature of the relationship between the stated mandated "at-risk" variables and a second set of variables which were determined to indicate "failure"?

(2) What proportion of "academic failure" can be predicted by the set of "at-risk" factors?

The data were analyzed using procedure CANCOR of the SAS system. The purpose of canonical correlation analysis is to determine the nature of the relationship (Rc) between a mathematically derived linear composite of a set of predictor variables and a linear composite of a set of criterion variables. These composites are formed by weighing the variables in such a way as to maximize the relationship between them. Based on the results of this analysis it appears that the mandated "at-risk" variable was indeed related to the "failure" of students and that this relationship can be quantified by an additive weighted function. Because the legislative mandate prohibits weighing of any one "at-risk" variable by more than 50%, it was an equitable compromise to weight FAM as 50%, and to divide the remaining 12% between EDL and POV according to their relative contribution to the explanation of variability in "failure". Therefore, the final weights should be .50 for FAM, .185 for EDL, and .315 for POV. Because these weights were based on a mathematically derived linear composite definition of "at-risk", a linear weighing system can be used to determine equitable allocation of funds. The calculation of a school district's "fair share" of funds should then be accomplished through the following steps:

(1) Calculate an "at-risk index" (ARI) for each school district using the following formula: ARI = .50 (FAM) + .185 (EDL) + .315 (POV) x (enrollment)
(2) Calculate a "total state at-risk index" (TSARI) for the state by adding the individual corporation ARI's.
(3) Determine a school's "fair share index" (FSI) by dividing the ARI by the TSARI. FSI = ARI / TSARI
(4) Determine the dollar amount ($) to be awarded to each district by multiplying the total dollars available (TDA) by the fair share index (FSI). $ =TDAxFSI (Perture, 1987).

An additional Department of Education task group was formed within the Department of Education to outline parameters and implement the legislative atrisk initiative. This task group was comprised of state level staff members who have had experience working with established programs often associated with at-risk students. Representatives were included from Chapter I, Language Minority, Adult and Vocational Education, Educational Equity, Special Education and Student Services. The goal of the task force was to address the educational deficiencies of the at-risk youth and examine how to create positive environments conducive to the promotion of academic success.

WHO ARE THE YOUTH AT-RISK IN INDIANA

The task group began the search for a definition with an extensive review of the literature and current practices. Initial review found that definitions of at-risk children varied tremendously across the country. A number of comprehensive definitions did emerge to provided educators with some degree of understanding of students who carry the label "at-risk of academic failure". The most useful information was derived from studies by Ginzberg, Berliner, and Ostow (1988) Levine (1988), McCann and Austin (1988), Whelage and Potter (1986) and Hilliard (1986).

In *Young People At Risk*, Ginzberg, Berliner and Ostow (1988) used the term "ineffective performers" in their attempt to describe at-risk adolescents. Here the term referred to young people who would not be able to support themselves or their dependents, would get into trouble with the law, would not be able to sustain a long term marital relationship, or serve in the armed forces. In their writings these authors continue to stress the point that a new class of "untouchable" is emerging in our inner cities, in this social fringes of suburbia, and in some rural areas: Young people who are functionally illiterate, disconnected from school, depressed, prone to drugs, and early criminal activity, and eventually, parents of unplanned and unwanted infants. These are the children who are at high risk of never becoming responsible adults (Ginzberg, 1988).

In his book *Structuring Schools for Greater Effectiveness with Educationally Disadvantaged or At-Risk Students* (1988), Levine supplied a reasonably simple and inclusive definition for at-risk children. He noted specifically that "the educationally at-risk population consists of students who lacked the home and community resources to fully benefit from conventional schooling practices." He further indicated that these at-risk students are especially concentrated among minority groups, immigrants, non-English-speaking families and children from economically disadvantaged families (Levin, 1988).

McCann and Austin (1988), in their paper for Research for Better Schools developed a list of criteria used to define the at-risk population. Their list identified specific sets of behaviors:

- not attending school regularly; being truant;
- not engaging in classroom and school activities;
- not succeeding in daily learning tasks and on local and state achievement measures;
- using drugs and alcohol;

- committing disruptive and delinquent acts;
- becoming pregnant and having to take care of a baby;
- attempting suicide (McCann, 1988).

It is suggested by Whelage and Potter (1986) that by identifying potential dropouts through certain predisposing social characteristics these characteristics will almost inevitably single out low income, minority students. Furthermore, directing special programs and additional funds at this group would only reinforce the middle class educational biases (Wehlage, 1986).

Finally with regards to the problem of a definition of at-risk children and youths, Hilliard (1989) states that "the greatest risk poor and minority children may face is that which comes from our incorrect perception of the problem. Such a perception causes us to blame the child for what we have failed to provide and the search for solutions through an examination of children rather than systems" (Hilliard, 1989).

Taking into account all of the various factors that could conceivably be used to identify at-risk children and youth, the task group focused on a definition. This definition was designed to facilitate the development of a common vision for Indiana's educators, not to be the "official" definition. The definition developed by the task group states:

> *"Any student who runs the risk of not acquiring the knowledge, skills and attitudes needed to become a productive adult...is at-risk. Therefore, the term 'student at-risk' refers to any child who has been adversely affected by one, or more, of the factors associated with poor health, economic status, family conditions, linguistic mismatch, social maladjustment, and community change/upheaval. It is the inability to cope with these adversities (whether they be short or long-term) that negatively affects school performance and attendance. Indicators of risk may include: underdeveloped language skills, drug and alcohol abuse, disruptive and/or delinquent behavior, inattentiveness, chronically withdrawn behavior, excessive school absence, dropping out of school, and low academic achievement"* (Indiana D.O.E.).

In addition to the task groups development of a functional definition of "at-risk students", the statute directed the task group to develop an application and administrative guidelines for school corporations to apply for funds for programming. Although this was not to be a competitive grant program, school corporations were required to submit a proposal that 1) defined their at-risk population to be served; 2) described the type of program that will be offered; and 3) outlined how the program will be evaluated.

From the at-risk program's very inception the legislators were very sensitive to the idea that some students are difficult to educate following the traditional educational model. The statute stressed that the at-risk grants must focus on assisting the local school corporation in creating programs for children who are at-risk of failing in school and dropping out. One strategy was to focus on early identification and intervention strategies. Alternative educational approaches were also needed in the areas of techniques of instruction, establishment of responsive learning environment, design of alternative curriculum and the enhancement of the child's self concept. Following this line of thinking lawmakers identified nine categories of programs for funding in the statute. A tenth program category "Mentoring", was added during the 1990 General Assembly session. Within the primary program categories there were five sub-sets of programs that were also created to maximize a school corporation's potential for meeting the needs of those children and youth most in need of services. The five sub-sets of programs were: alcohol and drug abuse, school/home advisor, after school enrichment, vocational emphasis and student health program. The ten program categories to be funded by the legislators were:

(1) Preschool programs

(2) Full-day kindergarten

(3) Parental and community involvement programs

(4) Transitional programs

(5) Tutoring programs

(6) Remediation programs

(7) Expanded utilization of school counselor
- alcohol and drug abuse
- school/home advisor (who serve as liaison between families and school personnel

(8) Individualized programs

(9) Model alternative education programs for students who are determined by the department to be at risk of withdrawing from school before graduation.
- after-school enrichment
- vocational emphasis
- student health, and

(10) Mentoring programs.

The language of the legislation did not exclude other types of programs. The two critical elements for any program to be funded are 1) the program must be a new one and/or 2) an expansion of a current one and that the program serve identified at-risk students.

The task group created a "draft" program application, administrative guidelines, program guidelines and the estimated cost for program implementation documents. After the first drafts of these documents were written, a series of five forums were held throughout the state. These forums were held to insure that the application and guidelines were clearly written and realistic and that school officials could provide feedback and ask questions about the at-risk legislation. As soon as the task group digested comments and incorporated necessary changes for clarity into each document, approval was given to print the material. The task group invested a tremendous amount of time and energy into developing both the "Guidelines for Developing an Educational Program for At-Risk Students" and the "At-Risk Program Costing" document. To insure that all school corporations started at the same point regarding the development of their at-risk program, the program guideline document contained essential elements to be included in the program proposal to the Department of Education. Those components were: Administrative, Program, Instruction, Curriculum, and Goals and Evaluation.

A description of each of the ten program categories was also included in this document (Tables 1.1 and 1.2 provides examples of two of the ten program categories).

Table 1.1
Example #1 of Program Categories

Parental and Community Involvement

Researchers of effective schools reported a positive correlation between parent involvement with the school and higher student achievement of all children. The evidence is clear that parental involvement, encouragement, interests, and active participation in a variety of roles positively affect children's achievement, attitudes, and aspirations regardless of the student's ability or family's socioeconomic status.

Parents are the child's first teachers. The attitudes they instill in their children during the preschool and early school-age years influence the children's success throughout life. Children whose parents encourage them and participate in their educational endeavors achieve more academically and have healthier self-concepts than do children of parents who are not supportive.

(Table 1.1 Continued)

Elements to Consider in Program Planning:

Develop a comprehensive parent involvement policy.

Prepare a parent involvement plan outlining goals, objectives and strategies. Determine resources needed to supplement the existing channels for parent involvement.

- Analyze and develop new channels.
- Establish a procedure for using them effectively.
- Survey community attitudes and interests.
- Develop parent newsletters.
- Ensure program accessibility to all parents (e.g., language minority, single parents, parents of special needs children).
- Form committees of administrators, teachers, and parents to develop common goals for children.
- Provide parent education training.
- Encourage staff involvement; make them aware that parent involvement is a school priority.
- Encourage positive interaction between parents and administrators.
- Identify new ways parents can be involved.
- Make sure parents feel appreciated for their efforts.
- Convince parents that their services/advice/recommendations will be considered. Assist parents in the understanding of process skills used for twoway decision making.
- Communicate to parents the scope of a committee charge, the time commitment expected of them, and that what they will be doing is important to the school and to their children.

Table1.2
Example #2 of Program Categories

Mentoring Programs For At-Risk Students

Mentor was entrusted with the education and sponsorship of Telemachus during the travels of his father Odysseus. The term mentor has come to connote a one-toone helping relationship in which one person, usually older, more skilled, or more experienced works in an on-going relationship to enhance the personal and professional development of another person. When single-session workshops for teachers or classroom instruction for students do not produce adequate results, research has shown that adding a mentor program does produce results in teacher or students being able to improve and succeed.

(Table 1.2 Continued)

Elements to Consider in Program Planning:

- Does the program provide a one-to-one relationship?
- Does the program provide feedback in a non-threatening atmosphere?
- Does the program help the person to analyze activities and problems and create new strategies?
- Does the program allow practice to achieve new beneficial habits or techniques in a safe environment?
- Does the program allow the mentor relationship to be sustained over time without changing mentoring pairs (a minimum of one semester)?
- Has the program carefully matched the mentors and the recipients?

The Matching Process:

Matching can be accomplished through identifying specific interest areas. The following are a few examples of how this can be accomplished.

1. Individual Sports
   roller/ice skating
   horseback riding
   swimming
   martial arts
   others
2. Special Interests
   board games
   small animals
   reading
   kite making/flying
   collections
   computers
   others
3. Outdoor Activities
   hiking
   boating/fishing
   sightseeing
   camping/backpacking
   archery
4. Skill Activities
   auto mechanics
   wood working
   cooking/baking
   building models
   arts/crafts
   fixing things
   music
   gardening
   photography
   other
5. Group Sports
   (spectator or participant)
   base/softball
   basketball
   football
   scoccer
   coaching
   other

Program Examples:

(1) Students several years older who have successfully overcome difficulties or solved problems paired with younger ones on a regular basis during a study period or after-school meeting each week.

(2) Teacher assigned to a small group of students over an extended time to guide their development generally and be available on a one-to-one basis as a student faces problems or makes decisions.

(3) Teachers successful with at-risk children serving as mentors for new or inexperienced teachers whose experience did not include at-risk children or whose work with at-risk children has not been successful.

(4) Agency personnel, parents or adults may serve as mentors
**(Mentoring programs are not substitutes for counseling programs.)

The "At-Risk Program Costing" document reflects a "bench mark" for program review purposes and should not be considered as an absolute cost. The costs that were presented in the document were to be viewed more in terms of "generic" program cost only (Table 2.1).

Table 2.1
A Costing Summary

Parental and Community Involvement Programs

To have a meaningful parent involvement program, a staff person should be designated for community relations. The cost involved would include the salary of the staff person and miscellaneous expenses incurred as a result of developing newsletters, handbooks, programs, etc. The staff person is not considered to be a "certificated" person. The travel component is necessary to permit the community relations person to meet with community leaders and groups throughout the school corporation.

Cost Components

Staff Salary (1 full-time staff person including fringes)	$ 20,000
Supplies and Materials	1,000
Purchased Services (Contracted services for printing of newsletters and programs, radio spots, newspaper advertisement and as needed secretarial support)	6,000
Travel (50 miles/week x .25/mile x 36 weeks)	450
TOTAL	27,450

The Department then held a second series of workshops throughout the State to inform administrators and local program coordinators about the application procedure, administrative guidelines, estimated cost of program implementation and program development guidelines. It was the Department's intent to provide local schools approximately six months to apply for funds which will be available after July 1,1988.

Table 3.0 is an example of the summary of the At-Risk Student Program for the school year 1988-89. This summary provides an excellent profile of the total number of programs for each of the ten at-risk program categories approved by the legislators. The term "programs" specifically refer to the type of program a school corporation chooses to implement in addressing their at-risk student population. An example would be a school corporation would like to implement a "Parent and Community Involvement Program" for their at-risk children and parents in two elementary schools and a middle school. If the programs that the corporation implemented in the two elementary schools were identical with regards to program characteristics, instructional and curriculum components, that would constitute a single elementary program and one middle school program for that school corporation. However, if the two elementary school programs were significantly different regarding the program characteristics (i.e., philosophy, mission, goals, parent and community participation), instructional, curriculum components, the school corporation would then submit three separate program applications. Two separate atrisk program applications for the elementary schools and one at-risk program application for the middle school.

Table 3.0
A Summary of the At-Risk Student Program for 1988-89.

At-Risk Programs in Indiana	Programs
1. Preschool	20
2. Full-Day Kindergarten	13
3. Parental and Community Involvement	47
4. Transitional	45
5. Tutoring	142
6. Remediation	68
7. Expanded Use of School Counseling	185
• Alcohol and Drug Abuse	11
• Home School Advisor	10
8. Individualized	48
9. Alternative Educational Models	79
• After School Enrichment	83
• Vocational Emphasis	2
• Student Health	6
TOTAL	759

Indiana's At-Risk Student Population

The vast majority of school corporations tend to incorporate into their at-risk student definition and identification scheme the following characteristics of children and youth who are identified as needing additional supportive services. These children are described as "running the risk of not acquiring the knowledge, skills and attitudes needed to become a productive adult." About 17 percent of boys and girls are identified as fitting this description - that is they are "at-risk" of academic failure and/or dropping out of school.

Based on the local school corporation's identification and selection criteria the following table 4.0 provides a five year profile of the total number of at-risk programs per year, number of students involved in those programs per year, number of at-risk and non at-risk students involved in the programs per year, total number of students in Indiana's public schools per year, and the total amount of local and state funds used in the program each year.

Table 4.0
Five Year Summary Of Indiana's At-Risk Programs and Local Funding
1988-1993

	1988-89	1989-90	1990-91	1991-92	1992-93
Total Number of Students in Indiana Public Schools [1]	959,078	952,247	953,172	955,676	959,876
Number of State School Corporations	302	297	297	297	293
Number of Programs	759	723	642	681	606
Total Student Involved	211,118	220,424	242,938	211,697	228,382
At-Risk Students	124,460	124,529	163,893	156,372	169,002
Non At-Risk Students [2]	68,658	95,895	80,045	55,041	59,379
Total of Local Funding Added to State Grant	$2.5M	$7M	$135M	N/A [3]	$9.6M
State At-Risk Allocation	$20M	$20M	$20M	$20M	$20M

1. These figures do not include students enrolled in state operated schools
2. Some students not identified as at-risk may be served along with at-risk students in certain programs
3. Information not collected due to change in application process instituted by the Department

The department initially thought that the local funds that school corporations were adding might be in-kind contributions, such as lights, heat, rental space and administrative costs. Upon further investigation we were quite pleased to find that the local funds were coming out of the school corporations general operating budget. This money was being applied to the various programs in the areas of hiring additional staff, computer software or hardware, transportation for field trips, contracted services and additional resources and materials.

In the past five years the "at-risk student program" has identified and aided an annual average of 147,451 students who are most in need of additional resources and special assistance. A five year summary of program types, categories using percentages to indicate the top five program types implemented in the school corporations is provided in table 5.0. It should be noted that the top three programs types constitute close to 70% of the total type of programs implemented during the past five years.

The top three programs in 1992-93 also represented nearly 65% of all programs created that year and accounted for more than 14.5 million of the states 20 million dollar allocation.

Table 5.0
Most Common At-Risk Program Types in Indiana

	1988-89	1989-90	1990-91	1991-92	1992-93
Expanded Use of School Counseling	27%	33%	32%	37%	37%
Tutoring Programs	19%	19%	18%	15%	14%
Model Alternative Education Programs	22%	11%	13%	14%	12%
Remediation	9%	8%	7%	9%	8%
Transitional Classrooms	6%	6%	6%	6%	5%
Mentoring Programs			2%	4%	9%

Under the State statute mentoring programs were added in 1989-90 to the original nine program types designated by the State legislators.

Essential elements of an Effective At-Risk Program

The restructuring of curriculum and instruction is an area of high potential for ensuring success for children, but it is often not addressed in direct thoughtful ways. Many efforts to help children academically are merely designed to add more time,give attention to "the basics", or provide reinforcement for school work. These efforts do not necessarily constitute the kind of change needed to motivate and maximize the potential of the children.

The school literature is quite lengthy when it sets down recommendations for effective at-risk programs. The vast majority of experts and the various task forces and commissions do not always agree on the essential elements of effective at- risk programs. However. there appears to be a set of core characteristics found in programs with positive outcomes for youth. Dryfoos (1990), in her recent publication *Adolescents At Risk: Prevalence and Prevention* indicates a set of core elements which seem to be inherent in effective at-risk programs:

(1) No single approach or component has been demonstrated as most effective. The key concept is flexibility.

(2) Early intervention is of critical importance for the prevention of learn development problem.

(3) Early identification for high-risk students must be expedited and progress monitored through a longitudinal K-12 data system.

(4) Small size of school and classes appear to be beneficial to high-risk students.

(5) Individualized attention and instruction are necessary for children with problems.

(6) Program anonymity is very important.

(7) Committed teachers must have high expectations for students and be sensitive to gender, race, and cultural issues.

(8) Strong vocational components should make the link between learning and working using experiential education and out-of-class learning, community service projects and paid work experience.

(9) Intensive, sustained counseling is essential for high-risk students who need assistance with personal and family problems and, in many cases, on-site health and social services

(10) Positive school climate should be encouraged through a "family" atmosphere and a safe, secure and non-threatening environment.

(11) School- community integration is essential. Collaborative programs for educational, family, social, and health services as well as job placement must be planned and implemented (Dryfoos, 1990).

Manning (1993) referred to a similar core of essential elements. However, he places a major emphasis on improving a child's self concept. Additional elements which constitute effectiveness include placing challenging and rigorous expectations on atrisk students, and helping students to be successful in social interaction. He feel that programs should be developed to include deliberate and planned activities to address the at-risk students lack of social skills. Programs should also be developed to provide for the teacher and student with opportunities to agree on expectations, methods, and materials necessary for learning to occur. Finally effective programs place considerable responsibility on the learner to be motivated to succeed (Manning, 1993).

Effective Programs In Indiana

Programs that are successful take the essential elements to children and youth through day-to-day instruction and quality curriculum. Ongoing evaluation and monitoring, provide opportunities for documenting success while challenging and motivating the students. Providing more opportunities for application rather than drill and practice, planning lessons with attention to more content and context, not less, and demanding the children take an active responsibility for their learning are some of the activities observed in programs that have been carefully restructured to promote positive outcomes.

Since there is no one definition of "at risk," used exclusively in Indiana, there is also no one solution employed by all school corporations to reduce the at-risk student population in the state. The schools corporations that have been most successful are generally those that attack the problem on a holistic basis. They see it as a problem that begins before the child enters kindergarten and then increasingly manifests itself as the child advances, or becomes a potential dropout. Therefore, successful strategies attack the problem at many levels. The following Indiana school corporations have demonstrated a holistic approach in addressing the needs of their at-risk student population.

BARTHOLOWMEW CONSOLIDATED SCHOOL CORPORATION

This pre school program titled "Home School Partnership Program is designed to establish rapport with the parents, share educational ideas, activities, toys, newsletters, etc., to enhance the preschool development of the children ages 1-5. The program also provides a means of letting families know of other community services available, keeps the parents informed about school activities such as kindergarten registration, adult education opportunities and parent meetings. Parent meetings are set up twice a year to help develop a parent support network.

Through this program the school corporation helps the identified parents to realize the value and responsibility as their childs' first and most important teacher by affirming their role and helping them acquire age appropriate parenting skills. The school corporation's goal is to create an interactive link between school and home before the child enters school, and to assist the parents in acquiring an understanding of the formal school procedures and the need for parents to be involved in their childs' education. What the school corporation has realized from this program is that the children respond well when enrolled in school and that the parents continue their involvement with the school. In addition, the program is becoming an integral part of the community service network.

FORT WAYNE COMMUNITY SCHOOLS

The "Alternative Learning Program" is designed to provide either a short term or permanent alternative program for those students in grades 4-12 who have lost their privilege of attending their home school, who have shown they cannot function constructively in a traditional classroom setting, or who have exhibited a need for a specialized program in order to be able to continue their education. The Alternative Learning Program uses alternative strategies structured within a positive school environment to teach these students the academic, decision making, and pro-social skills they need to be successful as students, worker and citizens. This program uses two methods to alter negative student behaviors. Students are scheduled into special needs (substance abuse, impulse control, etc.) individual and group counseling sessions that fit their individual needs. Secondly, the staff deals with affective behavior of students by using the concepts of reality therapy as developed by Dr. William Glasser. One of the most unique and effective components of this program is the "Aftercare" program (unique in the nation) is extremely valuable and is felt to be instrumental in the fact that approximately 80% of their program graduates are still in their home schools. A full-time aftercare person was added to the staff to provide students who have returned to their home school with a strong, more effective support system.

WESTFIELD-WASHINGTON SCHOOLS

The services offered through Westfield-Washington's SAFARI (Student Assistance for At-Risk Individuals) program are multi-faceted and comprehensive. This comprehensive program has been firmly established as a staff development program for impacting teacher attitude and behavior toward the at-risk student. This program has received national recognition from the Council of States on Inservice Education in 1992. The services of this program are available at all grade levels K-12 and are adapted to fit the needs of that grade level. SAFARI provides staff with guidance and procedures for identifying the at-risk student, as well as training in recognizing and addressing at-risk behaviors. Building level core teams assess and place students according to identified needs. Students find support through components including Adopt-a-Teacher, support groups. individual counseling, referral to and support of outside counseling, prevention clubs, teacher support and attendance incentives Students, parents, staff,and the community are provided with periodic informational programming designed to reduce at-risk behaviors and attitudes.

Business/community partnerships are encouraged through programs such as *Textbooks and French Fries* and the *Attendance Program. Textbooks and French Fries* is a recent SAFARI component involves a partnership between school, student, parent, and student employers. The program brings participants together in a informal, non-threatening format to discuss what is best for the working student.

REFERENCES

Charles Stewart Mott Foundation. (1988). *American's shame, america's hope: twelve million youth at risk.* Chapel Hill, N.C. : The Charles Stewart Mott Foundation Press.

Committee for Economic Development, (1987). *Chidren in need: investment strategies for the educationally disadvantaged.* New York: CED Research and Policy Committee

DryFoos, J. (1990). *Adolescents at-risk : prevalence and prevention.* New York: Oxford University Press.

Ginzberg, E. Berliner, H., and Ostous, M. (1988). *Young people at risk: is prevention possible?* Boulder, Colorado: Westview Press.

Hilliard, A.C. (1989). *Public support for successful instruction practices for at risk students.* From D.W. Horbeck (Eds) *School Success for Students At-Risk.* Orlando: Harcourt Brace Jovanovich.

Hodgkinson, H. (1991). Reform Versus Reality, *Phi Delta Kappan*, September, 9-16.

Indiana Department of Education, (1987). *A progress report to the citizens of Indiana, Indianapolis*: D.O.E. Publications.

Indiana Department Of Education, (1987). *Development of the formula for the educational opportunity program for at risk students*, Indianapolis, D.O.E. Publications.

Indiana Department of Education, (1987). *Identification of at at-risk students*, Indianapolis D.O.E. Publications.

Levin, H. (1988) Structuring schools for greater effectiveness with educationally disadvantaged or at-risk students, *Educational Leadership*, 44: 13-16

Lilly Endowment Inc. (1993). *The state of the child in Indiana II*, Indianapolis: Lilly Endowment Inc.

Manning, L. (1993). Seven essentials of effective at-risk programs. *The Clearing House*, January/February, 66 (3).

McCann, R. and S. Austin (1988). At-risk youth: definitions, dimensions, and relationships. *Family Relations*, 37, 247-254.

National Commission on Excellence in Education (1983). An open letter to the american people; a nation at-risk : the imperitive for educational reform. *Education Week*, 2 (31) : 12-16.

National School Board Association (1989). *An equal chance: educating at-risk children to succeed*, Alexandria, Va.: N.S.B.A. Publications.

Wehlage, G.G. and R.A. Rutter (1986). Dropping out : how much do schools contribute to the problem? *Teachers College Record*, 87 (3) : 374-392.

INDEX

A

B

C

D

E

O

P

Q

R

S

T

U

V

W

Y